Partners or Rivals?

RACE, ETHNICITY, AND POLITICS

Luis Ricardo Fraga and Paula D. McClain, Editors

Partners or Rivals?

POWER AND LATINO, BLACK, AND WHITE RELATIONS
IN THE TWENTY-FIRST CENTURY

Betina Cutaia Wilkinson

University of Virginia Press
CHARLOTTESVILLE AND LONDON

University of Virginia Press
© 2015 by the Rector and Visitors of the University of Virginia
All rights reserved
Printed in the United States of America on acid-free paper

First published 2015

9 8 7 6 5 4 3 2 1

Library of Congress Cataloging-in-Publication Data

Wilkinson, Betina Cutaia, 1981–
  Partners or rivals? : power and Latino, black, and white
relations in the twenty-first century / Betina Cutaia Wilkinson.
    pages   cm. — (Race, ethnicity, and politics)
  Includes bibliographical references and index.
  ISBN 978-0-8139-3773-1 (cloth : alk. paper) —
ISBN 978-0-8139-3774-8 (e-book)
  1. United States—Race relations. 2. Minorities—United
States—Attitudes. 3. Hispanic Americans—Race identity.
4. African Americans—Race identity. 5. Whites—Race
identity—United States. I. Title.
  E184.A1W453 2015
  305.800973—dc23

                          2015010839

To Gabriel, Rosario, and Jason

Contents

Acknowledgments

I have been thinking about and examining the questions in this book since I was an undergraduate student at Loyola University New Orleans. It was there where my interest in race relations and racial inequality was ignited and developed. Thus, I want to thank my sociology undergraduate advisors and mentors, Laurie Joyner and Ed McCaughan, for taking me under their wing and giving me significant attention, academic support, and encouragement to succeed in my undergraduate studies and beyond. I also want to extend a special thanks to my advisors and peers at Louisiana State University where I completed my graduate work. Jim Garand, my major professor, has provided me with a tremendous amount of intellectual and emotional support necessary to succeed in graduate school (and get the dissertation done), in the job market, and as an assistant professor. I would not have become the scholar that I am today without Jim. He has taught me how to be a great researcher, professor, colleague, mentor, and friend. I am also indebted to Johanna Dunaway, who read countless drafts of my dissertation chapters (which were later modified to blossom into this book project) and provided me with significant encouragement and support to complete this project. I also want to thank Robbie Hogan and Kirby Goidel, whose enthusiasm toward my research were unwavering. Special thanks go to Natasha Bingham for her friendship and encouragement all these years as well as for helping me to conduct several focus groups whose findings are presented in this book.

The research and financial support that I have received from Wake Forest University helped to make this project a reality. I would like to begin by thanking the Dean's Office and the Office of Research and Sponsored Programs, which supplied funds to collect data used in this project. I am also appreciative of the advice and support from Sara Dahill-Brown, Neil DeVotta, Katy Harriger, Sarah Lischer, Michael Pisapia, Peter Siavelis, Kathy Smith, and Will Walldorf. I am particularly appreciative of the assistance of Emily Earle for her help with some last-minute editing and revisions. Students from my Latino Political Behavior and Racial and Ethnic Politics courses have also provided insightful comments on several of the chapters in this book project, so I would like to acknowledge the students enrolled in these courses.

Outside of the institutions where I have studied and worked, I would like to express my appreciation to several individuals. Thank you, Ansley Abraham, for helping me to succeed as a scholar through your faculty diversity program's commitment to the professional development and success of minority graduate students and professors. I want to thank Vince Hutchings for providing me with county geocodes for the 2004 National Politics Survey (NPS) and for 2004 contextual data at the county level. I am also indebted to Marisa Abrajano, Matt Barreto, Christina Bejarano, Ben Bishin, Vanessa Cruz, Martin Johnson, Jane Junn, Jessica Lavariega-Monforti, Taeku Lee, Jennifer Merolla, Melissa Michelson, Karthick Ramakrishnan, Ricardo Ramirez, Rene Rocha, Gabe Sanchez, Gary Segura, and Sophia Wallace. This book is a better project because of my interactions with them and their insights. I am also appreciative of Marcela Garcia-Castanon, Francisco Pedraza, Stella Rouse, and Ping Xu for their consistent support and friendship, which has been at the crux of my development as a researcher and teacher. I would like to thank Dick Holway at the University of Virginia Press for his early interest in this project, as well as the solid support of Luis Fraga and Paula McClain, the Race, Ethnicity, and Politics series editors.

I express my deepest gratitude to my family. My husband, Jason's, continuous encouragement and patience throughout my graduate school experience and now life as an assistant professor has not gone unnoticed. He has listened to my conference presentations, read over my papers, assisted me in developing my research interests, and kept himself busy for many weekends and weeknights while I finished this manuscript, all with an encouraging smile. I am thankful for the continuous love and encouragement of my sisters, Clarisa (now Sister Maria Victoria) and Marina, as well as Domingo, Rosa, and Vicente. Lastly, I want to thank my parents, Rosario and Gabriel, who came to this country to create a better future for their daughters and who have made many sacrifices for their well-being. Their continuous advice to be genuine, polite, hard-working, determined, and courageous has carried me very far in my academic career and life in general. I am grateful for and reminded of their strength and courage every day.

Portions of chapter 2 appeared in Betina Cutaia Wilkinson, "Perceptions of Commonality and Latino-Black, Latino-White Relations in a Multiethnic U.S.," *Political Research Quarterly* 67, no. 4 (2014): 905–16.

Partners or Rivals?

Introduction

His father is white, neighbors say. His mother is Latina. And his family is eager to point out that some relatives are black.
　　　　　　　　　　　　—*The* Washington Post *on George Zimmerman*

On the evening of February 26, 2012, Trayvon Martin, an unarmed black teenager with a hoodie, was shot and killed in Sanford, Florida, by George Zimmerman.[1] Martin left the house he was visiting to purchase a few things from the local 7-Eleven, including a bag of Skittles and a can of iced tea. Zimmerman, a neighborhood watch volunteer and resident of Sanford, saw Martin walking back from the 7-Eleven and called the police. A recording of the 911 call made by Zimmerman illustrates that he thought that Martin looked suspicious and that Zimmerman was instructed not to follow Martin. What occurred afterward is not completely clear, though Martin was left fatally shot while Zimmerman suffered a bloody nose and a laceration to the back of his head (Alvarez 2012; Blow 2012). Once the mass media published details of Trayvon Martin's shooting, hundreds of individuals (led predominantly by African American community leaders) participated in rallies and protests in the city of Sanford and throughout the United States in efforts to have Zimmerman arrested. Such was the support for Martin that a national "wear a hoodie day" was declared in late March resulting in thousands sporting hoodies to work, school, and in public settings (Preston and Moynihan 2012). In April 2012, Zimmerman was charged with second-degree murder for fatally shooting Martin, and in July 2013, a six-person jury found that Zimmerman was not guilty of second-degree murder or manslaughter because he could have been justified in shooting Martin since Zimmerman feared great bodily harm or death (Horwitz 2012; Alvarez and Buckley 2013).

What remained unclear a few weeks after the shooting was the race and ethnicity of George Zimmerman. Some news reports stated that he was white, others stated that he was white and Latino, and many did not provide any racial information. With a last name of Zimmerman, some may have perceived him as Jewish and white. When his picture was presented to the nation, some believed that he was Latino, though this may not have been completely apparent given his light complexion. What we do know about the man charged with second-degree murder is that his mother is Peruvian, his father is white, he was raised Catholic, and he has a strong interest in law enforcement (Roig-Franzia et al. 2012). A letter from Zimmerman's father a few weeks after the shooting emphasized that George Zimmerman was a minority. The letter stated that Zimmerman is Hispanic and a member of a multiracial family, and would therefore be the last person to discriminate against anyone. Zimmerman's father also stressed that the media's portrayal of his son as a racist was far from the truth (Stutzman 2012). Since race and ethnicity can influence the lens through which individuals interpret the facts of a case, it was critical for Zimmerman and Martin supporters to emphasize the backgrounds of these men.

Undoubtedly, the fatal shooting of Trayvon Martin reveals the ongoing racial tensions that exist among whites, blacks, and Latinos, as well as Latinos' complex identity, as noted by the chapter-opening quote. Given that Latinos are establishing an emerging presence throughout this country as one of the fastest growing groups and the largest minority group (Lopez et al. 2013), our discussion of inter-race relations in this country is incomplete if it does not include Latinos. In efforts to obtain a comprehensive understanding of Latino/white and Latino/black relations in the 21st century, this book addresses two main questions: Do Latinos, African Americans, and whites perceive each other as allies or rivals? Additionally, what explains Latinos', blacks', and whites' perceptions of commonality, closeness, and competition with each other? I begin this chapter by outlining questions that the book addresses, then discuss what we know about Latinos and how they relate to African Americans and whites. Finally I describe this study's main theory and the chapters that make up this project.

Goal of the Book

The aim of this book is twofold. First, I examine whether whites, blacks, and Latinos regard each other as partners or rivals by exploring perceptions of closeness, commonality, and competition among the three groups. These perceptions reflect the intricate racial dynamics that exist among blacks, whites, and Latinos, and they are commonly thought to be precursors of coalition formation. While perceptions of commonality and closeness can bring racial and ethnic groups together to form political coalitions, perceptions of competition can inhibit two groups from forming alliances (Kaufmann 2003; Barreto and Sanchez 2008; Abrajano and Alvarez 2010).

The political science research on perceptions of commonality and competition among whites, blacks, and Latinos has increased considerably in the past decade. This work has advanced our understanding of how similar and distinct Latinos are from whites and blacks. It has examined how having a minority status (experiencing substantial socioeconomic struggles and having limited power, mostly associated with African Americans and Latinos) and having a majority status (having significant sociopolitical clout, mostly associated with whites) impact race relations. Still, it is not clear as to whether Latinos and blacks, and Latinos and whites view each other as partners or competitors. Numerous key questions remain: Do Latinos regard blacks as greater allies than whites? Do blacks view Latinos (a group with comparable experiences and power) as neighbors or rivals? Do whites regard Latinos like African Americans since they are both minority groups with less power than whites? In order to unearth these complexities and gaps, I analyze what I call a "triangle of perceptions"—how members of each group perceive the other two and also their own group. Thus, I examine Latino attitudes toward blacks and whites in comparison to their attitudes toward their co-ethnics, African Americans' views of Latinos and whites in relation to their views of other blacks, and whites' dispositions toward Latinos and blacks relative to their attitudes toward other whites. In so doing, I challenge the conventional practice of examining one racial/ethnic group's attitudes toward another by (1) comparing one group's views toward another group with their attitudes toward a third group, and (2) analyzing how one group regards members of their own race or ethnicity. As Jason L. Morin and colleagues (2011) state, one group's perceptions of another group cannot be understood without also having at least one additional group for comparison (104). Analyzing racial attitudes in this way allows me to determine whether some individuals may have greater affinity with a racial group of a distinct status than another of a similar status, and to establish whether individuals may feel closer and/or more competition with members of their own race/ethnicity than any other group.

Before going further, it is critical to mention that there are several reasons why this project does not include Asian Americans. First, I have been unable to access national survey data that covers the specific questions that I seek to answer as well as one that has a large representative sample of Asian Americans similar in size to other minority groups. Second, African Americans and Latinos as a whole are distinct from Asian Americans. They are the two largest minority groups in the country; they participate politically at considerably higher levels than Asian Americans (Lopez and Gonzalez-Barrera 2013); and Latinos and blacks are significantly disadvantaged relative to whites, while Asian Americans as a whole are not (Wong

2012). Third, my research builds heavily on previous literature exploring the power dynamics that exist among whites, blacks, and Latinos through perceptions of closeness, commonality, and competition, and Asians have been largely absent from this research (Sanchez 2008; Kaufmann 2003; McClain et al. 2011). Lastly, given the wide economic and social diversity of Asian Americans (Wong 2012), members of this racial group do not easily fall into a particular status, minority or majority, making it quite challenging to develop theories that capture this racial group as a whole.

The second goal of this book is to determine under what conditions Latinos, blacks, and whites perceive closeness, commonality, and competition with each other. Today, Latinos have established a strong presence in urban and rural communities nationwide, and, more recently, they are moving to areas in the Midwest and South where many established residents have not had previous interaction with them. Some are for the first time calling Latinos their neighbors, coworkers, and even friends. The destinations where Latinos reside vary significantly in context as well. Some areas have established educational and employment infrastructures where the unemployment rate is lower than the national average and the education levels of the residents are significantly high, though in many counties, the socioeconomic opportunities for Latinos and other minorities to climb the social ladder are limited, often placing Latinos as a social and economic threat to established residents. Some counties are racially mixed and others are predominantly white or black, influencing the degree to which a burgeoning Latino population is noticed and the extent to which the residents feel that Latinos are "taking over" their towns. In some parts of the country, such as major metropolitan areas like New York, Los Angeles, Miami, and Houston, where Latinos have established a considerable presence over time, many of these tensions remain. Racial hostility and conflict has even extended into the political sphere since in many traditional Latino areas, Latinos make up a significant portion of the electorate with Latino political representation at numerous levels.

While Latinos' presence and influence has been felt in different ways, existing approaches have not given us a clear understanding of the conditions under which Latinos and blacks, and Latinos and whites view each other as allies or competitors. We have not reached a conclusive stance on the circumstances in which Latinos and blacks are likely to have affinity or cooperate with each other, when they are likely to believe that they are allies experiencing the same struggles and working toward the same causes, or when they are rivals who pose direct threats to each other in securing greater socioeconomic opportunities and political power. Further, it is not evident under what circumstances whites feel close to Latinos or when they regard them as political and cultural threats. Secondarily, this study seeks to further examine how the addition of Latinos to the black/white racial structure affects each of the three groups' attitudes toward and disposition to cooperate with either or both of the other two groups.

This book argues that there are three major categories of predictors that structure black, white, and Latino racial dispositions: social contact, context, and identification with one's racial/ethnic group or others. The main theory of the book is the Triangular Theory of Contact, Context, and Identification (TTCCI), which argues that unequal levels of power exist across and among African Americans, Latinos, and whites fostering an "us versus them" perspective, yet this mentality is shaped by these groups' social networks, sense of power (established by their social, political, and economic environments), and identification with members of their own group and others. This study overcomes the limitations of extant studies by exploring the effects of these three major determinants with a multitude of measures. I examine institutional context through the ideological climate of a congressional district, the race of its representative, whether or not the congressional district is a majority-minority district (Barone and Cohen 2005; Barone et al. 2009) and whether a state has provisions for direct democracy (State Initiative and Referendum n.d.). I analyze racial context by examining objective context (the percentage of blacks, whites, and Latinos in one's county) as well as subjective context (one's perception of the racial makeup of one's county). A county's unemployment rate, poverty rate, and education level define economic context. Social contact is measured in terms of one's friends, neighbors, and coworkers and the racial makeup of one's social and political organizations.[2] Identification with one's own racial/ethnic group or others is examined through perceptions of closeness and commonality with whites, blacks, and Latinos.

In addressing these goals, I rely on national survey data (2004 National Politics Survey, 2006 Latino National Survey, 2010 Cooperation Congressional Election Study) as well as focus group data to study the degree to which feelings of identification, social contact, and context structure perceptions of closeness, commonality, and competition among the three groups. Focus groups are a research method focused on data collection where a researcher has an active role in fomenting a discussion in a group setting (Morgan 1996). Some of the questions that I analyze in this project include: Does social contact with one group also affect attitudes toward other groups? For instance, does having black friends expand Latinos' sense of commonality with blacks *and* whites? Regarding institutional context, does being represented by a minority legislator decrease blacks' sense of competition with

Latinos and whites? When it comes to economic context, does living in a county with high unemployment and poverty rates and a low education rate expand whites' competition with Latinos and blacks? Does identifying with blacks increase whites' sense of closeness with Latinos? Since variations exist in both the amount of social interaction individuals have with others and the context that surrounds them, their environment structures how individuals perceive themselves and other racial groups. Further, whites', blacks', and Latinos' preconceived notions of other racial/ethnic groups, which in turn affect whether they identify with them or not, influence how they regard other groups regardless of whether they have interacted with them.

An Addition to the Black/White Dynamic of Race Relations in the United States

Before engaging in a full description of this project's main theory, I would like to provide a comprehensive discussion of who Latinos are and what we know about how they compare and relate to African Americans and whites.

Latinos have surpassed African Americans and are now the largest minority group in the United States, comprising 16.6 percent of the population according to the latest census. The top four national origin groups among Latinos are Mexican, Puerto Rican, Salvadoran, and Cuban (Lopez et al. 2013). Some come as political refugees, others as migrants, and many come as immigrants for improved employment and educational prospects for their children. From 2000 to 2010, Latinos comprised more than 50 percent of the nation's population growth (Passel et al. 2011) and by the year 2050, they are projected to make up at least 30 percent of the U.S. population (Passel and Cohn 2008). Consequently, it is not surprising that native-born Latinos account for 9.9 percent of the total U.S. population, and foreign-born Latinos comprise 5.9 percent. Foreign-born Latinos make up 37.4 percent of the total Latino population with 10.9 percent of immigrants holding U.S. citizenship and the rest being noncitizens (26.5%). Latinos also differ in geographic residence. Although they remain heavily concentrated in traditional Latino areas such as California, Texas, New Mexico, and Florida, a substantial number have relocated to nontraditional Latino areas in the South including South Carolina, North Carolina, West Virginia, Louisiana, and Arkansas (Pew Hispanic Center 2011).

Latinos and African Americans

While Latinos may differ from African Americans when it comes to national origin and immigrant status, Latinos are comparable to African Americans in several ways. Both groups have lower education and income levels (average for Latinos is $20,000; average for blacks is $23,000) than their white and Asian American counterparts. When it comes to unemployment, both Latinos (11.2%) and blacks (15%) have substantially higher rates of unemployment than whites and Asians (Kochhar 2012). Further, similar to blacks, some Latinos experience discrimination in their neighborhoods, grocery stores, schools, and other public places. Recent legislation in response to the burgeoning Latino immigrant population has not made a college education accessible to all Latinos. As of the time that this book was written, only seventeen states (California, Colorado, Connecticut, Florida, Texas, Illinois, Kansas, Maryland, Minnesota, Nebraska, New Jersey, New Mexico, New York, Oregon, Oklahoma, Utah, and Washington) allow undocumented immigrants to receive in-state tuition rates, and three states (Arizona, Georgia, and Indiana) completely bar undocumented immigrants from paying in-state tuition rates. South Carolina and Alabama go so far as to exclude undocumented immigrants' entry into state colleges (National Conference of State Legislatures 2014).

With regards to political affinity and influence, Latinos may be closer to African Americans than other racial groups. Recent restrictive immigration legislation (e.g., Arizona's S.B. 1070 law, Alabama's H.B. 56 law) has made it more difficult for undocumented Latinos to search for employment and work, as well as heightened their fears and distrust of law enforcement, possibly augmenting Latinos' identification with and affinity toward other minority groups, including blacks. Given that many Republicans have largely supported this prohibitory legislation, Latinos are identifying less with the Republican Party and expanding their support of the Democratic Party, an organization with substantial ties to the black community (see Barreto 2012). Latino voters actually broke a record in the 2012 presidential election with 75 percent of Latino voters casting their ballots for President Barack Obama (Latino Decisions 2012b). When it comes to political power, Latinos are attractive contenders for political parties and candidates, yet their voter registration and turnout rates are lower than those of whites and largely similar to those of African Americans. Still, Latinos' political participation can be smaller than that of blacks in the United States for two obvious reasons. First, not all Latinos are U.S. citizens and thus not all are eligible to vote. Second, since Latinos' average age is considerably lower than that for whites, blacks, and Asian Americans, they are less likely to be of voting age. This is not surprising based on their significant contribution to the growth of the U.S. population in the last decade.

Given that Latinos' socioeconomic struggles and limited power are largely congruous to blacks, some might expect that the two groups have become minority allies who understand each other and who seek to work together to expand their sociopolitical clout. The last part of the quotation at the beginning of this chapter, "And his family is eager to point out that some relatives are black," alludes to this possible bond and understanding among minorities. George Zimmerman's family wanted to emphasize his minority roots in order to quell his image, as portrayed by some media sources, as a "Jewish" racist who deliberately killed an unarmed African American teenager wearing a hoodie.

Despite Latinos' and African Americans' similar status and struggles, however, being related to a member of a minority group and/or being a member of a minority group does *not* make one less susceptible to adopting negative views toward another minority group. Actually, what often brings blacks and Latinos together can also tear them apart. The fact that Latinos and African Americans generally have lower socioeconomic status and are more likely to seek blue-collar positions than whites and Asian Americans automatically places them as competitors for jobs, government services, and even the national spotlight. Blacks have been the largest minority group in the United States for numerous decades, and now that Latinos have surpassed them in size and socioeconomic prospects in some cities, some blacks may regard Latinos as adversaries who have completely yanked the rug out from under their feet. African Americans' attitudes toward Latinos are often explained by fear of economic displacement due to the possible loss of certain social and economic powers. Blacks who are surrounded by more economically advantaged Latinos are more likely to adopt negative stereotypes of Latinos and view black/Latino interests as incompatible (Gay 2006). Furthermore, blacks who are less established in a society (based on population size) feel the greatest economic threat from a growing Latino population (McClain et al. 2009).

Although some blacks may perceive Latinos as socioeconomic threats, African Americans do not view Latinos and whites similarly. Actually, when comparing blacks' opinions of Latinos with those of whites, Paula D. McClain and Joseph Stewart, Jr. (2002) find that African Americans identify more with Latinos than their white counterparts. A plausible explanation for this is that blacks are cognizant of the disparities in power that exist between whites and minority groups (including Latinos), naturally placing them closer to Latinos than whites.

Latinos and Whites

Besides revealing current interracial tensions, the Trayvon Martin shooting also highlights the extensive diversity that exists within the Latino population. After looking at George Zimmerman's picture, some thought that he was Latino while others were not so certain. This may not come completely as a surprise since Latinos differ considerably in skin tone, such that individuals like Argentines and Cubans can resemble whites (e.g., having fair skin, blonde hair, and blue eyes) much more than Puerto Ricans or Dominicans, who often resemble blacks due to their dark skin tone and phenotype (Bonilla-Silva 2004). The 2010 U.S. Census reveals that 53 percent of Latinos identify as white alone, a number higher than in 2000 when 47.9 percent of Latinos identified as white (Passel et al. 2011). This racial identification may be a result of Latinos' general partiality toward whites over blacks based on negative perceptions of dark skin tone carried from Latin America, or Latinos' general desire to identify with the racial group in the United States that has the most sociopolitical clout (see Johnson et al. 1997). Interestingly, Latino racial attitudes can be explained by their variances in skin tone. Latinos who identify as light-skinned are more likely to sense commonality with whites than dark-skinned Latinos, and dark-skinned Latinos are more prone to feel closer to blacks than their light-skinned counterparts (Wilkinson and Earle 2013).

On the other hand, it is uncertain as to whether whites perceive more commonality with one minority group than another. Since minorities may not pose any major threat to whites' economic and political power, whites as the majority may not relate at all to blacks and Latinos nor even differentiate blacks from Latinos when it comes to perceptions of commonality and competition. Then again, the racial tensions and conflict between blacks and whites in the past several decades may influence whites to harbor greater affinity toward Latinos than African Americans. Marisa A. Abrajano and R. Michael Alvarez (2010) actually find that whites sense slightly greater commonality with Latinos than with blacks. Still, whites have noticed Latinos' burgeoning presence in the United States, and, like blacks, some perceive Latinos as a group that has taken over their country and that poses a considerable socioeconomic and cultural threat resulting in fervent support for restrictive immigration policies.

The Argument

The various contexts, opportunities, and attitudes that whites, blacks, and Latinos have do not seemingly lead us to believe that they are allies or enemies. What is more, the emerging Latino population, with its differences and complex identity, makes for an intricate puzzle of racial dynamics. This situation notwithstanding, race relations among Latinos, blacks, and whites today can best be explained by my Triangular Theory of Contact, Context, and Identification (TTCCI), which asserts that social contact, context (institutional, economic, and racial), and identification with one's racial/ethnic group or others largely determine what whites, blacks, and Latinos think of each other, as measured through perceptions of closeness, commonality, and competition. I argue that while unequal levels of power among whites, blacks, and Latinos create an "us versus them" mentality, this mentality is moderated by social contact with other groups, the level of power that individuals perceive themselves to have based on their environment, and feelings that one identifies with others. Research on interracial attitudes assists in discerning the relationship among social contact, racial context, and perceptions of closeness, commonality, and competition. The social contact hypothesis states that greater social contact with a group augments one's affinity toward the group; the racial threat hypothesis asserts that a growing out-group population (a group not part of one's own racial group) heightens the socioeconomic threat that the in-group (a group from one's own racial group) senses resulting in negative views toward the out-group; and the group position theory posits that as individuals feel that another group is encroaching upon their status, they view others as competitors and adversaries (Bobo and Hutchings 1996; Welch and Sigelman 2000; Rocha and Espino 2008).

As the findings of this book illustrate, variations in social contact, context, and feelings of identification produce considerably divergent results for perceptions of closeness, commonality, and competition among blacks, whites, and Latinos. My findings regarding the effects of social contact on interracial attitudes support the social contact hypothesis as well as bolster the notion that minorities view the world in terms of either siding with whites or with those of minority status (less power). With regards to racial context, I find that the racial threat hypothesis explains Latino and black racial attitudes. In accordance with the group position theory, blacks and Latinos who reside in weak economic and political environments are often less prone to feel close to another minority group and are more likely to regard the other minority group as competitors. Residing in generally threatening economic and political environments does not seem to have comparable effects on whites' racial attitudes. While one might expect that low socioeconomic status would correlate with increased hostility to minorities, the opposite finding is not surprising given whites' greater sociopolitical power. As for the effects of identification, identifying with one racial/ethnic group increases the likelihood that one perceives commonality with another of a different status. For instance, Latinos who identify with blacks sense greater commonality with whites, and African Americans who feel close to Latinos are more likely to perceive commonality with whites. The more whites identify with Latinos/blacks, the more they feel close to blacks/Latinos, respectively.

Additionally, while identifying with one group may improve relations with another, whites, blacks, and Latinos may not consider race when reflecting on whether they perceive commonality with another group.

The normative implications of these findings are threefold. First, I present evidence for the social contact hypothesis *and* the racial threat hypothesis as they relate to black, white, and Latino attitudes: while contact with a particular group heightens individuals' sense of closeness with a group, being surrounded by an outside group intensifies competition with them. Second, I also show that perceiving commonality and competition with a group is *not* mutually exclusive, particularly for minority groups. The more blacks and immigrant Latinos perceive commonality with each other, the greater their sense of competition. Lastly, I offer evidence demonstrating that the three major political players in the United States do not always adopt an "us versus them" mentality toward those who differ in power and status, and certain circumstances trigger this perspective.

Implications of Perceptions of Closeness and Competition

The research presented here is critical to obtaining a complete understanding of the racial attitudes that exist today in a country where racial dynamics vary significantly from the past. When it comes to Latinos, if members of this group perceive as much commonality and competition with blacks as they do with whites, then they may not necessarily differentiate whites from blacks and are likely to view both groups as the insiders or "Americans." If Latinos, however, perceive greater commonality and sense less competition with blacks than whites, they may embrace that they are a minority group with similar struggles as blacks and thus become more predisposed to forming mass political coalitions with blacks. If Latinos feel closer to and perceive less rivalry with whites, then unlike other minorities, they may view whites as the group that they aspire to be like, hence augmenting the likelihood that they favor whites over blacks as coalition partners.

Similarly, African Americans' attitudes toward Latinos compared to their attitudes toward whites can provide profound insight on blacks' racial attitudes and future coalition behavior. If blacks sense more commonality and less competition with Latinos than whites, then African Americans may perceive Latinos as a minority group like them, increasing the likelihood that they join Latinos in advocating for a particular policy and/or endorsing a candidate. Nonetheless, blacks may sense strong closeness *and* competition with Latinos given Latinos' relatively comparable socioeconomic status and search for similar jobs and opportunities as blacks, thus challenging the notion that perceptions of commonality and competition are opposing attitudes. On the other hand, if blacks perceive more commonality and less competition with whites, then blacks may perceive Latinos as outsiders who are infringing on African Americans' "piece of the pie" of opportunity, heightening blacks' preference of whites over Latinos as political coalition partners.

Exploring whites' closeness, commonality, and competition with blacks and Latinos meaningfully augments our understanding of whites' views toward minorities and perceptions of power. If whites sense as much closeness and competition with Latinos as with blacks, then they may not necessarily differentiate one group from another and may perceive both groups as minorities who would not be potentially beneficial as coalition partners. In contrast, if whites perceive greater commonality and less rivalry with African Americans than Latinos, then whites may be predisposed to thinking of blacks as more like themselves and viewing Latinos as "outsiders" who are distinct from them, increasing the possibility that whites favor blacks over Latinos as coalition partners. Conversely, if whites feel closer to Latinos and view them with less hostility than blacks, then whites may favor Latinos over a racial group with which they share an extensive history of racial tensions and conflict. Thus, under these circumstances, whites may form political coalitions with Latinos over blacks.

Examining the effects of identifying with one group on attitudes toward another has strong implications for comprehending the extent to which individuals distinguish the majority (those who have a sizable amount of power) from minorities (those who have substantially less influence). If having a considerable amount in common with Latinos increases the likelihood that blacks perceive commonality with whites, then blacks may not vastly distinguish Latinos from whites and, hence, not take an "us versus them" mentality regarding the majority and a minority group like Latinos. Also, if whites who identify with Latinos sense greater closeness with African Americans, then whites may not greatly differentiate Latinos from blacks and/or not view individuals as members of a group but as individuals who happen to be part of a racial or ethnic group. If Latinos' identification with blacks, however, augments their employment competition with blacks, then being part of a minority group does not automatically result in greater affinity with other minorities and can actually provoke hostilities and tensions with those who share a comparable status.

Policy Implications

Besides helping to uncover the complexity of racial attitudes and account for the social, political, and economic diversity that exists among whites, blacks, and Latinos today, exploring the relationships among social contact, context, and identification with one's group or others are critical for our understanding of how laws and political infrastructures can shape inter-race relations. The relationship between social contact and perceptions of commonality, closeness, and competition has broad implications for the influence of desegregation and zoning laws on race dynamics. In general, if we know that social contact with one group expands one's perceptions of commonality with that group, then we could say that desegregation laws are successful in pacifying racial conflict and improving race relations among various groups. On the other hand, if social contact heightens racial tensions across groups (such as if Latinos' emerging presence in a new immigrant destination and a traditional Latino area poses a demographic and economic threat to whites and blacks, particularly) then increased desegregation may depress the prospects of peaceful race relations among blacks, whites, and Latinos. Additionally, my findings regarding the effects of economic context on racial attitudes have implications on the importance of policies that foster economic growth. If I find that individuals who feel economically threatened are more likely to regard another group with antagonism, then enactment of policies that promote job growth and increase the minimum wage and funding for public schools have the potential to encourage interracial alliances.

Exploring the effect of political context on interracial attitudes also illustrates how individuals respond to changes in power. If a minority group resides in a predominantly minority district (of their own race or ethnicity) that is predominantly liberal in ideology and represented by a minority legislator, then that group may feel substantially powerful and thus may not perceive other racial groups as a threat to their sociopolitical power. If a minority group, however, does not have a significant amount of social or political clout (i.e., not descriptively represented, residing in a majority-minority district, and in a largely Democratic district), then they may be less likely to form coalitions with other groups. Then again, whites who are represented by a minority legislator and who live in a majority-minority district that is predominantly liberal in ideology may feel threatened socially, politically diminishing their desire to form alliances with other minority groups. My analyses also shed light on the extent to which Latinos, blacks, and whites may form coalitions with others to elect minority officials into office, a growing phenomenon. While it may not be surprising that whites, blacks, and Latinos join others to elect candidates of their same race or ethnicity, it may not be as evident whether these groups can come together to elect minority candidates. Given blacks' and Latinos' marginal political clout, they may not regard voting for a minority candidate of a divergent race or ethnicity in the same way as voting for a candidate of their same background. Latinos may be more willing to seek and vote for Latino representatives than blacks, and blacks may be more inclined to promote support for and vote for African American representatives than Latinos (Kaufmann 2007). Further, blacks and Latinos who are represented by a minority candidate of a divergent race may be more likely to regard the other minority group as a threat. Thus, my analyses examining the relationship between political context and racial attitudes shed light on the implications the makeup of a congressional district and the race of a political candidate have on future race relations.

Organization of the Book

In chapter 1, I present the particular framework of my central arguments. After emphasizing the disparities in context, attitudes, and opportunities among whites, blacks, and Latinos, I provide an in-depth explanation of and motivations behind the Triangular Theory of Contact, Context, and Identification. The testable predictions from my theory as they specifically relate to Latinos, African Americans, and whites are also presented in this chapter.

Chapter 2 begins by discussing Latinos' current sociopolitical presence and clout, and the disparities that exist among Latinos. Using the 2006 Latino National Survey (LNS) (Fraga et al. 2006) and the 2010 Cooperative Congressional Election Study (CCES) (Ansolabehere 2010), I take advantage of the most recent and comprehensive data sets available to assess the intricacies of Latinos' perceptions of commonality and competition with blacks and whites. The 2006 LNS is a unique data set with a sample of 8,636 Latinos of various national origins and geographical locations. While the 2010 CCES does not have as vast a sample of Latinos as the LNS, this data set extends beyond the LNS and examines perceptions of competition with whites and the number of individuals that Latinos perceive to be residing in their county. Using these data, I examine the effects of social contact, context, and identification with other Latinos and other groups on foreign-born and native-born Latinos' perceptions of commonality and competition with blacks and whites. To assess economic and racial context, I rely on data individually collected from U.S. Census estimates for the years 2006, 2007, 2008, and 2006–10. To examine the effect of institutional context, I use data collected from U.S. state congressional districts in 2006 and 2010.

Chapter 3 takes a qualitative approach to exploring Latinos' racial attitudes with a focus on Latinos' social networks and sense of closeness and rivalry with whites and blacks in a new Latino destination, the New Orleans metro area.[3] I begin with a discussion of intergroup relations in the South and why New Orleans is an appropriate setting to explore Latino/black and Latino/white race relations in this region of the United States. I then analyze emerging themes from focus group discussions with Latino residents placing an emphasis on how these results increase our understanding of intergroup relations and can better explain some perplexing findings from the previous chapter.

Chapter 4 details African Americans' perceptions of closeness and competition with Latinos in comparison to their attitudes toward whites. It begins by describing the possibility of the formation of a rainbow coalition where Latinos and blacks form political partnerships out of necessity due to little sociopolitical power and generally parallel struggles and experiences. The chapter examines blacks' sense of closeness and rivalry with Latinos, whites, and other African Americans. The second part of the chapter tests the TTCCI on African Americans' sense of closeness and competition with Latinos and whites. I rely on the 2004 National Politics Survey (NPS) (Jackson et al. 2004) and the 2010 CCES to test my main theory. Both national surveys have a significantly large sample of African Americans, and the 2004 NPS particularly covers an extensive number of questions that engage poignant topics central to racial attitudes and race relations in the United States. To assess economic and racial context, I rely on data collected from U.S. Census estimates for the years 2000, 2004, 2007, and 2008. I examine U.S. state congressional district data from 2004 and 2010 to gauge the effects of institutional context.

In addition to relying on national survey data to test my TTCCI on blacks' racial attitudes, I dedicate chapter 5 to analyzing African Americans' attitudes toward whites and Latinos using focus group data of black residents in New Orleans. I begin with a brief discussion of the history of blacks in New Orleans and then analyze emerging themes from focus group discussions regarding social networks, perceptions of commonality and competition, and the relationship between social interaction and racial dispositions. I center the discussion of my focus group results on gaining a deeper understanding of black/Latino and black/white relations and addressing a few unanswered questions from my previous chapter's quantitative analyses.

Chapter 6 discusses whites' attitudes toward Latinos and African Americans. It begins detailing whites' responses to the growing immigrant population from Latin America and the disparities in clout and experiences that exist among whites. Using the 2004 NPS and the 2010 CCES, I survey in this chapter the majority group's perceptions of closeness and competition with Latinos and blacks as well as their perceptions of these minority groups compared to their perceptions of other whites. Afterward, in order to attain a broad comprehension of whites' racial dispositions, I test the TTCCI on whites' sense of closeness and competition with Latinos and African Americans. As in chapter 4, I rely on U.S. Census estimates for the years 2004, 2007, and 2008 to assess economic and racial context, and I use state congressional district data from 2004 and 2010 to measure institutional context.

Chapter 7 takes a qualitative approach to studying whites' dispositions toward blacks and Latinos in the South. I begin with a brief discussion of whites' responses to the recent influx of Latinos in New Orleans and then examine emerging focus group themes centered on whites' social networks and their sense of commonality and competition with Latinos and African Americans. The purpose of this chapter is to explore white racial attitudes in an emerging Latino area while further delving into any perplexing quantitative results from chapter 6.

The conclusion summarizes the major findings of the research and emphasizes the theoretical and empirical contributions to extant research on racial attitudes and racial dynamics among whites, blacks, and Latinos. In this section, I also discuss various policy implications. It ends with a discussion of the current state of racial alliances using 2012 Latino Decisions poll data.

1

A Triangular Theory of Contact, Context, and Identification

A recent Pew Research Center study finds that Millennials (individuals who are part of a generation born after 1977) are more supportive of interracial dating than the generations who came before them (Taylor 2010). Further, the number of interracial marriages has more than doubled since 1980, from 6.7 percent to approximately 15 percent in 2010 (Wang 2012). These findings provide some hope for improved inter-race relations in the future. Nonetheless, some individuals' responses to a recent Cheerios cereal commercial of a biracial family reveals that multiracial relations may not be improving as fast as some may think. The commercial features a biracial daughter asking her white mom about Cheerios's health benefits, and once she is told that Cheerios is good for the heart, she dumps a batch of Cheerios on her black father's chest while he is resting on the couch (Stump 2013). While some have applauded Cheerios for its efforts to illustrate that it is inclusive and up to date on the demographic changes in this country, others' responses were quite negative and toxic. Some found the commercial "disgusting," even stating that it makes them "want to vomit." A few negative comments referenced racial genocide and Nazis. Other commentators even mentioned that they were shocked to see that a black man stayed with his family (Goyette 2013).

Although these are individuals' responses to a commercial, the previous example reveals that racial discrimination persists and that disparities in attitudes toward race exist across the country. In this project, I attempt to examine black, Latino, and white attitudes toward each other with my Triangular Theory of Contact, Context, and Identification (TTCCI). The theory is "triangular" in that it seeks to explain not one but three groups' racial attitudes. The crux of my argument is that power disparities exist among black, white, and Latino groups, triggering an "us versus them" mindset among all groups, *yet* this outlook is moderated by their social networks; level of clout as determined by their racial, political, and economic environments; and their attitudes toward others. In this chapter, I provide an in-depth explanation of my TTCCI as well as the predictions that emerge from it for whites, blacks, and

Latinos. The chapter begins with a discussion of how this study compares and contrasts from Claire Jean Kim's (2000) discussion of racial order and power. Next, I provide a thorough analysis of differences that exist within groups of whites, African Americans, and Latinos, highlighting how racial, economic, and institutional contexts shape their levels of power. Finally, I explore key factors that influence perceptions of closeness, commonality, and competition, and provide predictions for their effects on these racial attitudes individually for Latinos, blacks, and whites.

Racial Power and Order

In her book titled *Bitter Fruit*, Kim (2000) argues that a triangulated racial order is the result of white dominance, what she coins racial power, leading to conflict between African Americans and Koreans. She states that "racial power operates not only by reproducing racial categories and meanings per se but by reproducing them in the form of a distinct racial order" (10). That is, racial power generates conflict among minority groups by producing a racial order that contrasts one group with another, making conflict between the two groups with limited social, political, and economic influence, such as Koreans and blacks, highly probable. Kim presents a triangulated racial order with an axis of superiority/inferiority where whites are superior to blacks, the extreme underclass, and Asians are triangulated between blacks and whites. Asian Americans are more favorable and powerful than blacks by being self-sufficient and motivated, less dominant than whites since they are often ostracized, and more distinct than both racial groups due to their immigrant ties.

The author of *Bitter Fruit* provides a compelling and important argument illustrating race relations and racial conflict in the United States today. It is undeniable that each group's position is considerably defined relative to other groups. Whites outpace other racial and ethnic groups in terms of economic, political, and social clout, and blacks have been and continue to be one of the least influential groups. African Americans are segregated in politically powerless settings with scant resources and opportunity for upward mobility. Individuals constantly compare themselves to whites, and many seek the same amount of power and opportunities that whites have. For some, this desire can result in pursuing relationships and political alliances with whites, obtaining employment positions that are predominantly occupied by whites, and desiring to have a lighter skin tone, regrettably even going so far as to bleach one's skin. Many minority groups, particularly Latinos and blacks, perceive that the amount of power and opportunity in the

United States is limited. Whites have the most power, and others have to fight for what remains (Gay 2006). Therefore, it is inevitable that minority groups constantly draw parallels between themselves and others in order to get a sense of where they stand relative to other groups. Kim is also accurate in asserting that Koreans (and I would say Latinos and many other immigrant groups) are perceived as outsider groups and generally superior to blacks by our society, particularly by the news media and our political and social institutions today. Additionally, African Americans differ from other racial groups based on the existing parameters enforced due to continuing experiences with discrimination and oppression.

Although I concur with Kim on several assertions regarding racial power and racial order, the general race dynamics and relations that exist in the United States today are not as simple as she describes. While racial power is not congruent across the United States, and racial order does account for racial conflict between groups, I argue that variances in social, contextual, and attitudinal factors considerably structure how whites, blacks, and Latinos perceive themselves and others as mentioned in the introduction of this book.

Variances among Whites, Blacks, and Latinos

Racial, economic, and institutional contexts generate differences in power among racial groups. Whites have significant dominion in the United States, yet, like many other groups, vast differences exist within the white population. For instance, whites in the South have considerably higher levels of poverty and lower median incomes, and are less likely to have health insurance than whites in other regions. Besides differences in region and socioeconomic influence, whites differ in political clout. More whites today than ever before are represented by minority legislators and live in majority-minority districts. While this environment may simply influence whites to believe that their political influence is diminishing, whites' political clout may indeed decrease in this context. Moreover, the Great Recession has greatly depressed the socioeconomic status, employment opportunities, and general prospects for upward mobility for numerous white households across the country in the past few years (DeNavas-Walt et al. 2011).

There are also several discrepancies in power across the African American population, and context is a critical determinant of these variances. While racial segregation persists and incarceration rates continue to be high, the poverty rate among African Americans is declining, and a substantial number of blacks throughout the country have joined the middle class in the last few decades (Dawson 1994; Tate 2010). The political opportunities for African Americans have also increased (e.g., the growing number of black legislators in the House of Representatives becoming almost proportional to the U.S. black population, and the election and reelection of the first African American president), thus expanding blacks' political influence and power (Tate 2010). Then again, a considerable number of blacks, like other minority groups in the United States, have less than a high school level of education, are unemployed, and are not registered to vote in U.S. elections. Blacks in numerous southern cities have been economically disadvantaged in relationship to an emergent Latino population in their places of work and neighborhoods, resulting in a decline in employment opportunities and a rise in racial tensions (McClain et al. 2007; McClain et al. 2009).

While Latinos are the largest minority group and are quickly gaining more attention and clout than blacks in numerous settings, not all Latinos have the same amount of influence and opportunities. Context significantly explains these variances. Latinos in some states such as New Mexico, California, and Florida are attaining more political clout due to a growth in the number of Latino legislators in the last few decades (Casellas 2011). Yet, in nontraditional Latino areas such as the Midwest and South, where employment opportunities for Latinos have surged, Latinos' emerging presence has resulted in greater conflict and discrimination from whites and African Americans (Marrow 2011). Furthermore, recent restrictive immigration legislation passed in Alabama and Arizona has spurred substantial fear and anxiety among Latino residents resulting in vast seclusion and distrust of local law enforcement (Gomez 2012; Planas 2012). Latinos who reside in predominantly Latino counties such as Los Angeles and Miami-Dade have attained far greater social and political power than those who reside in less "Latino-friendly" areas such as rural regions in the Midwest and South (see Marrow 2011).

Triangular Theory of Contact, Context, and Identification

In this book, I recognize the disparate influences of blacks, whites, and Latinos, and contend that various factors shape the experiences and clout of these individuals. Racial, economic, and institutional contexts temper individuals' levels of power, subsequently influencing interracial attitudes and race relations (Segura and Bowler 2005; Telles et al. 2011). Furthermore, social context in the form of formal and informal social networks (Segura and Bowler 2005) and feelings of identification with one's own group or others shape the attitudes and behavior of these groups. In the next few paragraphs, I provide a thorough explanation of these determinants.

The Role of Social Contact

Social contact can be defined in terms of the social networks that individuals have such as their friends, neighbors, coworkers, and those whom surround them in social, civic, and political organizations. The social contact hypothesis has been tested extensively to gauge the effect that social networks have on racial attitudes. It asserts that direct contact with a group increases the likelihood that individuals perceive the group in a positive way and decreases the hostility that exists between members of the two groups (Ellison and Powers 1994; Welch and Sigelman 2000; Rocha and Espino 2008). While Gregory W. Allport (1954) stated that the necessary conditions for the positive effects of contact to occur are direct equal-status contact, cooperation, and opportunities for socializing, several studies (Sigelman and Welch 1993; Pettigrew 1998; Welch et al. 2001; Oliver and Wong 2003) suggest that all of these conditions do not need to be met in order for contact to counteract negative attitudes. Lee Sigelman and Susan Welch (1993) contend that the primary psychological mechanism that mediates the relationship between interracial contact and positive racial attitudes is availability of information about another racial group. They state that "whites' perceptions and expressions of racial hostility should be materially affected by personal contact with blacks, because such contact is a key source of positive information about blacks; in the absence of this source, whites must fall back on other information sources . . . which are more likely to be negative" (783). Sigelman and Welch also argue that availability of information is the mechanism that facilitates the effect of social contact, particularly friendship, on blacks' hostility toward whites. They claim that "interracial friendship may deter racial stereotyping by providing blacks with counterexamples to the stereotype of whites as prejudiced and hostile" (783). J. Eric Oliver and Janelle Wong (2003) declare that even casual exposure to out-groups can decrease the in-group's racial resentment and competition.

The social contact hypothesis has been tested extensively in the literature on racial attitudes to increase our understanding of complex race relations among blacks, whites, and Latinos. In particular, it has been significantly analyzed with perceptions of commonality and competition. With regard to Latino attitudes toward whites and blacks, there is some support for the social contact hypothesis. Tatishe M. Nteta and Kevin Wallsten (2007) and Michael Jones-Correa (2011) find that contact with blacks/whites heightens Latinos' sense of commonality with blacks/whites, respectively. The social contact hypothesis also explains other racial group's perceptions of commonality and competition. Oliver and Wong (2003) suggest that interethnic closeness in neighborhood contexts decreases intergroup resentment and competition. Still, support for the social contact hypothesis has not remained consistent. Jones-Correa (2011) and Jason L. Morin and colleagues (2011) find that greater social interaction with blacks in the workplace heightens Latinos' sense of competition with blacks. Morin and his coauthors explain this finding by stating that it is only natural for individuals to regard those with whom they work as competitors (109). Hence, social interaction can have a positive effect on white, black, and Latino racial attitudes, but this does not happen under all circumstances.

In this project, I argue that prevailing research provides too narrow an approach to testing the social contact hypothesis. To obtain a contemporary, comprehensive understanding of its relevance today, we must test it on multiple groups and the broader contexts in which contact occurs. One way that I address gaps in the racial attitudes literature is by testing the social contact hypothesis with Latino, African American, and white perceptions of closeness, commonality, and competition, thereby improving our knowledge of the precursors of coalition formation.[1] With the growing minority population in urban areas and the rising migration of Latinos to nontraditional immigrant areas including the South and rural locations, more individuals throughout the United States have opportunities to be in contact with minorities. Hence, this study takes into account these increasing opportunities and provides a more in-depth understanding of racial dynamics and attitudes among several racial and ethnic groups that only recently have emerged. The findings of this project also have strong implications for explaining future race relations. A second contribution of this study is that it tests the social contact hypothesis with various forms of social contact: friends, neighbors, coworkers, and participants in social or civic groups. Social networks develop not only in neighborhoods or through friendships, and I take this into account. Third, this study explores the interactive effect of social contact by examining how social contact with one group influences attitudes toward another. Analyzing the effects of social contact on one group's views toward another does not give us a sense of the relations and, consequently, cannot give us a real idea of the viable options for the formation of alliances. Now more than ever, race relations are complex, and our interactions with one racial/ethnic group can significantly affect our perceptions of others.

I hypothesize that social contact structures white, black, and Latino racial attitudes in the following ways. First, the social contact hypothesis explains white, black, and Latino perceptions of closeness, commonality, and competition with others: the more social contact one has with members of a distinct racial or ethnic group, the more positive his or her views are toward them. Second, I contend that the relationship between social contact and racial attitudes is mediated by an individual's sociopolitical clout, and social contact with one group has divisive effects on their views toward another (see Wilkinson 2009). Given the significant disparities in sociopolitical struggles and clout between whites and minorities, blacks and Latinos are influenced to feel that they have to either side with whites (the majority) or with other minorities. Social interaction with a certain racial/ethnic group structures this feeling. For instance, while blacks' and Latinos' greater social contact with other minorities decreases their perceptions of closeness yet heightens their sense of rivalry with whites, social interaction with whites depresses blacks' and Latinos' identification and competition with other minorities. Since whites' sociopolitical position is more established and generally higher than those of minorities, increased social interaction with other whites depresses whites' predisposition to both identify with minorities *and* sense competition with them.

The Role of Racial Context

Context and contact theories are intertwined and have similar elements, yet the processes associated with them are not the same. The social contact hypothesis relates to the direct interaction and physical proximity with a particular racial group or members of that group. On the other hand, context involves more diverse forms of connection with a group or immigrant culture. It can include (1) the ethnic composition of one's community or even individuals' perceptions of who lives in his or her county; (2) the headlines of local news stories revealing the political culture of a particular city or town; or (3) political climate and the various economic and political resources and opportunities that county residents have to move up the socioeconomic ladder swiftly. In this project, I explore racial, economic, and institutional contexts.

With regard to racial context, a key theory in the contextual effects literature is the racial threat hypothesis (also known as the power threat hypothesis), which suggests that members of the majority may perceive a threat by the aggregation of minority members in their home contexts. As the size of the minority population increases, the perception of socioeconomic threat by members of the majority also increases, resulting in greater negative perceptions of the minority population (Rocha and Espino 2008, 1). The racial threat hypothesis can be seen as a counter to the social contact hypothesis insofar as the racial threat hypothesis suggests that contact has a negative effect on racial attitudes. Yet, it is critical to recognize that unlike the social contact hypothesis, the racial threat hypothesis does not explicitly discuss the effects of racial contact. This theory was designed to provide an explanation as to how whites respond when the black population expands and they become threatened and concerned about losing political, economic, and social power. Thus the causal mechanisms for these two theories are distinct. For the social contact hypothesis, the causal instrument is contact between members of the in-group and those of the out-group. For the racial threat hypothesis, the causal mechanism is the perceptions of in-group members that they are losing majority status—and therefore social, economic, and political power—to the out-group.

In the racial attitudes literature that assesses perceptions of commonality and competition, support for the racial threat hypothesis is mixed. John Mollenkopf (1997) examines the determinants of the formation of biracial coalitions in the city of New York and concludes that a growing Dominican population results in competition and severe tensions between Puerto Ricans and Dominicans, and African Americans and Dominicans. These tensions have even caused some Puerto Ricans and blacks to support banning Dominicans from voting in New York City elections. Similar to the tensions and competition in New York, the city of Miami has experienced tensions among Cubans, whites, and African Americans due to the rising Cuban population (Warren 1997). Nevertheless, in a study on Latinos' perceptions of commonality and competition with whites and blacks, Jones-Correa (2011) finds conflicting support for the racial threat theory: the greater the number of African Americans who are in Latinos' census tract, the more predisposed Latinos are to sensing economic commonality with blacks. Moreover, Jones-Correa does not find that Latinos' racial surroundings structure their sense of competition with blacks and whites.

While the literature on the effects of racial context on perceptions of commonality and competition is limited, there are several implications for the findings above. Although being surrounded by an out-group can heighten whites' sense of threat and negative perceptions of Latinos, an emerging Latino population does not automatically generate into negative views toward Latinos since various factors (e.g., Latinos' nativity, social contact, and positive views toward Latinos) affect whites' views toward immigration and Latinos. Further, the racial threat hypothesis can explain not only white racial attitudes but black and Latino dispositions as well. Not only can status disparities (between whites and blacks as originally described by the power threat hypothesis) but status similarities can be a basis for conflict (McClain and Karnig 1990; Bobo and Hutchings 1996). Additionally, the power struggles described by the racial threat hypothesis can also illustrate how racial and ethnic groups respond to those within their own group. A growing Latino national origin group can influence other Latinos of diverse origins to respond negatively toward the new Latino group. Hence, individuals, regardless of status and—for Latinos—national origin, respond negatively to an emerging group because they sense that the new group threatens their status.

Although extant research consistently analyzes the relationship between racial context and interracial attitudes, it does not lack shortcomings. First, we know relatively little about the extent to which a growing Latino population shapes whites' and blacks' perceptions of competition *and* closeness with the largest immigrant group in the United States. Will a heavily Latino area lead whites to feel that Latinos are threatening their status and power, subsequently depressing their sense of closeness and heightening their competition with Latinos? Does being surrounded by Latinos deepen blacks' regard for Latinos as aggressors of their territory and status, therefore diminishing blacks' perceptions of closeness and augmenting their sense of competition with Latinos? A second limitation of previous research is that we know relatively little about the interactive effects of racial context on interracial attitudes. To what extent does being surrounded by one racial group structure one's own attitudes toward another?

This project addresses these gaps and shortcomings by testing the racial threat hypothesis through racial context as measured by percentage of Latino, black, and white residents in one's county. Although some may argue that analyzing racial context at the county level has several weaknesses, Regina P. Branton and Bradford Jones (2005) posit that exploring racial dynamics at the county level has solid practical and theoretical reasons. Individuals' social environment is not confined within their zip code or neighborhood and can very well branch out to the county level. Individuals regularly branch out for social and employment reasons on a daily basis. In addition, county governments are often in control of delivering resources and overseeing programs that considerably affect residents, including policies associated with race (361–62). Through these measures of racial context, I take a broad approach to testing the racial threat hypothesis since in one project, I assess the effects of racial context on white, Latino, and black perceptions of closeness, commonality, and competition. In line with the racial threat theory, I posit that the greater the number of racially/ethnically diverse residents individuals have in their county, the more predisposed they are to perceive these residents as a sociopolitical threat. These perceptions of threat, however, are moderated by position and influence. For instance, when Latinos reside in a predominantly white county, they are more prone to view whites favorably due to whites' considerable status and clout. When blacks are surrounded by Latinos, they are less likely to perceive closeness with them and more likely to regard them as a threat.

Another way that this study develops our comprehension of the relationship between racial context and racial dispositions is by exploring the interactive effects of racial context. For Latinos, I examine the effects of being surrounded by whites on their dispositions toward African Americans. I argue that the causal mechanism presented by the racial threat hypothesis is moderated by perceptions of power established by racial context. When Latinos are in a predominantly white environment, they are less prone to perceive closeness and competition with blacks since they are surrounded by those of a generally higher status and, thus, less likely to identify with those of lower socioeconomic clout. Yet when whites are surrounded by other whites in their county, they are less inclined to perceive Latinos negatively since they do not feel threatened by Latinos.

The Role of Economic Context

Context plays a critical, multifaceted role in shaping a variety of racial attitudes. Besides exploring the relationship between racial context and perceptions of closeness, commonality, and competition, I analyze the effects of economic context on African American, Latino, and white perspectives. A prevailing theory heavily tested in the immigration attitudes and racial politics literature is the economic self-interest theory, which asserts that individuals who are negatively affected (such as through wages, household income, employment opportunities, etc.) or sense that they are being adversely affected by immigration and/or immigrant groups adopt more stringent attitudes toward immigration and less affinity toward immigrant groups (Fetzer 2000; McClain et al. 2009).

Although research on economic self-interest and perceptions of closeness and competition is scant, economic context has been considerably discussed as to African Americans' and whites' perspectives on immigration and immigrants. James H. Johnson, Jr., and colleagues (1997) examine race relations in Los Angeles and find that blacks' limited power and considerable struggles influence them to feel threatened economically and politically by Asians and Latinos. Additionally, the scholars find that a significant number of blacks in Los Angeles sense that they would experience a loss in economic and political power if immigration continues at its current rate, and they would be at an employment disadvantage if Asians and Latinos were to have access to better jobs (1061–62). In a later study using survey data from Durham,

North Carolina, Paula D. McClain and colleagues (2007) conclude that blacks who think that Latinos place them at an employment disadvantage are more concerned about the rapid growth of the Latino population. Besides perceptions of economic and social displacement, a more specific measure of economic self-interest—income level—shapes black views toward Latinos. These scholars find that African Americans with lower income levels perceive greater competition with Latinos than those with higher incomes.

In addition to blacks' incomes, perceived employment, and social displacement, Latinos' socioeconomic status and population growth structure African Americans' views toward Latinos. Relying on survey data from the city of Los Angeles, Claudine Gay (2006) finds that as Latinos' wealth and education increase, blacks' prejudice against Latinos heightens. A growing Latino population in one's surroundings also accounts for blacks' prejudice toward Latinos. An explanation for this finding is that "the size of the Latino population affects black attitudes primarily by amplifying African Americans' sensitivity to the economic disparities between the groups" (990).

Nonetheless, support for economic self-interest as a robust predictor of blacks' views of Latino immigrants is not consistent. Michael C. Thornton and Yuko Mizuno (1999) find that economic factors are uncertain predictors of blacks' attitudes toward Latinos. Alluding to the rainbow coalition theory, they speculate that Latinos' and blacks' comparable socioeconomic struggles and limited power lead blacks to view whites as their true economic, social, and political competitors (38). This assertion is supported by Vincent L. Hutchings and colleagues (2011). Thomas J. Espenshade and Katherine Hempstead (1996) also present a comparable explanation regarding blacks' attitudes toward Latinos by declaring that African Americans are more predisposed to expressing pro-immigration views than non-Hispanic whites. They speculate that blacks' generally favorable attitudes are due to their low concern regarding employment competition and high affinity toward Latinos because of shared socioeconomic status (548–49).

On the other hand, economic self-interest is a critical predictor of white racial attitudes. J. Eric Oliver and Tali Mendelberg (2000) find that socioeconomic contexts, particularly an area's education level, significantly influence whites' perceptions of threat. When economic disparities between whites and minorities are high, whites are likely to respond negatively to an emergent minority population. Branton and Jones (2005) argue that the influence of racial context on white attitudes toward racial policies is conditioned by the socioeconomic context of the environment. They conclude that whites who reside in a county that is racially diverse and highly educated are more likely to adopt positive views toward minorities and support liberal policies in comparison to whites who reside in lower educated, racially diverse counties.

There are several strengths associated with the prevailing literature on economic context. Economic environment is measured not only at the individual level, through the assessment of blacks' and whites' socioeconomic status, but also in social and economic settings such as county education level. Another significant contribution of current research is the examination of another group's level of wealth and education (such as that of Latinos in studies of black attitudes) to explore individuals' animosity toward that group. By examining another racial/ethnic group's socioeconomic opportunities and status, we are able to gauge the extent to which other individuals' positions heighten a group's level of social and economic threat, better understand the racial dynamics between the two groups, and broaden our understanding of the group position theory.

Although the prevailing literature on economic self-interest and context develops our understanding of racial dynamics and attitudes, it has several weaknesses. Current research provides too narrow an approach to testing the economic self-interest theory. While economic self-interest is significantly discussed in the immigration attitudes literature, we know very little about the relationship between economic context and perceptions of commonality and competition among whites, blacks, and Latinos. Further, recent studies significantly focus on the effect of economic self-interest on African American attitudes toward Latinos, greatly ignoring the extent that economic context moderates whites' and Latinos' sense of closeness and competition with each other. Hence, how do we reconcile black and white attitudes toward the largest minority group, Latinos, as they establish themselves in white and black areas and begin to compete for social, political, and economic influence?

This project addresses these significant shortcomings and distinguishes itself from current research in several ways. First, it takes a comprehensive perspective to testing the economic self-interest hypothesis since in one project, I assess the effects of economic context on white, black, and Latino perceptions of closeness, commonality, and competition. Second, given these racial/ethnic groups' diverse positions and experiences, this project takes a broader, more contemporary approach to understanding racial dynamics today. I measure economic context by examining county level education levels and poverty and unemployment rates from 2000, 2004, 2007, 2008, and 2006–10. Our knowledge of black/Latino and white/Latino relations at the national level has greatly relied on national survey data from ten to thirty years ago, when blacks' and Latinos' clout and opportunities were not as significant as they are today. Thus, this study provides a more accurate representation of the extent that economic threat explains current interracial dynamics.

Third, this study contributes to our understanding of Herbert Blumer's (1958) group position model, including the significant extensions of this theory introduced by Lawrence Bobo and Vincent Hutchings (1996). Blumer attempted to explain whites' (the in-group) attitudes toward African Americans (the out-group) by asserting that as whites feel that blacks are encroaching on their status and level of power (based on context), they begin to view blacks as competitors and adversaries. A central component of Blumer's theory is whites' subjective idea of where they "ought" to stand in relation to African Americans. As Bobo and Hutchings describe, "feelings of competition and hostility emerge from historically and collectively developed judgments about the positions in the social order that in-group members should rightfully occupy relative to members of an out-group" (1996, 955). Meanwhile, Bobo and Hutchings extend Blumer's group position model to explain minorities' attitudes and posit that individuals who regard their group as oppressed and disenfranchised within society, as established by their environment, are more likely to perceive out-group members as competitors (957). In this study, I build on Blumer's and Bobo and Hutchings's theories and contend that when individuals (Latinos, blacks, and whites) are in a setting with limited economic power, their understanding of where they should stand relative to others is triggered, resulting in negative views toward the other group. The effects of the economic measures allow me to gauge under which circumstances whites begin to perceive Latinos and African Americans as encroaching on their status and under what conditions minorities feel racially alienated and no longer perceive each other and whites as allies but as competitors.

The Role of Institutional Context

Although often ignored, institutional context is another form of context that can significantly structure race relations and racial attitudes. Kevin Wallsten and Tatishe M. Nteta (2011) assert that a limitation of current research on the precursors of coalition formation is its extensive focus on individual-level explanations. They call for interracial attitudes research to "bring politics back in" to understand intergroup relations (22). Political behavior and attitudes should not be examined separately from the contexts in which they form. Thus, like racial and economic context, it is critical to comprehend how the overall political environment that surrounds individuals shapes their perceptions of their sociopolitical status in society and, thus, their attitudes toward others who compare or contrast in that power.

While the number of studies examining political context and racial attitudes is scant, we have some knowledge about the effect of institutional context on race relations in the United States. Kenneth R. Mladenka (1989) finds that greater Latino and black representation in city councils promotes more and better jobs for blacks and Latinos, possibly resulting in depressed competition between the two groups. On the other hand, McClain and Albert K. Karnig (1990) assert that political competition may emerge between Latinos and African Americans when there is a small number of white residents in majority-minority cities and when blacks or Latinos succeed politically.

Moreover, there are specific measures of institutional context that structure political attitudes. Ballot initiatives are a dimension of institutional context that only recently have been studied. There is a debate as to whether ballot initiatives increase whites' and not minorities' political power and efficacy. While some claim that referenda capture white voters' discriminatory beliefs and fears, thus alienating minority voters, others declare that ballot initiatives and political referenda actually augment minorities' political knowledge and participation in the long run. Rodney E. Hero and Caroline J. Tolbert (2004) address the issues in this debate and find that individuals, regardless of race, who live in states with frequent use of direct democracy provisions are more likely to perceive that government is responsive to their needs. Still, they do find that in comparison to whites and Latinos, African Americans and Asian Americans are less confident that government is receptive to their necessities. Besides ballot initiatives, descriptive representation (i.e., being served by a legislator who shares similar demographic attributes as one), often correlated with the presence of majority-minority districts, also shapes attitudes about government. Susan A. Banducci and colleagues (2005) find that being represented by a black legislator heightens voter turnout and improves African Americans' views toward government responsiveness. In particular, the effects of descriptive representation are most pronounced among less-educated blacks, whereas the effect of being represented by a black legislator on perceptions of government responsiveness declines as blacks' education levels rise.

Research on institutional context has considerably focused on its effect on political behavior and attitudes, like voter turnout and government responsiveness. While analyzing these relationships is important, institutional context may have other effects that warrant consideration in a political arena where minorities are steadily gaining political power and racial tensions are prominent. Given minorities', particularly blacks' and Latinos', growing presence in seats of Congress, at voting booths, and in marches and protests, racial tensions between whites and minorities are developing in the political arena. Whites no longer completely dominate political institutions and agencies, giving way for power shifts and animosity between whites and minorities that may not be easily understood. Moreover, though Latinos and blacks are gaining political clout, they are considerably less powerful than whites. Not only do many minority legislators have less political influence and fewer resources than their white counterparts, white voters significantly surpass minorities in influence. Furthermore, racially polarized bloc voting occurs frequently, and majority-minority districts may actually impede minorities' political sway (Segura and Bowler 2005). These narrow opportunities and barriers can essentially heighten political competition between blacks and Latinos, resulting in substantial hostilities between these two groups.

Therefore, in this project, I attempt to better comprehend the power dynamics that exist among the three main political players in politics, as well as the implications that these dynamics have on race relations, by examining the effect of institutional context (as measured by residing in a majority-minority district, the ideological climate of a congressional district, the race of the representative, and opportunities for direct democracy) on perceptions of commonality and competition among whites, blacks, and Latinos. Another main contribution of this study is that I rely on Blumer's (1958) group position model and Bobo and Hutchings's (1996) modification of the group position model to analyze the relationship between institutional context and white, black, and Latino racial dispositions. I posit that those who perceive declining shifts in their group's (whether it be African Americans', Latinos', or whites') political clout are more aware of where they ought to stand relative to others, resulting in antagonistic views toward others. My measures of institutional context permit me to explore the circumstances in which whites begin to perceive Latinos and African Americans as encroaching on their status, and the conditions wherein minorities feel racially alienated and no longer perceive each other and whites as allies but as competitors. I theorize that when whites feel that they have significant political clout, they are less likely to relate to minorities and regard them as rivals. When Latinos and blacks perceive that they have substantial political power, they are less likely to identify and sense competition with other minorities and sense less closeness but *more* competition with whites.[2] With emerging influence, minorities sense that they are less close to whites (who surpass blacks and Latinos in socioeconomic and political clout) yet also perceive whites as a threat to their emerging political power.

Besides analyzing the power dynamics of the three main political players and relying on the group position theory to explain the effects of institutional context, I examine specific measures of institutional context that moderate groups' political power and, thus, shape their perceptions of others. For instance, how a congressional district is drawn and the racial composition of a district influence whether and how majority/minority views are reflected in policy, which affect the level of influence that district residents have. Individuals' perceptions of their clout then structure their attitudes toward others who compare and contrast in political power. The same dynamics would apply for those who are descriptively represented. Another dimension of institutional context that I consider is the ideological climate of a district as measured by the district's Democratic vote share in the last presidential election. This climate tempers black, Latino, and white racial views. Although living in a district that highly favors Democratic candidates can affect blacks' and Latinos'(groups that largely identify as Democratic) perceptions that other minority groups are threatening, the effects of residing in a predominantly Democratic environment for whites may not be as simple to explain. While some whites who reside in a significantly Democratic district may adopt greater affinity toward nonwhites, others who reside in a similar setting may adopt more hostile views toward Latinos and African Americans.

I also explore institutional context through provisions for direct democracy, that is, whether states adopt ballot initiative and/or referendum processes. These provisions can also structure individuals' perceptions of power since ballot initiatives and political referenda can expand the political influence of all individuals by allowing them to shape policymaking more directly. Consequently, this project allows me to account for all of these potential consequences of political context and address several unchartered domains in the racial attitudes literature.

The Role of Identification

Attitudes and behavior cannot be studied separately from context since economic, racial, and political contexts considerably affect individuals' predispositions and behavior. But what about the extent that feelings of identification with one racial or ethnic group shape views toward another? We do not live in an isolated world, and the emerging presence of minorities in racially homogenous and diverse settings increases individuals' opportunities for interaction with those who differ considerably from them. These opportunities can significantly structure individuals' opinions toward others in many ways.

Some have taken note of the recent demographic and regional changes in the United States and in turn have assessed the effect of individuals' dispositions toward one group on their perceptions of others. Latinos who identify with other Latinos perceive greater commonality with African Americans, suggesting that adopting a pan-ethnic identity improves Latinos' prospects of forming coalitions with African Americans (Kaufmann 2003; Wallsten and Nteta 2011). Then again, whites who identify with other whites are more likely to express competition with other groups and view blacks as a threat to their current power and status (Blumer 1958; Bobo 1999; Nteta 2006, 199). In addition to studying the relationship between identification with individuals' own racial group and views toward others, several studies evaluate the effect of Latinos' sentiments toward a group besides theirs on their perception of others. Latinos who identify with blacks are more predisposed to perceive commonality with whites (Kaufmann 2003; Wallsten and Nteta 2011). A possible explanation for this finding is that Latinos do not significantly differentiate whites from blacks and perceive both groups as out-groups who are distinct from their own. Latinos may also view blacks and whites in similar ways since many experience socioeconomic adversity and alienation resulting in a strong suspicion of others who do not share their ethnicity (see Morin et al. 2011).

Furthermore, a contemporary assertion in the prevailing racial attitudes literature is that Latinos' perceptions of closeness/commonality with a racial group actually intensify their sense of competition with the group (Jones-Correa 2011; Morin et al. 2011; Wallsten and Nteta 2011). Although this may seem counterintuitive, since identification with a racial group can provide the basis for coalition formation and because perceptions of competition can cause deterioration of racial alliances, this phenomenon is expected. Latinos who have established social networks and, thus, feel close to a certain group are predisposed to perceiving competition with members of that group. On the other hand, those who are not socially integrated do not have the opportunity to perceive commonality or competition with others. In a study of Latinos' attitudes toward blacks and whites, Jones-Correa asserts that "closeness, in a sense, breeds competition" (2011, 90). In addition, Morin and colleagues argue that Latinos who share a disadvantaged sociopolitical position with blacks are prone to competing with them for limited resources: "Perceived competition is not racially motivated or necessarily negative, but rather a realistic observation of a political and social environment" (2011, 119). As a result, being socially integrated and having a disadvantaged status can not only result in greater affinity with other groups but might also provoke hostilities and tensions with others, particularly those who share a comparable status.

Although the number of studies analyzing individuals' identification with one group on views toward another are limited, existing research is strong in many ways. Current studies take a fundamental and up-to-date approach to understanding racial sentiments. As minorities enter racially diverse and homogenous settings, the racial dynamics of a city or town change, prompting individuals to compare one racial group with another. Hence, comparing views toward one racial/ethnic group with those of another depicts the racial encounters and relations that are occurring today. Another advantage to comparing the views toward one group with those of another is that these attitudes are examined in several ways. Not only do we know the effects that Latinos' views toward other Latinos and whites/blacks have on their sentiments toward African Americans/whites (respectively) but we also have an understanding of the influence of Latinos' commonality with African Americans on their perceptions of competition with blacks.

Notwithstanding this, our knowledge of the relationship between identification with one group and sentiments toward others is substantially limited. First, we know relatively little about the influence of whites' and African Americans' sentiments toward one group on those of another. More attention needs to be centered on comprehending perceptions of closeness and competition of residents who are experiencing changes to the racial makeup of their neighborhoods. A second gap in our understanding of the effects of identification is lack of theory. The explanation for examining the effects of Latinos' identification with blacks on attitudes toward whites and vice versa is often absent. Additionally, there are very few theoretical justifications for the correlation between Latinos' identification with whites and Latinos, and their increased sense of commonality with blacks. The most developed theoretical explanation for Latinos' attitudes is the relationship between Latinos' perceptions of commonality and competition with blacks.

This project addresses the aforementioned shortcomings by analyzing the effects of identifying with whites, blacks, and Latinos on these individuals' perceptions of commonality and competition with each other. To clarify, some of the questions that I pose in this project are: Does identification with Latinos expand whites' sense of commonality with African Americans? Does perceiving commonality with blacks heighten Latinos' sense of competition with blacks? Are blacks who identify with Latinos more predisposed to viewing Latinos as competitors? Do African Americans who identify with Latinos also feel that they are close to whites? Thus, this project takes a comprehensive approach to studying the effects of perceptions, since I assess the effects of racial attitudes on white, black, and Latino perceptions of commonality and competition with each other. I also account for individuals' attitudes toward their own racial group on their views toward others, and compare groups' sentiments toward one group with those of another. Further, I examine the relationship between identifying and sensing competition with one group.

Another way that this project addresses the gaps in our knowledge of interracial attitudes is through its theoretical contribution. I examine the extent to which Blumer's (1958) group position theory can explain the relationship between individuals' attitudes toward one group and their sentiments toward others. His theory asserts that individuals place their own racial/ethnic group in one category and others in distinct classifications. This differentiation of categories influences how individuals perceive and respond to others. For instance, when individuals think about blacks, they inevitably make direct or indirect comparisons with whites (Bobo 1999). I assert that when individuals think about one group, they inevitably make indirect or direct comparisons to their group and others, which subsequently affect their views toward other racial groups. These comparisons illustrate when individuals take an "us versus them" mentality. For instance, if whites who identify with Latinos perceive more closeness with blacks, then whites may perceive those with limited clout similarly and not adopt a restrictive perspective as to who their allies are. If blacks who identify with whites are more likely to feel close to Latinos, however, then blacks may not place whites and Latinos in separate categories, providing less support for the group position theory. Furthermore, if Latinos who identify with blacks sense greater commonality with whites, then they may not differentiate those with limited clout from those with greater power and opportunities, keeping them from adopting a restrictive perspective as to who their allies are. Then again, if Latinos' identification with blacks augments their competition with blacks, then commonality with blacks heightens Latinos' perception of where they ought to stand relative to a group with similar struggles and clout. Hence, similarities can incite hostilities and tensions with those who share a comparable status.

Although I do not make direct assertions as to how and under what circumstances the group position theory explains racial attitudes, I develop two general hypotheses that I discuss in greater detail in the next few paragraphs. Given the decreasing social distance and relations among individuals of diverse races and ethnicities, I contend that regardless of race or ethnicity, individuals' feelings of identification with one group shape their views toward another. Also, the more individuals identify with another group, the less prone they are to perceive competition with that group. The more individuals identify with a group, the greater their affinity toward that group, resulting in depressed competition toward members of the group.

Explaining Latino Attitudes

In addition to presenting the general theoretical contributions of this project, I provide a summary of specific hypotheses on how contact, context, and feelings of identification structure Latino, black, and white perceptions of closeness, commonality, and competition toward each other. On the whole, there are numerous parallels among my hypotheses that explain Latino and African American racial attitudes since these two groups share a minority status and thus compare in socioeconomic interests and experiences. Table 1 presents a visual summary of the hypotheses that I pose to explain Latinos' racial dispositions. More developed hypotheses are presented in the theory section of each empirical chapter.

In order to obtain a more thorough understanding of Latinos' racial attitudes, I examine Latinos' perceptions of commonality and competition with blacks, whites, and other Latinos. First, I begin with hypotheses accounting for Latino attitudes. In general, I contend that Latinos' limited sociopolitical clout and opportunities prompt them to feel that they have to side with either whites (the sociopolitical majority) or blacks (the minority), yet this mindset is shaped by Latinos' social interaction with other groups, sense of clout based on their surroundings, and perceptions of blacks and whites. Regarding the relationship between social contact and perceptions of commonality and competition, I posit that the relationship between Latinos' contact with blacks and whites and their racial attitudes comport with the social contact hypothesis—the more contact Latinos have with another group, the more commonality and less competition they perceive with members of that group. Notwithstanding this theory, I also argue that social contact has divisive effects on racial attitudes. Given the discrepancies in experiences and socioeconomic struggles among Latinos, blacks, and whites, Latinos who interact with a group of a certain position are less likely to sense commonality and more likely to perceive competition with those of a different position. Thus, Latinos who have significant black social networks are less likely to perceive commonality with whites but more predisposed to sense competition with whites. Additionally, the more Latinos interact socially with whites, the less prone they are to feel close to blacks. On the other hand, Latinos who have significant social contact with whites sense less competition with blacks because their interactions with those of a higher status decrease the likelihood that they view those with less clout as a threat.

When it comes to the effects of racial context on Latinos' racial attitudes, I posit that Latinos' perceptions of power structure their attitudes toward African Americans and whites. For instance, in accordance with the racial

TABLE 1. Directional hypotheses for Latino models

	Commonality with		Competition with	
	blacks	whites	blacks	whites
Social contact with blacks	+	−	−	+
Social contact with whites	−	+	−	−
Percentage of blacks in county, perception of the number of blacks in county			+	
Percentage of whites in county, perception of the number of whites in county	−	+	−	−
Education level (county)	−	+	−	−
Poverty rate (county)	−	−	+	−
Unemployment rate (county)	−	−	+	−
Latino legislator	−	−	+	+
Democratic congressional district		−	−	+
State ballot initiatives, political referenda		−	−	+
Identification with blacks		+/−	−	
Identification with whites	+/−			

Note: The signs displayed above indicate whether I hypothesize a positive or negative relationship between the two variables. The absence of a sign indicates that I do not predict a relationship.

threat hypothesis, when Latinos perceive that they are powerless (i.e., being surrounded by African Americans, more than likely residing in a low socioeconomic environment), they are likely to view African Americans as social and economic competitors. Furthermore, when Latinos sense that they are in a position of power, such as by residing in a predominantly white environment (more than likely a high socioeconomic setting), they view whites more favorably and, hence, perceive more commonality and less competition with whites. Moreover, being surrounded by whites depresses Latinos' identification with blacks as well as their sense of rivalry with them, since Latinos are less likely to relate to African Americans and view them as a threat.

Similarly, I suspect that Latinos' perceptions of influence structure the effects of economic and institutional contexts on their sense of commonality and competition with whites and blacks. When Latinos are in economically powerful settings, they are more likely to feel close to whites and less close to African Americans. In these settings, Latinos are less prone to regard blacks and whites as economic threats. Nonetheless, when in a high-threat environment, Latinos perceive greater competition with African Americans, less competition with whites, and less commonality with both groups. As to institutional context, Latinos who are in politically influential settings perceive less commonality and greater rivalry with whites. Latinos who are represented by a Latino and who have the opportunity to voice their opinions through ballot initiatives and/or political referenda sense less closeness with blacks.[3] As to Latinos' perceptions of competition with blacks, I hypothesize that Latinos who are represented by a Latino sense higher competition with blacks, though I suspect the opposite for the effects of residing in a largely Democratic district and in a state with provisions for direct democracy.

With regard to the relationship between attitudes toward one racial group and sentiments toward another, I theorize that Latinos who identify with blacks perceive less competition with African Americans. While Latinos and African Americans compare greatly in sociopolitical struggles and experiences, their commonality may not directly result in greater competition and may depress hostility between both groups. I also hypothesize that Latino perceptions of commonality with blacks influence their views toward whites and vice versa. Latinos are well aware of the sociopolitical disparities between blacks and whites, and their views toward one group structure their perceptions of the other.

Explaining Black Views

Similar to my explanations for Latinos' perceptions, I develop power-based hypotheses to explain the effects of contact, context, and perceptions on African Americans' attitudes toward whites and Latinos. African Americans generally parallel Latinos in low socioeconomic status and clout, which heighten their awareness of the discrepancies in power that exist among individuals. This cognizance then structures how they perceive themselves and others. In comparison to my examination of Latino attitudes, I analyze African Americans' attitudes toward whites, Latinos, and other blacks in order to achieve a more comprehensive understanding of African Americans' racial views. Table 2 presents a visual synopsis of my hypotheses pertaining to blacks' racial dispositions.

With regard to the effect of social contact on black attitudes, I adopt two hypotheses. First, I argue that the social contact hypothesis considerably accounts for black attitudes—the greater contact African Americans have with Latinos and whites, the more prone they are to sense closeness and less competition with these groups. I also posit that social contact has divisive effects. As blacks socially interact with Latinos, they are less likely to perceive closeness with whites. Furthermore, blacks' social contact with whites depresses their sense of rivalry with Latinos.

TABLE 2. Directional hypotheses for black models

	Closeness with		Competition with	
	Latinos	whites	Latinos	whites
Social contact with Latinos	+	–	–	
Social contact with whites		+	–	–
Percentage of Latinos in county, perception of the number of Latinos in county	–		+	
Percentage of whites in county, perception of the number of whites in county		+		+
Education level (county)	+	+	–	+
Poverty rate (county)	–	+	+	+
Unemployment rate (county)	–	+	+	+
Black legislator		–		+
Latino legislator	+		+	
Democratic congressional district	–	–		+
State ballot initiatives, political referenda	–	–		+
Identification with Latinos		+/–	–	
Identification with whites	+/–			–

Note: The signs displayed above indicate whether I hypothesize a positive or negative relationship between the two variables. The absence of a sign indicates that I do not predict a relationship.

I also provide several explanations for the relationship between racial, economic, and institutional contexts and African Americans' sentiments toward whites and Latinos. As to racial context, I suspect that African Americans who reside in a predominantly Latino county perceive less closeness yet greater competition with Latinos in accordance with the racial threat hypothesis. Comparable to my hypotheses for Latinos' racial attitudes, blacks' perceptions of their racial, economic, and political power explain the relationship between contact and their perceptions of whites and Latinos. Blacks who are surrounded by whites are more prone to feel close to whites and regard them as a sociopolitical threat. African Americans in a predominantly Latino environment are more likely to regard Latinos as competitors than those who do not.

Similarly, I theorize that blacks' perception of influence moderates the effects of economic and institutional contexts on their sense of commonality and competition with whites and Latinos. Residing in either a high-threat or low-threat economic setting increases the likelihood that blacks feel closeness *and* rivalry with whites. Still, when blacks are in an economically weak setting, they identify less and perceive greater competition with Latinos. Residing in a poor area can increase the likelihood that they attribute their socioeconomic mobility to race. This perception then makes African Americans more prone to viewing other minorities such as Latinos as encroaching on their status (Telles et al. 2011, 7). The effects of residing in a low-threat environment are not the same. When African Americans reside in an economically strong setting, they are more prone to perceive closeness and less competition with Latinos. As to institutional context, I develop three main hypotheses. First, as blacks gain more political power, they are less likely to identify with whites and Latinos yet perceive more competition with whites. Second, when blacks are represented by a black legislator, they sense less closeness but more competition with whites. Descriptive representation develops blacks' sense of empowerment and depresses their identification with the majority group. Yet, since competition between whites and blacks considerably involves electoral power, blacks who gain some clout through descriptive representation are more prone to regard whites as competitors. Third, African Americans who are represented by a Latino perceive more closeness with Latinos and sense greater rivalry with Latinos. Blacks with a Latino legislator feel closer to Latinos because of their increased familiarity with and understanding of Latinos, yet blacks represented by a Latino are more likely to perceive that Latinos as individuals are infringing on their status because of the consistent competition that exists between the two minority groups.

When it comes to the effects of attitudes toward one racial group and sentiments toward another, I hypothesize that African Americans who identify with Latinos and whites perceive less competition with them. Additionally, I theorize that blacks' feelings of identification with whites shape their views toward Latinos and vice versa.

Explaining White Dispositions

Due to whites' majority status, my explanations for the relationship between contact, context, and perceptions and whites' attitudes toward minorities do not completely parallel those of African Americans and Latinos. Whites' generally high sociopolitical position alters their perceptions of who they are and their sentiments toward others. Notwithstanding this, whites' status can alter based on their racial, economic, and political settings. These contexts then shape their perceptions of power, which structure the amount of threat that blacks and Latinos pose for whites. I explore whites' sense of closeness and rivalry with blacks, Latinos, and other whites to obtain a

TABLE 3. Directional hypotheses for white models

	Closeness with		Competition with	
	Latinos	blacks	Latinos	blacks
Social contact with Latinos	+		−	
Social contact with blacks		+		−
Social contact with whites	−	−	+	+
Percentage of whites in county, perception of the number of whites in county	−		−	
Low percentage of Latinos in county × High percentage of high school degree in county	+		−	
High percentage of Latinos in county × Low percentage of high school degree in county	−		+	
Low percentage of blacks in county × High percentage of high school degree in county		+		−
High percentage of black in county × Low percentage of high school degree in county		−	+	
Education level (county)	+	+	−	−
Poverty rate (county)	−	−	+	+
Unemployment rate (county)	−	−	+	+
Black legislator		−		+
Latino legislator	−		+	
Reside in a majority-minority district	−	−	+	+
Democratic congressional district	+	+	−	−
State ballot initiatives, political referenda	−	−	−	−
Identification with Latinos		+	−	
Identification with blacks	+			−
Identification with whites			+	+

Note: The signs displayed above indicate whether I hypothesize a positive or negative relationship between the two variables. The absence of a sign indicates that I do not predict a relationship.

broader comprehension of whites' racial dispositions. Table 3 presents a visual summary of the hypotheses that I pose to explain whites' racial dispositions.

Contact structures whites' perceptions of closeness and competition with blacks and Latinos. In accordance with the social contact hypothesis, I theorize that the more whites integrate Latinos and blacks into their social networks, the greater whites' sense of closeness and the lesser their competition with blacks and Latinos, respectively. I also suspect that social contact has several divisive effects on whites' attitudes toward minorities. When whites interact socially with other whites, they are less prone to sense closeness yet more likely to perceive competition with Latinos and blacks. Whites' social interactions with those who have a generally higher status than minorities decrease their affinity and augment their antagonism toward those of minority status.

In terms of racial context, whites' context affects their sense of power, significantly structuring their reactions to African Americans and Latinos. In accord with the racial threat hypothesis, I hypothesize that whites who are in predominantly African American and Latino settings perceive less closeness and greater rivalry with blacks and Latinos. Residing in a predominantly white setting also structures whites' dispositions. Whites who are surrounded by other whites are less prone to perceive closeness and competition with blacks and Latinos. Residing in a largely white context influences whites to feel less close to those who have a lower socioeconomic status. Further, in accord with Branton and Jones (2005), I hypothesize that high education and low diversity contexts are associated with greater perceptions of commonality and lesser perceptions of competition with blacks and Latinos. On the other hand, low education and high diversity contexts are associated with lower perceptions of closeness and greater antagonism toward both groups.

Additionally, whites' perceptions of their own influence moderate the relationship between economic and institutional context and whites' racial attitudes. Whites who reside in an economically sturdy environment are more likely to perceive closeness yet less likely to perceive rivalry with blacks and Latinos. Still, whites who reside in a high-threat economic setting are less prone to sense closeness and more inclined to perceive competition with both groups. The rationale for these hypotheses centers on the extent to which whites feel threatened by minority groups. Whites in a high education setting are more likely to adopt greater affinity toward blacks and Latinos and not view them as a threat. Yet, whites in counties with high poverty and unemployment rates are more likely to regard blacks and Latinos with antagonism. As to the effects of institutional context, I hypothesize that the more politically powerful whites are, the less prone they are to feel close to and sense rivalry with minorities. On the other hand, when whites are in a politically vulnerable district (i.e., represented by a black or Latino legislator, residing in a majority-minority district), they are less likely to perceive closeness with blacks and Latinos yet are more prone to view them as competitors (see Glaser 1994). Based on African Americans' and Latinos' ties to the Democratic Party, I posit that whites who reside in a predominantly Democratic district feel closer to and less threatened by these two groups.

Regarding the effect of perceptions on racial attitudes, I hypothesize that whites' sense of closeness with one racial/ethnic group structures their views toward that group and another. In line with Blumer's (1958) group position theory, when whites think about one group, they inevitably make direct or indirect comparisons to their group and others influencing their racial attitudes. Given whites' significant social, economic, and political clout, their identification with a minority group does not incite competition with that group. Actually, feeling close to African Americans and Latinos depresses whites' sense of rivalry with these two groups. As whites identify more with Latinos and African Americans, they are more likely to perceive closeness with blacks and Latinos, respectively. Still, given minorities' generally distinct sociopolitical status from whites, whites' identification with other whites increases the likelihood that they regard black and Latinos with hostility.

Summary

This chapter presents an explanation of and motivations behind the Triangular Theory of Contact, Context, and Identification. Since this theory is grounded in the disparities in context, attitudes, and opportunities of and among whites, blacks, and Latinos, I first describe the differences among these three groups. Next, I provide background information on the effects of social contact, context (racial, economic, and institutional), and racial attitudes on perceptions of commonality and competition. Then I discuss my expectations for these predictors on Latino, black, and white racial attitudes. The empirical tests of these predictors are presented in chapters 2–7. Chapter 2 begins with a quantitative approach to testing my theory as it applies to Latinos.

2

Latinos' Perceptions of
African Americans and Whites

A QUANTITATIVE ANALYSIS

Latinos are now the largest minority group in the United States with a burgeoning influence in various social and political institutions. Today more
than ever, Latinos are entertaining us through television programs, movies,
and music. Latinos are bringing innovative ideas, values, and customs to
the United States. The Spanish language is prevalent in many public places
throughout the country and is spoken by so many non-Latino residents that
it comes as no surprise that applicants for employment who are fluent in
both English and Spanish often have an advantage over other applicants in
employment positions at various levels. In the past few years, Latinos have
also made significant political inroads. Today, a Latina of Puerto Rican descent is a member of the U.S. Supreme Court. President Barack Obama has
appointed numerous Latinos to positions on his presidential staff. Susana
Martinez is the first Latina governor in U.S. history. Further, the practices of
political organizations and leaders heavily reveal that Latinos are a key electoral group that cannot be overlooked. The 2012 Republican and Democratic
National Conventions targeted Latinos in order to win their votes with a
Latino convention chairman and several Latino keynote speakers, including
an undocumented immigrant speaker at the Democratic convention (Barreto 2012). Recently, Latino voters were heavily recruited and turned out in
record numbers for the 2012 presidential election, with Latinos considerably
influencing the election results in several battleground states (Latino Decisions 2012b).

The Complexity of the Latino Population Today

While U.S. residents cannot ignore the considerable changes that Latinos
have brought to this country, as well as their emerging presence and sociopolitical strength, Latinos are generally limited in their opportunities and positions. As a group, Latinos have a meaningfully lower socioeconomic status
and level of political clout than many other racial and ethnic groups. Many
Latinos continue to have lower incomes and education levels and higher high

school dropout rates than their black, white, and Asian counterparts (Pew Hispanic Center 2011). Further, there are considerable disparities within the Latino population that make this group difficult to define and understand. When it comes to nativity, there are numerous divergences in experiences and levels of understanding of race relations. In comparison to native-born Latinos, foreign-born Latinos may not have fully developed opinions of African Americans and whites, given these Latinos' recent arrivals to the United States. Additionally, while we know that the number of native-born Latinos is larger than foreign born, differences among the foreign born influence the social and political clout that immigrants from Latin America have in the United States. Not all foreign-born Latinos are of legal status. A 2008 U.S. Census report asserts that the percentage of undocumented immigrants encompasses approximately 4 percent of the U.S. population (Passel and Cohn 2009). Undocumented immigrants cannot vote and live in great fear of deportation. Recent restrictive immigration legislation has made it more difficult for undocumented Latinos to search for employment and has increased the amount of racial profiling that they, as well as all Latinos, experience. Thus, their limited sociopolitical opportunities and power increase their propensity to feel and be socially, politically, and economically disenfranchised from society. Furthermore, generational differences among Latinos affect their assimilation behavior. Second- and third-generation Latinos are more likely than their first-generation counterparts to adopt American culture, values, and the English language, and to build relationships with non-Latinos. On the other hand, first-generation immigrants are more prone to reside near non-Hispanics than other generations (Wilkinson 2007).

Besides differences in nativity, legal status, and generation, discrepancies in Latinos' geographic location, skin tone, and positions exemplify their varied contingencies and experiences. Some Latinos reside in traditional Latino areas with established Latino social networks and significant prospects for political participation and influence, as found by the number of Latino political leaders and political organizations in cities such as Los Angeles, Miami, San Antonio, Chicago, and Santa Fe (Casellas 2011). Others live in new immigrant areas such as the South, with a small but escalating number of Latinos with some opportunities for upward mobility, particularly given the increased employment opportunities in the agriculture, construction, food processing, and service industries (McClain et al. 2007; Marrow 2011). Some Latinos have numerous opportunities to form social networks with whites and blacks due to a high level of desegregation in a city or town and an amicable and receptive surrounding environment. Others do not because they choose not to or are simply limited by their recent arrival. Latinos also differ in skin tone and socioeconomic power. While some Latino national origin groups resemble whites in status and skin tone—and some Latinos even identify racially as white alone—other Latinos strongly compare to African Americans in skin tone and education and income levels, and thus identify more with blacks than whites (Bonilla-Silva 2004; Passel et al. 2011; Wilkinson and Earle 2013).

This chapter captures central disparities among Latinos by taking a quantitative approach to examining the effects of social contact, context, and feelings of identification with other groups on Latinos' sense of commonality and competition with whites and blacks. The subsequent chapter takes a qualitative approach using focus group data of Latinos in an emerging Latino area to delve deeper into the intricacies of Latinos' racial sentiments. My focus in this chapter is multifaceted. I analyze how Latinos regard African Americans and whites in relation to their views of their co-ethnics using the most recent, comprehensive data sets, the 2006 Latino National Survey (LNS) and the 2010 Cooperative Congressional Election Study (CCES).[1] In accordance with my Triangular Theory of Contact, Context, and Identification (TTCCI), I contend that Latinos' generally low socioeconomic clout and opportunities due to status, discrimination, and insecurity pressure them to perceive that they need to side with either whites (the sociopolitical majority) or blacks (the minority), *yet* this mindset is shaped by Latinos' social interactions with other groups, sense of clout based on their surroundings, and identification with blacks and whites. Focusing on the effect of this theory on native-born and foreign-born Latinos' racial attitudes advances what we know about Latinos' assimilation behavior and their experience with those of distinct races and statuses from the moment they arrive in the United States to later generations.

Social Contact, Context, and Latinos

Although most of the literature exploring Latinos' perceptions of blacks and whites focuses on the effects of linked fate, commonality with other racial groups, the time Latinos spend in the United States, and demographic attributes (McClain et al. 2006; Nteta and Wallsten 2007; Barreto and Sanchez 2008), we have some knowledge of the extent to which social networks and context shape Latinos' attitudes toward non-Latinos. In the next few paragraphs, I discuss what we know about the effects of contact and the relationship between context and Latinos' racial attitudes.

Increased social interactions with non-Latinos can structure Latinos' perceptions of blacks and whites. Paula D. McClain and colleagues (2006) find strong support for the social contact hypothesis in their analyses of Latinos' adoption of negative stereotypes of blacks. They find that Latinos who have more social contact with African Americans are less predisposed to espouse negative stereotypes of blacks than those who do not have a lot of contact. Similarly, Matt Barreto and Gabriel Sanchez find that dark-skinned Latinos with black friends are less likely to perceive competition than Latinos with no black friends (2008, 32). Tatishe M. Nteta and Kevin Wallsten also find support for the social contact hypothesis in their study of Latinos' commonality with blacks and whites. They conclude that having black friends has a positive effect on native-born Latinos' commonality with blacks (2007, 58). Still, support for the social contact hypothesis has not remained consistent. Vincent L. Hutchings and colleagues (2011) do not find that increased social contact has positive effects on Latinos' perceptions of blacks. Further, Michael Jones-Correa (2011) and Jason L. Morin and colleagues (2011) find that increased interaction with blacks in the workplace actually heightens Latinos' sense of competition with them.

Although not as extensive as social contact, the effects of racial context have also been examined on Latinos' perceptions of blacks, whites, and other Latinos. In a study of biracial coalitions in New York, John Mollenkopf (1997) concludes that an emerging Dominican population heightens competition and tensions between Puerto Ricans and Dominicans. Hutchings and coauthors (2011) also find that Latinos in a segregated neighborhood are more likely to sense rivalry with Afro-Caribbeans. Yet, when it comes to Latinos' attitudes toward whites and blacks, Hutchings and colleagues and Jones-Correa (2011) find that racial context does not influence Latinos' perceptions of competition with blacks and whites.

The Triangular Theory of Contact, Context, and Identification for Latinos

Although several studies have made some headway in our understanding of the determinants of Latinos' perceptions of blacks and whites, these studies have left several unanswered questions. Do Latinos regard whites and blacks analogously? Under what conditions do Latinos regard whites and African Americans as allies and rivals? How does the heterogeneity of the Latino population structure their racial attitudes? This study closes several gaps in our knowledge of Latinos' racial attitudes. It is one of the first to examine Latinos' perceptions of blacks, whites, and other Latinos, thus providing insight as to how similarly Latinos regard blacks and whites and how they view other groups in relation to their co-ethnics. This chapter also develops our awareness of whether and under what conditions Latinos perceive commonality and competition with African Americans and whites. Another contribution of this study is that it directly addresses Marisa A. Abrajano and R. Michael Alvarez's (2010) call for more studies to explore the heterogeneity of the Latino community and examine how intragroup disparities structure Latinos' attitudes and behavior (181–82).

To explain Latinos' racial dispositions, this study develops a theory of contact, context, and identification that builds on the social contact, racial threat, and group position theories. I posit that Latinos' perceptions of commonality and competition with African Americans and whites are structured by their social networks, sense of clout created by context, and identification with whites, blacks, and Latinos. There are several parallels between my hypotheses that explain Latino racial attitudes and those than explain African Americans', since both groups compare in socioeconomic status, experiences, and opportunities.

Social Contact

Research on the relationship between social contact and Latinos' perceptions of blacks and whites is quite narrow, and this study overcomes several limitations of extant studies. Jones-Correa (2011) asserts that it is not clear as to whether the social contact hypothesis or the racial threat hypothesis (somewhat opposing theories) better explain Latinos' views toward blacks and whites. In this study, I address the extent to which social contact structures Latinos' perceptions of non-Latinos in several ways. I test the social contact hypothesis by examining the effects of socially interacting with one group on Latinos' sentiments toward that particular group. I posit that the more contact Latinos have with another group, the more commonality and less competition they perceive with members of that group. This study also examines the divisive effects of social contact. Latinos do not live in a vacuum and are interacting more with those of a distinct race and ethnicity than before; thus, I analyze how Latinos' social interactions with one racial group structure their attitudes toward another. Given the considerable sociopolitical disparities that exist between blacks and whites, Latinos are influenced to feel that they have to side either with whites or with blacks. Social interaction with a certain group affects this feeling. These assertions lead me to hypothesize:

Social contact hypothesis: The more contact (i.e., friends, neighbors, coworkers, or fellow participants in a civic or social group) Latinos have with another group, the more commonality and less competition they perceive with members of that group.

Divisive effects hypothesis: Latinos who interact with whites are less likely to sense commonality and competition with blacks. Latinos who interact with blacks are less prone to perceive commonality yet more prone to perceive competition with whites.

Racial Context

In addition to social networks, another primary category of variables used to test my main theory is racial context. Similar to the literature exploring the relationship between social contact and Latino racial attitudes, we have a narrow understanding of the effects of racial context on Latinos' perceptions of blacks and whites.

This study addresses this weakness in several ways. I analyze the effects of racial context through the percentage of whites and African Americans who reside in the counties of surveyed Latinos and whom Latinos perceive to reside in their counties. Further, in accordance with the racial threat hypothesis and Herbert Blumer's (1958) group position theory, I posit that Latinos' perceptions of their levels of social, political, and economic power in their communities structure their attitudes toward blacks and whites. When Latinos perceive that they are powerless (i.e., being surrounded by African Americans and thus more than likely residing in a low socioeconomic environment), they are more predisposed to regard blacks as socioeconomic competitors and view other Latinos as lesser competitors. When Latinos sense that they are in a position of influence, such as by residing in a predominantly white environment (more than likely a high socioeconomic setting), they regard whites more favorably. Further, I posit that racial context can have divisive effects on Latinos' racial attitudes. Latinos who are largely surrounded by whites are less likely to feel close to blacks. When Latinos reside in a largely white environment, which for some can mean establishing a secure, dominant status in society, they are less likely to relate to African Americans. Hence, these theoretical discussions lead me to propose:

Racial threat and blacks hypothesis: When Latinos are surrounded by African Americans, they are more predisposed to regard blacks as socioeconomic competitors. Also, being largely surrounded by whites depresses the likelihood that Latinos perceive closeness and competition with blacks.

Racial threat and whites hypothesis: When Latinos reside in a predominantly white environment, they are more likely to perceive commonality and less likely to perceive competition with whites.

Economic Context

Another form of context that I examine is economic context, as measured by a county's unemployment rate, poverty rate, and education level. While the dialogue as to whether Latinos pose an economic threat to whites and blacks (particularly) has not diminished, we know relatively little about the relationship between Latinos' economic prospects and context and their perceptions of blacks and whites. To foster our understanding of this relationship, I rely on the group position theory and Lawrence D. Bobo and Vincent Hutchings's (1996) modified group position theory. I hypothesize that Latinos in a high-threat environment (with limited economic clout and opportunities) sense less closeness yet greater competition with blacks since they perceive that blacks in these settings are not their allies and can infringe on their opportunities to ascend the socioeconomic ladder. When it comes to whites, Latinos in a high-threat environment are less predisposed to sense commonality and competition with whites since they regard their experiences in this setting as far removed from those of the majority group. The results would not be the same for Latinos who reside in low-threat settings. When Latinos are in economically powerful settings, they are more prone to perceive commonality with whites and less inclined to sense commonality and competition with African Americans. Further, I suspect that Latinos in a high education setting sense less competition with whites. Latinos in strong fiscal environments perceive less commonality and competition with blacks given that Latinos in this setting may be less likely to relate to African Americans and regard them as a threat. Still, the hypothesis for Latinos' attitudes toward blacks is not parallel to those for whites since Latinos in high education settings may adopt greater affinity toward whites. Thus, I hypothesize:

Economic threat and whites hypothesis: Latinos in a low-threat environment (residing in a county with a high percentage of high school graduates) are more prone to perceiving commonality and less prone to perceiving competition with whites. Latinos in a high-threat environment (high unemployment and poverty rates) are less predisposed to sense commonality and competition with whites.

Economic threat and blacks hypothesis: Latinos in a low-threat environment (residing in a county with a high percentage of high school graduates) are less inclined to sense commonality and competition with African Americans. Latinos in a high-threat environment (high unemployment and poverty rates) are less likely to feel close to blacks yet more likely to sense competition with them.

Institutional Context

Another form of context that has been relatively absent in analyses of Latinos' racial attitudes is institutional context. As Latinos establish a political presence at the local, state, and national levels, the various dimensions of their political clout and opportunities must be examined. Further, in this study, I adopt a power-based approach to explain Latinos' perceptions of blacks and whites. I posit that Latinos' perceptions of their own level of political influence, in addition to their perceptions of blacks' and whites' power, structure their views toward these two racial groups. When Latinos are in a low-threat environment (and thus politically influential settings), they are less likely to perceive closeness and more likely to perceive competition with blacks and whites. The exception to this hypothesis applies to the relationship between residing in a largely Democratic district, in a state with ballot initiatives, and Latinos' sense of rivalry with blacks. Given that Latinos and African Americans strongly identify with the Democratic Party and have limited political clout relative to whites, I posit that Latinos who reside in predominantly Democratic districts and states with direct democracy provisions are less inclined to regard blacks as rivals. These assertions lead me to hypothesize:

Political context and blacks hypothesis: Latinos who are descriptively represented and who have the opportunity to voice their opinions through ballot initiatives and/or political referenda are less likely to perceive closeness with blacks. Latinos who are descriptively represented sense higher competition with blacks, yet Latinos who reside in largely Democratic districts and in states with provisions for direct democracy are less inclined to regard blacks as rivals.

Political context and whites hypothesis: Latinos who reside in low-threat environments (i.e., represented by a Latino legislator, residing in a largely Democratic setting, or residing in a state with direct democracy provisions) are less likely to perceive commonality yet more likely to sense rivalry with whites.

Identification with Other Groups

To further test the ttcci, I analyze the effects of Latinos' identification with blacks and whites. While a number of studies evaluate the effects of Latinos' commonality with other Latinos on their perceptions of blacks and whites (Kaufmann 2003; Sanchez 2008; Wallsten and Nteta 2011), little attention has been paid to the role that identifying with one group may play in influencing Latinos' perceptions of that same group, as well as the perceptions of others. To overcome these gaps in our knowledge, I rely on Blumer's (1958) group position theory and previous research. A component of Blumer's theory asserts that individuals place their racial/ethnic group in a category and others into distinct classifications. Still, Wallsten and Nteta (2011) find that Latinos may not greatly distinguish blacks from whites, since the greater their identification with whites/blacks, the greater their sense of commonality with blacks/whites, respectively. Thus, I hypothesize that Latinos' identification with whites/blacks structures their perceptions of commonality with blacks/whites. Latinos are aware of the sociopolitical disparities that exist between blacks and whites, and these discrepancies may influence their views toward these groups. Besides analyzing the relationship between identifying with one racial group on Latinos' perceptions of commonality with another, I posit that Latinos who identify with blacks are less likely to perceive competition with blacks. While some research suggests that perceptions of commonality and competition are not necessarily conflicting attitudes, I contend that identifying with blacks decreases the likelihood that Latinos regard blacks as rivals. These assertions lead me to hypothesize:

Identification hypothesis: Latinos' identification with whites/blacks structures their perceptions of commonality with blacks/whites, respectively.

Identification and competition with blacks hypothesis: Latinos who identify with blacks sense lesser competition with blacks.

Other Predictors of Latino Racial Attitudes

While this chapter's central contention is that Latinos' perceptions of commonality and competition with blacks and whites are structured by their social networks, their sense of clout as shaped by their surroundings, and their identification with blacks and whites, other explanations for Latinos' racial attitudes certainly exist. Commonality and linked fate with other Latinos, skin tone, region of residence, and social integration are leading determinants of Latinos' views toward whites and African Americans.

Commonality with other Latinos (i.e., internal commonality) is considered a key predictor of Latinos' perceptions of closeness with blacks and whites. Sanchez asserts that Latinos' identification with other Latinos is an essential precursor for establishing a meaningful relationship with another group (2008, 431–32). Increased commonality with other Latinos heightens Latinos' commonality with both African Americans (Kaufmann 2003; Nteta and Wallsten 2007; Sanchez 2008) and with whites (Nteta and Wallsten 2007). Based on these findings, I expect that Latinos who sense commonality with their co-ethnics are more likely to sense closeness with blacks and whites.

Linked fate with other Latinos is also a determinant of Latinos' perceptions of commonality and competition with blacks. It is important to recognize that linked fate and commonality are normally treated as conceptually distinct (Sanchez and Morin 2011), in that linked fate examines the extent to which individuals feel that their fate is linked with a racial group and predicts group consciousness (McClain et al. 2006), whereas commonality with other Latinos is a measure of group consciousness. Internal linked fate has been found to augment Latinos' solidarity with African Americans (Mc-Clain et al. 2006). Regarding perceptions of competition with blacks, Latinos with high levels of linked fate sense greater rivalry with blacks, yet linked fate with other Latinos is negatively related to Latinos' sense of competition with blacks relative to other Latinos (Morin et al. 2011, 111). I hypothesize that Latinos who perceive that their fate is associated with individuals who share their ethnicity are more prone to identify with blacks and whites, and increased linked fate with other Latinos depresses Latinos' sense of rivalry with blacks.

Latinos differ in skin tone, and these physical disparities can shape how they regard whites and African Americans. Individuals with dark skin tones regardless of race often perceive and experience more discrimination and socioeconomic struggles than light-skinned individuals (Hunter 2002; Levin and Banaji 2006). Barreto and Sanchez analyze the extent to which shared status and experiences structure Latino racial attitudes, and they conclude that Latinos who classify themselves as dark-skinned and have origins in countries with a large African ancestry population sense greater competition with blacks than those who do not (2008, 20). Additionally, Emily Earle and I (2013) find that variation in Latinos' skin tone leads to distinct attitudes toward these two groups. Latinos who identify as light skinned sense greater commonality with whites and lesser commonality with blacks than dark-skinned Latinos. We assert that individuals who compare in skin tone to whites considerably parallel whites in socioeconomic status and opportunities, depressing their identification with a minority group such as blacks, who are often discriminated against and have a considerably lower sociopolitical position than whites. Hence, the shared experiences and struggles that Latinos have with whites or blacks of comparable skin tone affect their perceptions of commonality with whites and African Americans. Given the findings of the aforementioned studies, I expect that light-skinned Latinos sense more commonality with and hostility toward whites and less closeness and competition with blacks.

Latinos' geographic location has been found to play a significant role in shaping their racial attitudes. In the last few decades, more Latinos have been relocating to the South at much faster rates than in other regions of the United States due to increased employment opportunities in the manufacturing, agricultural, and construction industries, fields that previously employed a significant number of African Americans. In this region, Latinos have been exposed to a racialized class structure that is not as prevalent as in other localities, and in some southern cities and towns with a significant portion of black residents, Latinos have been received with more antagonism and suspicion than in other areas (Marrow 2011). Thus, the racial dynamics between whites, blacks, and Latinos may be somewhat unique to the South. With regard to Latinos' perceptions of competition with blacks in the South, we do know that Latino immigrants perceive greater competition with blacks than those who do not reside in the South, and Latinos in southern states are more likely to perceive competition with blacks than with other Latinos (Morin et al. 2011, 114). I expect that Latino residents in the South are more inclined to perceive competition with blacks.

Social integration into the United States also has been found to shape Latinos' perceptions of blacks and whites. Extant research reveals that English-speaking Latinos sense greater commonality with blacks and whites than those more comfortable with the Spanish language. Interestingly, English-speaking Latinos perceive greater rivalry with African Americans regarding access to education (Jones-Correa 2011). Hence, I suspect that English-dominant Latinos sense greater commonality and competition with blacks and whites than Spanish-dominant Latinos. The effects of time in the United States have also been consistently examined, and I hypothesize that the longer Latinos spend in this country, the more likely that they perceive commonality with blacks and whites. The more time that Latinos spend in the United States, however, the more they become aware of racial inequalities and minorities' experiences with discrimination (Kaufmann 2003; Sanchez 2008). Thus, time in the United States is positively related to Latinos' perceptions of competition with whites and negatively related to Latinos' sense of rivalry with blacks.

Besides English proficiency and time in the United States, one of the main distinguishing factors that differentiates Latinos' experiences and perceptions of intergroup race relations is native status. Jones-Correa (2011) finds that first-generation Latinos are less prone to sensing commonality with African Americans yet are more likely to view blacks as rivals for employment than native-born Latinos. McClain and her colleagues (2006) conclude that foreign-born Latinos sense greater competition with blacks than their native-born counterparts. On the other hand, Morin and colleagues find some conflicting evidence: first-generation Latinos (in comparison to second-, third-, and fourth-generation) perceive less competition with blacks relative to Latinos (2011, 106). While Latinos born outside of the United States may have a sense of the racial structure and dynamics in this country, it is not until they have the chance to immerse themselves fully in their communities and develop a grasp of their standing relative to other racial/ethnic groups that they develop well-established views of who they are, how they compare to whites, and how they compare to other minority groups. Ben Bishin, Karen Kaufmann, and Daniel Stevens assert, "While it is fully understandable that many native-born African Americans see Whites as their primary oppressors, Latinos, especially new immigrants, do not necessarily come to this country holding these views" (2011, 114).

In this study, I further explore the effects of Latinos' nativity by analyzing Latinos' perceptions of blacks and whites among foreign-born and native-born Latinos. I contend that foreign-born and native-born Latinos' generally distinct experiences and comprehension (or lack of) of racial dynamics in the United States influence the degree to which social contact, context, and identification with other groups shape their attitudes toward blacks and whites. While I do not present specific hypotheses as to how the TTCCI structure the views of native-born Latinos and foreign-born Latinos divergently, I suspect that my main theory is better able to explain native-born Latinos' perceptions of commonality with whites/blacks and foreign-born Latinos' sense of rivalry with African Americans.

Data

This chapter analyzes Latinos' perceptions of African Americans and whites using 2006 LNS and 2010 CCES data. Both data sets are the most contemporary and comprehensive available that provide a broad understanding of Latino racial attitudes. There are several advantages to using the 2006 LNS data set. Unlike surveys used in previous studies on Latino public opinion and political behavior, the LNS is a national survey of 8,634 Latinos with a sizable number of Mexicans, Puerto Ricans, and Cubans. Table 4 presents the most popular national origins/ties of the survey respondents. Besides having such a large sample of Latinos from distinct national origins, the LNS is extremely useful to my study since it is one of the few national surveys with significant samples of foreign-born and native-born Latinos who are interviewed by bilingual interviewers, providing respondents the opportunity to answer questions in English or Spanish. Moreover, unlike many national surveys, the LNS explores a variety of topics that delve deeply into the complexities of Latino racial attitudes, touching on perceptions of economic and political commonality with African Americans and whites, social networks, interracial conflict, group consciousness, discrimination, and racial identification. The data set also covers Latinos in fifteen states and in the

TABLE 4. National origin/ties of 2006 LNS respondents

Nationality	Number	Percentage
Mexico	5,706	66.10
Puerto Rico	822	9.52
Cuba	420	4.86
El Salvador	407	4.71
Dominican Republic	335	3.88
Guatemala	149	1.75
Colombia	139	1.61
Spain	105	1.22
Honduras	87	1.01
Peru	65	0.75

Note: The percentages in this table do not add up to one hundred because it only includes the ten most common national origins of Latinos in the LNS sample.

Washington, D.C., metropolitan area. These states account for 87.5 percent of the U.S. Latino population, providing a large, national picture of Latinos in the United States.[2]

While the 2004 National Politics Survey (NPS) could be used as my primary data set to explore Latinos' racial attitudes, I rely primarily on 2006 LNS data for several reasons. The LNS is a more recent survey with a much larger sample of Latinos (LNS: 8,636, NPS: 810). Having a large sample size allows me to test all of my hypotheses in one model as well as control for the effects of leading determinants of Latino racial attitudes. Additionally, the foreign-born and native-born populations are much larger in the LNS (foreign-born: 6,186, native-born: 2,450) sample than in the NPS sample (foreign-born: 357, native-born: 453).

The 2010 CCES also provides a present-day understanding of the intricacies of Latino racial attitudes. The CCES includes a core set of common content questions as well as separate modules of survey questions developed by independent teams of scholars. The data used in this study is composed of variables from the common content portion of the CCES and variables from a module of questions on various aspects of interracial attitudes developed by the author and an investigator from Texas A&M University. The data consist of a total of 2,000 respondents, 174 of whom identify as Latino. While the 2010 CCES does not have as vast a sample of Latinos as the LNS, unlike the LNS it is a more current survey that assesses Latinos' sense of competition with blacks *and* whites as well as their perceptions of racial diversity in their county. A detailed description of the survey questions and coding as well as descriptive statistics of the LNS, CCES, and contextual variables are provided in the appendix.

The LNS data set includes several questions that assess Latinos' perceptions of commonality with blacks and whites. This data set includes questions that explore Latinos' perceptions of commonality with whites and blacks on two dimensions: economic (i.e., employment opportunities, education level, and income) and political (i.e., political power, representation, and government services). I create general indexes of commonality with blacks and commonality with whites since (1) Latinos are attaining more political power and attention at the local and national levels with significant repercussions on interracial attitudes; (2) I find that Latinos do not greatly distinguish between economic and political commonality with blacks and whites; and (3) the correlation coefficients and the Cronbach's alpha scores for Latinos' economic and political commonality for each racial group indicate that it is appropriate to create additive scales for commonality with whites and blacks using economic and political commonality variables.[3]

In order to assess how much competition Latinos sense toward blacks, I analyze the answers of several survey questions provided in the 2006 LNS. The LNS surveys Latinos' perceptions of competition with African Americans and Latinos in various ways: general employment competition, educational rivalry, employment competition in government jobs, and legislative competition. I create a general index of competition with blacks since (1) Latino/black relations can often be characterized by economic and political tensions; (2) there are few disparities in Latinos' responses to their educational, general employment, government employment, and political competition with blacks; and (3) the correlation coefficients and the Cronbach's alpha scores for all of the variables that compose the general competition with blacks measure reveal that it is appropriate to create an additive scale for Latinos' competition with blacks with these four variables. The additive index of Latinos' sense of competition with blacks ranges from 0 (no employment, government employment, educational, or political competition with African Americans) to 6 (a lot of competition). Unlike the LNS, the CCES data set only examines Latinos' perceptions of economic competition with blacks and whites.

Descriptive Results: Perceptions of Commonality and Competition with Blacks, Whites, and Latinos

The first stage of my analysis consists of examining the extent to which Latinos regard whites, African Americans, and Latinos in the same way through perceptions of commonality and competition. Prevailing research focuses heavily on whether Latinos perceive more commonality with African Americans than with whites (Kaufmann 2003; McClain et al. 2006; Jones-Correa 2011). While scholars have made significant progress in addressing this heavily contested question, with the exception of a few studies very little research has examined Latinos' sense of commonality and competition with whites and African Americans in relation to another racial/ethnic group. Furthermore, our comprehension of Latinos' perceptions of blacks and whites is quite limited unless we examine these attitudes relative to Latinos' views toward other Latinos (Morin et al. 2011, 104). Figure 1 summarizes Latinos' perceptions of general commonality with whites, blacks, and Latinos. This figure demonstrates that Latinos perceive more commonality with other Latinos than blacks and whites. Yet, when comparing their sense of commonality with blacks with those toward whites, I find that Latinos feel slightly closer to blacks than whites. On the other hand, analyses of CCES data reveal that Latinos sense greater economic commonality with whites than blacks. Thus, while these results do not provide robust support for the idea that Latinos regard blacks as greater allies than whites, these findings do reveal that Latinos distinguish their co-ethnics from blacks and whites and little difference exists in how Latinos regard whites and blacks.[4]

FIG. 1. Latinos' perceptions of commonality with blacks, whites, and Latinos

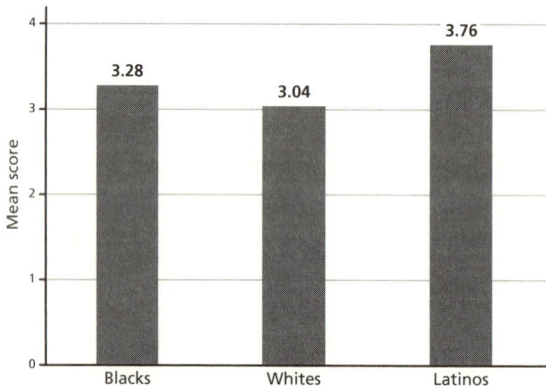

Source: Author's calculations using 2006 LNS data.

To what extent do Latinos perceive African Americans, whites, and other Latinos as competitors? Figure 2 summarizes Latinos' general competition with blacks and with other Latinos. The results shown in this figure illustrate that Latinos sense marginally greater competition with Latinos than with

African Americans as is also found by Morin and colleagues (2011). The LNS does not examine Latinos' perceptions of competition with whites, so I am not able to examine Latinos' sense of rivalry with whites. Nonetheless, the 2010 CCES explores Latinos' perceptions of employment competition with blacks and whites. When comparing Latinos' sense of rivalry with blacks with that with whites, I find that Latinos perceive a little more employment competition with whites than with African Americans.[5] These results suggest that Latinos may have greater affinity with blacks than whites, and that Latinos do not regard African Americans as serious competitors for jobs relative to whites and other Latinos.

FIG. 2. Latinos' perceptions of competition with blacks and Latinos

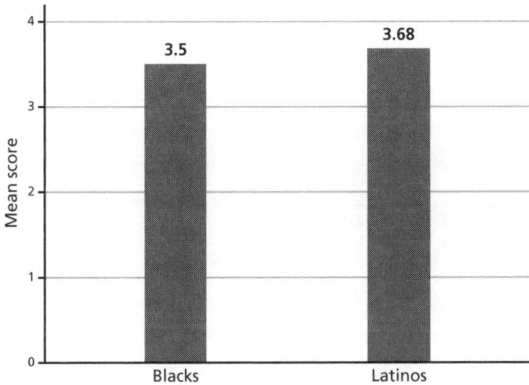

Source: Author's calculations using 2006 LNS data.

Given that native-born and foreign-born Latinos' relations with non-Latinos may be distinct (due to different experiences associated with different place of birth), I briefly examine Latinos' perceptions of commonality and competition with whites and blacks by native status. Descriptive statistics using 2006 LNS data illustrate that foreign-born Latinos perceive more commonality with Latinos and less with African Americans, whereas native-born Latinos sense approximately the same amount of commonality with blacks as their co-ethnics. When it comes to perceptions of commonality with whites in relation to those of Latinos, foreign-born and native-born Latinos' attitudes toward whites relative to other Latinos are nearly identical. When I juxtapose Latino immigrants' feelings of closeness with whites with those toward blacks, their attitudes toward these two racial groups are also very similar. Nonetheless, considerable differences exist between native-born perceptions of whites and blacks and between native-born and foreign-born Latinos' perceptions of African Americans. Latinos born in the United States exhibit greater commonality with African Americans than with whites as well as greater closeness with blacks than their immigrant counterparts. These findings suggest that Latinos' places of birth influence their racial attitudes and that Latinos born in the United States are more likely to adopt a minority status and affinity with blacks than foreign-born Latinos (Sanchez 2008).

In general, the findings discussed above do not provide robust evidence that Latinos regard blacks or whites as greater allies. Evidence regarding whether Latinos perceive more commonality with blacks than with whites, and whether Latinos regard blacks as greater threats than whites, is mixed. Still, my results reveal that Latinos regard other Latinos differently than they do blacks and whites, and they perceive greater commonality and competition with other Latinos than with blacks and whites. As to native-born and foreign-born Latinos' attitudes, Latinos' places of birth can translate into distinct racial attitudes. I turn to predictors of Latinos' sense of closeness and competition with whites and blacks to further explore Latinos' racial dispositions.

Testing the Triangular Theory of Contact, Context, and Identification for Latinos

In this section, I test my TTCCI on Latinos' views toward whites and African Americans in a multitude of ways. First, relying on 2006 LNS data, I analyze the effects of Latinos' social networks, sociopolitical power, and racial attitudes on their sense of commonality with blacks and whites as well as their perceptions of competition with blacks. I center my analyses on Latinos' distinct nativity and develop analyses for foreign-born and native-born Latinos. After each of the commonality and competition analyses using LNS data, I summarize my analyses of 2010 CCES data placing emphasis on the effects of subjective racial context and the correlation between sensing commonality and perceiving competition with a certain racial group. I test my hypotheses using ordered logistic regression given the ordered nature of my dependent variables.[6] I weight the Latino sample in all of my analyses so that it is proportionate to the Latino population in the United States.

Explaining Latinos' Perceptions of Commonality with Blacks and Whites

Table 5 presents the results of my LNS data analyses for Latinos' perceptions of commonality with whites and African Americans. The models in this table are also divided by native status.[7] In this section, I begin by discussing the determinants of Latinos' sense of commonality with blacks

TABLE 5. Ordered logistical regression results for Latino perceptions of commonality with blacks and whites, by nativity

	Blacks		Whites	
	Foreign born	Native born	Foreign born	Native born
SOCIAL CONTACT				
Black friends	0.34***	0.61***	−0.11*	−0.47***
	(0.10)	(0.12)	(0.08)	(0.14)
White friends	−0.14	−0.22***	0.21***	0.31***
	(0.12)	(0.09)	(0.08)	(0.11)
Black coworkers	−0.01	−0.19*	0.07	0.06
	(0.12)	(0.11)	(0.10)	(0.10)
White coworkers	−0.10**	0.22	−0.21	−0.34*
	(0.06)	(0.27)	(0.17)	(0.21)
Black group participation	0.18	0.22	−0.21	−0.34*
	(0.16)	(0.27)	(0.17)	(0.21)
White group participation	−0.02	−0.12	0.24***	0.36***
	(0.11)	(0.14)	(0.10)	(0.21)
RACIAL CONTEXT (COUNTY, 2006 ESTIMATE)				
Percentage white	−0.30	−1.02*	0.69***	0.80*
	(0.42)	(0.59)	(0.36)	(0.58)
ECONOMIC CONTEXT (COUNTY)				
Percentage with high school	−0.01	−0.04**	0.003	0.01
degree (2006–10 estimates)	(0.01)	(0.01)	(0.01)	(0.02)
Poverty rate (2007 estimate)	0.0001	−0.04***	0.01	0.02
	(0.01)	(0.02)	(0.01)	(0.02)
Unemployment rate (2008	−0.04**	−0.10***	−0.01	0.09***
estimate)	(0.02)	(0.03)	(0.02)	(0.03)
INSTITUTIONAL CONTEXT (COUNTY, 2006)				
Latino legislator	0.09	0.16	−0.08	−0.36**
	(0.14)	(0.15)	(0.10)	(0.17)
Majority-minority district	−0.12	−0.04	0.04	0.09
	(0.14)	(0.16)	(0.11)	(0.18)
Democratic candidate	−0.18	0.26	0.11	−0.09
	(0.45)	(0.54)	(0.38)	(0.74)
State provisions for direct	−0.10	−0.06	0.15*	−0.09
democracy	(0.10)	(0.11)	(0.10)	(0.13)
FEELINGS OF IDENTIFICATION				
Identification with blacks	—	—	0.53***	0.49***
Identification with whites	0.50***	0.45***	—	—
	(0.03)	(0.06)		

TABLE 5. (*continued*)

	Blacks		Whites	
	Foreign born	Native born	Foreign born	Native born
N	3,372	1,670	3,372	1,670
Pseudo-R²	0.07	0.07	0.07	0.06

Source: 2006 LNS.

Note: ***p < 0.01 level; **p < 0.05 level; * p < 0.10 level. Entries not in parentheses are unstandardized b coefficients; entries in parentheses denote the corresponding standard errors to the b coefficients and are clustered by county. Other control variables include commonality with other Latinos, linked fate with other Latinos, English language proficiency, skin tone, being Mexican, residing in the South, age, gender, education, income, and partisan identification.

and then discuss the key predictors of Latinos' perceptions of commonality with whites.

PERCEPTIONS OF COMMONALITY WITH BLACKS

In general, the results in the commonality with blacks analyses for foreign-born and native-born Latinos reveal some support for the TTCCI. In accordance with the social contact hypothesis, native-born and foreign-born Latinos with greater numbers of black friends are more likely to perceive commonality with African Americans (McClain et al. 2006). I also find some support for my divisive effects hypothesis. As expected, native-born Latinos with mostly white friends sense less commonality with blacks. While I find that Latino immigrants with white coworkers are less likely to sense commonality with blacks in support of my divisive effects hypothesis, I am surprised to find that native-born Latinos with a greater number of white coworkers are more likely to perceive commonality with blacks. A justification for these findings is that social interactions with non-Latinos can heighten native-born Latinos' identification with other non-Latinos, such as blacks, while the same would not apply for immigrants since they are still slowly becoming familiar with blacks and whites.

Although racial and institutional context do not systematically structure foreign-born and native-born Latinos' perceptions of African Americans, economic context does.[8] I find robust support for my economic threat and blacks hypothesis since my three measures of economic context have a statistically significant effect on native-born Latinos' attitudes toward blacks. Residing in a high-threat economic setting (i.e., a county with a high unemployment or poverty rate) is negatively related to native-born Latinos' sense of commonality with blacks. This finding is further supported by figure 3, which shows a strong decrease in predicted probability between a county's unemployment rate and native-born Latinos' perceptions of commonality with African Americans.[9] As the unemployment rate increases, perceptions of closeness with blacks moves from 0.13 to 0.04, suggesting that the probability of perceiving commonality with blacks is much smaller in high unemployment settings than in low settings. As expected, residing in a county with a high unemployment rate decreases the likelihood that Latino immigrants perceive commonality with blacks. Further, as I hypothesized, residing in a county with high levels of education decreases native-born Latinos' feelings of closeness to blacks.

FIG. 3. Probability of native-born Latinos' commonality with blacks by county unemployment rate

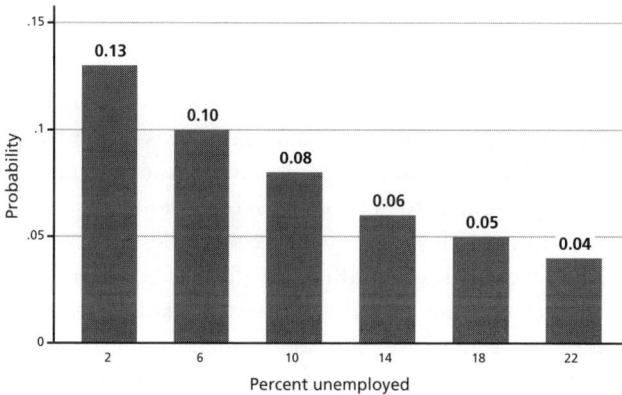

Source: Author's calculations using 2006 LNS data.

Feelings of identification with whites structure Latinos' perceptions of commonality with blacks. Wallsten and Nteta (2011) conclude that Latinos who sense commonality with whites also perceive commonality with African Americans. Based on the results, I can confidently confirm their results and also state that native-born *and* foreign-born Latinos who identify with whites are more likely to perceive commonality with blacks. Regardless of whether one is born in the United States or outside of this country, feeling close to whites heightens Latinos' sense of commonality with others who are non-Latinos, such as African Americans, and may decrease their perceptions of closeness with those who share their ethnicity. This finding is further examined in the next chapter.

    In addition to contact, context, and identification measures, I find that a few leading determinants of Latino racial attitudes have some significant effects on Latinos' perceptions of commonality with blacks.[10] As expected, foreign-born *and* native-born Latinos who perceive commonality with other Latinos and have linked fates with other Latinos are more likely to perceive commonality with blacks. I also find that length of time in the United States does not significantly explain Latino immigrants' attitudes toward blacks, thus providing less support for the notion that the longer Latinos reside in the United States, the more they feel close to African Americans. Yet, as hypothesized, foreign-born and native-born Latinos who are dominant in English sense greater commonality with blacks. As expected, light-skinned Latino immigrants are less likely to perceive commonality with blacks. With regard to regional location, somewhat as expected, native-born though not foreign-born Latinos who reside in the South are less likely to perceive commonality with blacks.

The results for my commonality with blacks analyses reveal some support for my TTCCI. Social contact and feelings of identification with whites strongly shape native-born and foreign-born Latinos' perceptions of closeness to blacks though not always in the direction that I expect. While immediate interaction with whites may influence Latino immigrants to perceive that they must side with blacks or whites, a more profound understanding of race relations and opportunities to network with blacks and whites may influence native-born Latinos to feel closer to blacks regardless of their contact with whites. Yet, my hypotheses regarding the effect of economic context more precisely predict native-born Latinos' views toward African Americans. Since native-born Latinos have more solid understandings of the racial structure and their opportunities and level of power in the United States, when they are in generally vulnerable economic settings they may be less predisposed to feel close to blacks and sense greater commonality with other Latinos.

PERCEPTIONS OF COMMONALITY WITH WHITES

Turning to my analyses of Latinos' sense of closeness with whites in table 5, I find some similarities between the results in the commonality with black analyses and those in these analyses. Social contact and identification with blacks significantly shape foreign-born and native-born Latinos' perceptions of whites. As expected, social contact with whites (i.e., friendship *and* group participation) augment Latinos' feelings of closeness to whites (Nteta and Wallsten 2007). In support of the divisive effects hypothesis, native-born Latinos with mostly black friends are less prone to perceive commonality with whites. Also, in accordance with my hypotheses, Latinos who identify with blacks are more inclined to perceive commonality with whites (Wallsten and Nteta 2011). The results in figure 4 further support this finding. As foreign-born *and* native-born Latinos' identification with blacks increases, so does their sense of commonality with whites. Again, these findings highlight the fact that Latinos' perceptions of commonality with one non-Latino group increases the likelihood that they perceive closeness with another non-Latino group.

FIG. 4. Probability of Latinos' commonality with whites by feelings of identification with blacks

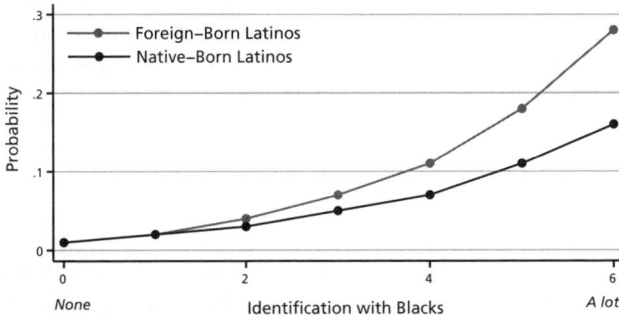

Source: Author's calculations using 2006 LNS data.

Unlike the results in the commonality with blacks analyses, racial and institutional context somewhat structure Latinos' attitudes toward whites, and economic context plays a more minor role. In accordance with my racial threat and whites hypothesis, Latino immigrants in a largely white county are more likely to perceive commonality with whites. Further, in accordance with what I hypothesized, native-born Latinos who are descriptively represented are less likely to feel close to whites. The only measure of economic context that significantly shapes Latinos' attitudes toward whites is unemployment rate. I find that native-born Latinos who reside in an economically vulnerable setting sense greater commonality with whites. A plausible explanation for this finding is that Latinos who reside in an area with high unemployment are more likely to feel close to whites, a group with generally higher socioeconomic clout than other groups.

Similar to my findings regarding the leading predictors of Latinos' sense of closeness to African Americans, I find that internal commonality, internal linked fate, skin tone, and age play critical roles in shaping Latinos' perceptions of commonality with whites. Latino immigrants with strong commonality and linked fates with other Latinos are more likely to feel close to whites. As expected, native-born and foreign-born Latinos who identify as light-skinned are more inclined to perceive commonality with whites. Older and less educated Latinos, regardless of native status, sense greater commonality with whites.

The results of the commonality with whites models as a whole illustrate that social networks, context (racial, economic, and political), and identification with blacks, as well as leading predictors of Latino racial attitudes, considerably explain Latinos' perceptions of closeness with whites. My findings also provide significant support for the social contact hypothesis and the group position theory. As expected, the TTCCI is better able to predict native-born Latinos' attitudes toward whites than those of Latino immigrants. Since native-born Latinos are more integrated and aware of the racial structure of the United States (who has power, who is less powerful, who has an opportunity to obtain more power), their perceptions of their own levels of influence are more likely to affect how they regard others who differ in status.

The 2010 CCES data allows me to take a more contemporary approach to examining Latinos' perceptions of blacks and whites. Further, this data set allows me to analyze the effects of subjective racial context (i.e., Latinos' perceptions of who surrounds them) on Latinos' racial attitudes, a topic about which we have relatively limited knowledge since most studies that examine racial threat center on objective racial context. The correlation between Latinos' perceptions of the number of whites in their county and the actual number of whites in their county reveals that the two measures are not related. I find comparable findings for the relationship between subjective and objective black context. Thus, Latinos' perceptions of who lives in their counties do not always reflect who actually lives in their counties. Table 6 presents analyses of Latinos' perceptions of economic commonality with blacks and whites. These analyses center on predictors that did not significantly explain Latinos' attitudes using 2006 LNS data and those whose effects have not been examined previously. Surprisingly, social contact with blacks is the only factor that structures Latinos' economic commonality with blacks. As expected, social interaction with blacks in the neighborhood is positively related to their commonality with blacks. When it comes to the determinants of Latinos' perceptions of commonality with whites, only social contact and political context structure Latinos' attitudes. Latinos with increased interaction with whites in neighborhoods and Latinos in states with direct democracy provisions are more likely to perceive economic commonality with whites than Latinos with little to no

TABLE 6. Ordered logistical regression results for Latino perceptions of economic commonality with blacks and whites

	Blacks		Whites	
SOCIAL CONTACT				
Black neighbors	0.70**	(0.42)	0.04	(0.31)
White neighbors	−0.39*	(0.27)	0.79***	(0.34)
RACIAL CONTEXT				
Perception of whites in county	0.24	(0.34)	0.54*	(0.43)
ECONOMIC CONTEXT (COUNTY)				
Poverty rate (2006–10 estimates)	−0.06	(0.04)	0.04	(0.06)
INSTITUTIONAL CONTEXT (COUNTY, 2010)				
Latino legislator	−0.01	(0.51)	0.12	(0.53)
State provisions for direct democracy	−0.39	(0.32)	0.77**	(0.45)
Cut 1	−2.48	(0.94)	−0.60	(1.42)
Cut 2	−1.03	(0.92)	1.44	(1.19)
Cut 3	1.18	(0.90)	3.87	(1.23)
N	131		114	
Pseudo-R^2	0.04		0.08	

Source: 2010 CCES.

Note: ***p < 0.01 level; **p < 0.05 level; * p < 0.10 level. Entries not in parentheses are unstandardized b coefficients; entries in parentheses denote the corresponding standard errors to the b coefficients and are clustered by county. Given the small sample of Latinos in the CCES, this model focuses on the determinants of Latinos' racial attitudes that were not explored by LNS data.

interaction with whites and Latinos who do not live in states with ballot initiatives.

Explaining Latinos' Perceptions of Competition with Blacks and Whites

In this section, I explore Latinos' perceptions of competition with African Americans and whites. I begin with a discussion of my analyses using LNS data and then discuss my findings using 2010 CCES data.

PERCEPTIONS OF COMPETITION WITH BLACKS

Table 7 presents the results of my analyses for Latinos' perceptions of competition with African Americans.[11] As is the case in table 5, the models in this table are divided by Latinos' native status. At the outset, the TTCCI seems

TABLE 7. Ordered logistical regression results for Latinos' perceptions of competition with blacks, by nativity

	Foreign born		Native born	
SOCIAL CONTACT				
Black friends	−0.14*	(0.09)	−0.11	(0.09)
White friends	−0.07	(0.07)	−0.15	(0.09)
Black coworkers	0.01	(0.10)	0.05	(0.11)
White coworkers	−0.001	(0.06)	0.04	(0.09)
Black group participation	0.40**	(0.19)	−0.18	(0.19)
White group participation	−0.12	(0.10)	−0.01	(0.11)
RACIAL CONTEXT (COUNTY, 2006 ESTIMATE)				
Percentage black	0.72**	(0.37)	0.72	(0.68)
ECONOMIC CONTEXT (COUNTY)				
Percentage with high school degree (2006–10 estimates)	0.02**	(0.01)	−0.02	(0.01)
Poverty rate (2007 estimate)	0.02***	(0.01)	−0.002	(0.02)
Unemployment rate (2008 estimate)	0.05***	(0.02)	−0.01	(0.04)
INSTITUTIONAL CONTEXT (COUNTY, 2006)				
Latino legislator	0.12	(0.12)	0.11	(0.16)
Majority-minority district	0.07	(0.14)	−0.37**	(0.20)
Democratic candidate	−0.51	(0.42)	0.51	(0.60)
State provisions for direct democracy	−0.26***	(0.13)	0.18	(0.14)
FEELINGS OF IDENTIFICATION				
Identification with blacks	0.11***	(0.02)	0.07*	(0.04)
Identification with whites	0.04	(0.03)	0.02	(0.03)
N	3,492		1,670	
Pseudo-R^2	0.01		0.01	

Source: 2006 LNS.

Note: ***$p < 0.01$ level; **$p < 0.05$ level; *$p < 0.10$ level. Entries not in parentheses are unstandardized b coefficients; entries in parentheses denote the corresponding standard errors to the b coefficients and are clustered by county. Other control variables include commonality with other Latinos, linked fate with other Latinos, English language proficiency, skin tone, being Mexican, residing in the South, age, gender, education, income, and partisan identification.

to better explain Latino immigrants' perceptions of competition with African Americans than those of native-born Latinos. In the model of foreign-born Latinos, I find that at least one predictor in each category of variables has a statistically significant effect on Latinos' sense of rivalry with blacks. In contrast to my social contact hypothesis, I find that foreign-born Latinos in largely black organizations are more likely to perceive competition with blacks. Further, as hypothesized and in accordance with the racial threat hypothesis, Latino immigrants who reside in a predominantly black setting perceive greater rivalry with African Americans than those who do not reside in a largely black county (see Sanchez and Morin 2011).

While economic and institutional contexts barely structure native-born Latinos' sense of rivalry with blacks, identification with blacks and several contextual measures structure Latino immigrants' perceptions. Latino immigrants who reside in an environment with a high unemployment rate, high poverty rate, and high education level perceive greater competition with blacks.

Figures 5 and 6 further explore the effects of economic context on foreign-born Latinos' sense of rivalry with blacks. Figure 5 demonstrates the progression in the predicted probability between a county's poverty rate and foreign-born Latinos' perceptions of competition with blacks. As the county poverty rate increases, the predicted probability moves from 0.09 to 0.17, showing that Latinos' sense of rivalry toward blacks is higher for those in high poverty settings than those in low poverty settings. Figure 6 presents how a county's education level affects foreign-born Latinos' sense of competition with African Americans. The results in the figure reveal that a rise in education level (percent high school graduates) coincides with an increase in perceptions of competition with blacks. Again, though these findings may seem contradictory, these results reveal that living in an economically weak *and* stable setting can influence Latinos to regard blacks as threatening. Since Latinos compete with blacks for educational resources (Borjas 1999), it may be that Latinos who are in an environment characterized by high education are more likely to sense that African Americans are encroaching on their status. Still, as hypothesized, Latino immigrants who do not live in a state with direct democracy provisions sense greater rivalry with blacks. Regarding the relationship between identification with blacks and whites, and Latinos' hostility with blacks, the only coefficient that reaches statistical significance is identification with blacks in the model of Latino immigrants. This coefficient contradicts my hypothesis yet supports Jones-Correa's (2011) assertion that Latinos who feel close to African Americans also regard them as competitors.

FIG. 5. Probability of foreign-born Latinos' competition with blacks by county poverty rate

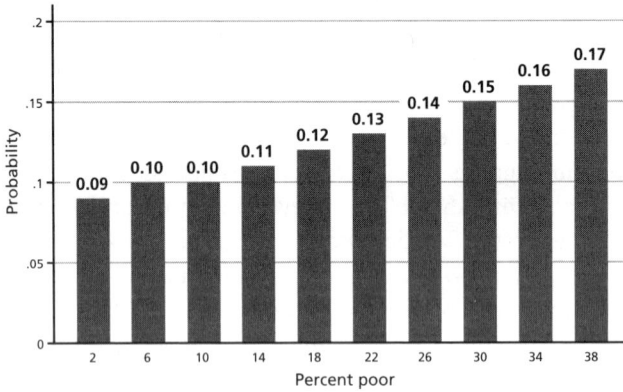

Source: Author's calculations using 2006 LNS data.

FIG. 6. Probability of foreign-born Latinos' competition with blacks by county education level

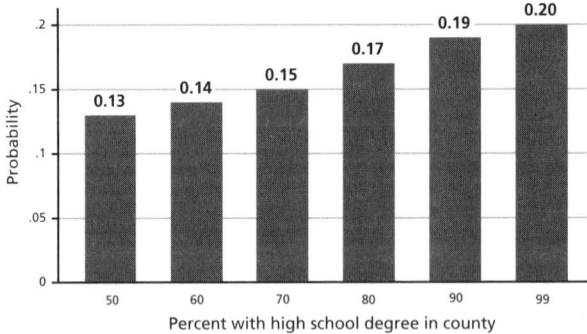

Source: Author's calculations using 2006 LNS data.

A few demographic characteristics and leading predictors of Latino racial attitudes shape Latinos' hostility with African Americans. Surprisingly, Latinos with linked fate with other Latinos are more likely to regard blacks as rivals. Interestingly, living in the South does not play a critical role in structuring Latinos' antagonism toward African Americans. As to the demographic factors, I find that Mexican and younger native-born Latinos are less likely to perceive competition with blacks thus providing some support for the idea that relations between blacks and certain Latino groups may improve.

The results of my analyses of Latinos' perceptions of competition with blacks illustrate some support for my TTCCI, particularly among foreign-born Latinos. As expected, this theory better explains foreign-born Latinos' perceptions of competition with blacks relative to those of native-born Latinos. Since Latino immigrants are less integrated into the United States and thus are less likely to adopt a fixed minority identity than their native-born counterparts (see Kaufmann 2003), residing in weak economic and political environments may prompt them to regard blacks as competitors.

The 2010 CCES data set provides me the opportunity to analyze the effects of contact and context measures that I have not previously examined. As the results in table 8 reveal, my measures of contact and context do not structure Latinos' sense of rivalry with blacks.

TABLE 8. Ordered logistical regression results for Latino perceptions of employment competition with blacks and whites

	Blacks		Whites	
SOCIAL CONTACT				
Black neighbors	0.52*	(0.33)	0.52*	
White neighbors	−0.10	(0.25)	−0.06	(0.25)
RACIAL CONTEXT (COUNTY)				
Perception of whites in county	−0.44*	(0.32)	−0.68***	(0.25)
ECONOMIC CONTEXT (COUNTY)				
Poverty rate (2006–10 estimate)	0.02	(0.06)	−0.06	(0.05)
INSTITUTIONAL CONTEXT (COUNTY, 2010)				
Latino legislator	0.06	(0.48)	0.24	(0.59)
State provisions for direct	0.13	(0.37)	−0.32	(0.43)
Cut 1	−2.35	(1.15)	−4.56	(1.13)
Cut 2	−0.94	(1.14)	−3.39	(1.11)
Cut 3	1.42	(1.08)	−1.51	(1.06)
Cut 4	2.00	(1.15)	−0.48	(1.09)
N	136		117	
Pseudo-R^2	0.02		0.04	

Source: 2010 CCES.

Note: ***p < 0.01 level; **p < 0.05 level; *p < 0.10 level. Entries not in parentheses are unstandardized b coefficients; entries in parentheses denote the corresponding standard errors to the b coefficients and are clustered by county. Given the small sample of Latinos in the CCES, this model focuses on the determinants of Latinos' racial attitudes that were not explored by LNS data.

PERCEPTIONS OF COMPETITION WITH WHITES

Unlike the 2006 LNS, the 2010 CCES allows me to test the TTCCI on Latinos' perceptions of competition with whites. While I am not able to assess Latinos' sense of rivalry with whites by Latinos' native status due to CCES data limitations, I take advantage of a very recent data set and center my analyses on questions that I have not been able to examine previously. Table 8 presents the analyses for Latinos' perceptions of employment competition with whites. The results of this table indicate that Latinos who sense that they reside near a large number of whites are less predisposed to perceive competition with whites.

To what extent does subjective context structure Latinos' perceptions of employment competition with whites? Much of the discussion regarding the relationship between racial context and Latinos' racial attitudes has centered on objective context: the actual percentage of racial/ethnic groups in one's neighborhood, county, census tract, and so on. Yet, since individuals' perceptions of their surroundings can shape their political attitudes (Wong et al. 2012), and attitudes toward race can often by structured by individuals' perceptions, I examine the degree to which subjective context shapes Latinos' antagonism toward whites without altering any previous hypotheses. It is important to note that prior to these analyses, I explored the effect of objective context (percent number of whites in one's county in 2011) on Latinos' perceptions of employment competition with whites controlling for the effects of other variables and found that objective context did not have a significant effect. Further, the correlation between Latinos' perceptions of the number of whites in their counties with the actual number of whites (based on 2011 U.S. Census estimates) was 0.07, suggesting that Latinos' perceptions of how many white neighbors they have is not related to the actual numbers of whites that surround them. While some may interpret this lack of correlation as a problem, I regard this finding as a contribution to our understanding of the effects of subjective context and how social desirability may affect Latinos' perceptions of who resides near them. Although a group of Latinos may live in a predominantly white county, it is their perception of the number of whites that surround them that considerably alters their predisposition to regard whites as competitors for employment. The findings shown in table 8 reveal that Latinos who perceive that they live near many whites are less likely to regard whites as economic rivals. In order to further delve into this finding, I examine the results shown in figure 7, which illustrates the progression in the predicted probability of sensing economic competition with whites when Latinos perceive that they have no whites in their county to having a lot of whites in their county.[12] The results appearing in figure 7 reveal robust support for my racial threat and whites hypothesis: as Latinos reside near a large number of whites, the predicted probability of perceiving employment competition with whites decreases. Hence, a rise in the number of whites that Latinos think surround them coincides with a decrease in the likelihood that Latinos perceive whites as a threat to their jobs.

FIG. 7. Probability of Latinos' employment competition with whites by number of whites in county

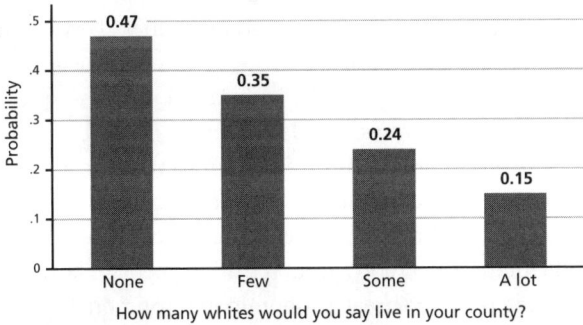

How many whites would you say live in your county?

Source: Author's calculations using 2006 LNS data.

Conclusion

In the past few decades, Latinos have become one of the fastest growing and most influential minority groups in the United States. While they are far from having the socioeconomic influence of whites, they are a distinct ethnic group with considerable disparities in social environment, opportunities for social and political progress, and racial attitudes. In this chapter, according to my TTCCI, Latinos' social networks, context (racial, economic, and political), and perceptions of whites and blacks largely structure their perceptions of commonality and competition toward Africans Americans and whites.

A key contribution of this chapter is my comparative approach to examining Latinos' racial attitudes. Not only do I analyze Latinos' perceptions of commonality and competition with blacks and whites but I also examine Latinos' perceptions of other Latinos. Given that Latinos at the national level sense greater commonality with Latinos than with their white and black counterparts, and that Latinos sense greater rivalry with their co-ethnics than with blacks, we can no longer overlook the importance of assessing Latinos' racial dispositions in light of their perceptions of other Latinos. It is critical to move beyond the "black/white attitudes box" when examining Latinos' perceptions of competition *and* commonality, and center our studies on considering Latinos' sentiments toward blacks and whites as well as those of their co-ethnics. I also find that native-born Latinos (relative to Latino immigrants) perceive greater commonality with blacks than whites and sense almost as much closeness with other Latinos as they do with blacks. This suggests that Latinos born in the United States are more inclined to adopt a minority status and have greater affinity with blacks than foreign-born Latinos.

Relying on comprehensive, contemporary survey data from the 2006 LNS and 2010 CCES, my analyses reveal several interesting trends in Latinos' attitudes that advance our understanding of how Latinos who differ in nativity regard their white and black counterparts and other Latinos. For instance, I find that foreign-born and native-born Latinos who interact socially with blacks and whites generally feel closer to these racial groups. These results reveal that the social contact hypothesis explains how Latinos regard other racial groups, regardless of Latinos' nativity. Still, I find that social contact has divisive effects on foreign-born Latinos' attitudes toward whites and blacks. Regarding the effects of context, I find fervent support for Blumer's (1958) and Bobo and Hutchings's (1996) group position theory. Native-born and foreign-born Latinos in high-threat economic environments (settings that make them feel powerless) are less likely to have affinity with blacks. Still, residing in a low-threat socioeconomic setting corresponds with higher levels of competition with blacks among foreign-born Latinos.

As to the effects of political context, I find that Latinos who have greater political power (i.e., reside in a majority-minority district or a state with provisions for direct democracy) are less likely to view blacks as threatening. While this work offers one of the first studies to examine the effect of political context on Latinos' perceptions of commonality and competition with blacks and whites, future studies on racial attitudes should analyze the effects of a type of context that has been largely ignored. When it comes to Latinos' racial surroundings, I find that differences exist in the effects of objective and subjective contexts on Latinos' antagonism toward whites. While residing in a mostly white county does not have a discernible effect on Latinos' employment competition with whites, Latinos who *perceive* that they live in a predominantly white county sense less employment competition with whites. These results contribute significantly to our knowledge of Latinos' attitude formation and thus challenge future studies to seriously assess the effects of subjective context on racial attitudes. As to perceptions, I conclude that Latinos' identification with one non-Latino group increases their sense of commonality with another non-Latino group. Could these results be a function of Latinos' assimilation behavior or can they be explained by another factor? This question is further examined in the next chapter examining Latinos' attitudes using focus group data.

Thus, based on these analyses, foreign-born and native-born Latinos' distinct social networks, environments, and feelings of identification with their co-ethnics and others influence them to regard blacks and whites in divergent ways. Besides further exploring the effects of perceptions of commonality, another question remains: given Latinos' recent emerging presence in southern cities, how do Latinos regard their black and white counterparts in an emerging Latino area in the South? Chapter 3 explores this question as well as the effects of social contact on Latinos' sense of closeness and rivalry with whites and blacks by examining focus group data of Latino residents in New Orleans, Louisiana.

3

Latinos Discuss Race Relations
in New Orleans

In addition to analyzing quantitative data to test the TTCCI, I take a qualitative approach to obtain a more complete understanding of Latino/black and Latino/white race relations. Previous research has significantly relied on survey data at the national, state, and local levels to analyze Latinos' views toward blacks and whites. Yet, solely relying on close-ended survey question answers to uncover Latino attitudes toward multifaceted, controversial topics that individuals may have deep-rooted views about may not allow researchers to disentangle fully the intricacies and intensity of Latinos' views toward blacks and whites (see Hibbing and Theiss-Morse 1995). In this chapter, I rely on focus group data of Latino residents in an emerging Latino area to obtain a deeper understanding of their racial attitudes and to address some of the unanswered questions from my quantitative analyses in the previous chapter.

Intergroup Relations in the South

Racial dynamics in the South are largely distinct from those of other regions. From 2000 to 2010, the Latino population in the South increased by 57 percent, "which was four times the growth of the total population in the South" (U.S. Census Bureau 2011). One of the primary reasons for Latinos' migration to the South was employment opportunities in numerous industries including agriculture, meat and poultry processing, manufacturing, construction, and service (Marrow 2011). African Americans in the South are largely employed in these industries, and many regard the new ethnic population as a threat to blacks' sociopolitical and employment status, especially since their life chances, opportunities to move up the social ladder, and daily experiences have been greatly defined by their race (McClain et al. 2011). Hence, it is not surprising that racial dynamics between whites, blacks, and Latinos are somewhat unique to the South. In her study of Latinos in two counties in North Carolina, Helen Marrow (2011) finds that Latinos' entrance in largely black areas is met with heightened tension between both groups in schools, neighborhoods, and places of work. These tensions result in greater distancing between blacks and Latinos due to conflict and discrimination, yet better relations between whites and Latinos. Additionally, Jason L. Morin and his colleagues (2011) conclude that Latino/black race relations in the South are distinct from other areas since Latinos who reside in southern states are more inclined to regard blacks as competitors than those who live outside of the South.

Therefore, in order to better understand the recent development of racial dynamics among blacks, whites, and Latinos in the South, I explore Latinos' perceptions of closeness and antagonism with their black and white counterparts in a southern city that has recently experienced a large influx of Latinos.

Why New Orleans?

The city of New Orleans is an emerging epicenter of black-brown racial tensions. Days after hurricane Katrina struck the Gulf Coast, the city received a large influx of Latinos due to a considerable demand for laborers to assist in rebuilding the city. The *Times Picayune* reported that a U.S. Census Bureau survey estimated that approximately 100,000 Hispanics arrived to hurricane-affected communities four months after Katrina hit the area (Waller 2006). Before Katrina, New Orleans was not known as a Latino immigrant region, yet in the last few years, African Americans, the majority of the population of New Orleans (Plyer and Ortiz 2009), and whites have noticed the strong presence of Latinos in their city. A recent report with data compiled by the Greater New Orleans Community Data Center indicates that as of 2011, Latinos comprised nearly 13 percent of the population in Jefferson Parish (7.1% in 2000) and 5.2 percent in Orleans Parish (3.1% in 2000) (Ortiz and Plyer 2012).[1] Moreover, from 2000 to 2010, the Latino population in the New Orleans metro area increased by 57 percent (greater than the 43% increase in the United States), suggesting that New Orleans is an emerging gateway metro area like Atlanta and Raleigh-Durham (Plyer 2011).[2]

Besides establishing a solid demographic presence, Latinos in New Orleans heavily occupied the blue-collar employment sector, a situation that yielded a fervent response by several residents. Many Latino newcomers obtained jobs in the construction and service industries, positions that were often occupied by African Americans before the storm. Blacks in New Orleans have noticed these vast fluctuations in demographics and employment, and many have not responded to these changes happily. Several have criticized and openly protested the presence of Latinos into the city's blue-collar workforce, and many perceive their presence as an economic and cultural threat (Eaton 2005). Moreover, several months after the hurricane, the city's African American former mayor even publicly suggested that there is a possibility that the city will be overrun by Mexican workers (Eaton 2006).

The shifting demographic landscape and the racial dynamics that occurred and continue to occur in New Orleans are not unique to the area, and there are several reasons why New Orleans is not the only setting for studying Latinos' attitudes. First, many cities throughout the United States have grappled with a surge in Latino population resulting in similar tensions between local residents and newcomers. In traditional Latino areas such as Los Angeles and New York City, racial strain and conflict between Latinos and blacks abound (Susman 2010; Guidi 2012). These tensions are greatly attributed to fiscal concerns by blacks that Latino workers are favored over African Americans, that Latinos depress wages for blacks, and that Latinos pose a cultural threat (Johnson et al. 1997; Susman 2010). Second, the tensions that existed and continue to exist among whites, blacks, and Latinos compare to several cities in the southern region of the United States. New Orleans, like many cities in the South, has an extensive history of discrimination against blacks and antagonism between African Americans and whites. Additionally, in New Orleans and in numerous southern cities, blacks are substantially less dominant economically and politically than whites. Hence, the black/Latino racial dynamics that exist in New Orleans may not be substantially distinct from those in other southern cities.

Methods

The data reported in this qualitative project derive from focus group interviews that I directed. While focus groups are not a common research method in political science, they are gaining popularity. Although there are limitations associated with focus group methodology, such as generally not capturing the breadth of various topics as provided by survey research (Morgan 1996, 138–39), focus group research has several strengths. First, unlike survey research, focus group methodology does not inhibit the number of topics that can be discussed. Although researchers can provide participants with guidance as to what topics to discuss through a set of questions, individuals' answers can and often times do diverge into a variety of subtopics. A second asset of focus group research is that participants have the opportunity to obtain background information regarding a particular issue with which they may not be familiar or understand (Hibbing and Theiss-Morse 1995), unlike survey research, which often encounters problems with respondents not answering questions accurately (Brians et al. 2010, 348–49) or stating "Don't Know." Third, focus groups allow researchers to capture the intensity and depth of participants' responses to particular topics (Hibbing and Theiss-Morse 1995; Morgan 1996). A fourth advantage of focus groups over surveys is that participants are able to interact with each other, permitting the researcher to examine the extent to which individuals concur or differ on various topics, which is especially critical for comprehending individuals' views toward controversial, intricate topics (Morgan and Krueger 1993; Morgan 1996, 139). Lastly, focus group data can greatly improve survey questions by targeting particular themes that arise when individuals' responses are not constrained in a specific way (Fraga et al. 2010). Thus, for such an intricate topic as Latinos' attitudes toward blacks and whites in New Orleans, focus group research is a critical and valuable research method.

The interviews were broadly conceived as an exploratory analysis of Latinos' perceptions of commonality and competition with African Americans and whites.[3] Given that this project is one of the first focus group studies that explore Latinos' perceptions of blacks and whites, there is very little research to rely on to model my questions. Nonetheless, I based my colloquial focus group questions on the 2006 Latino National Survey (LNS) and 2010 Cooperative Congressional Election Study (CCES) questions. My focus group questions centered on the levels of social interactions that Latinos have with blacks and whites, Latinos' sense of commonality and competition with these two groups, and the effects of social contact on Latinos' views of whites and African Americans. The questions for the focus groups of Latinos are found in the appendix.

The collection and analysis of focus group data are comparable to those of other studies in the field. Discussions were tape recorded and topically structured through the use of questions allowing for participants to discuss their attitudes unconstrained yet focused on social contact and perceptions of closeness and rivalry with blacks and whites. This approach is analogous to the minimalist strategy adopted by John R. Hibbing and Elizabeth Theiss-Morse (1995). Then the data were collected in a data display format. This format is commonly used to display large quantities of data in a reduced format allowing the researcher to easily identify appropriate variables. In order to ensure accurate findings, one researcher transcribed all of the focus groups, while another verified all of the transcriptions. Moreover, each researcher examined each transcribed focus group and extracted the themes individually. The commonality in the themes between the two researchers was approximately 90 percent. This means that the two researchers found the same themes while reading each transcribed focus group with the exception of two or three themes.

Data

Seven focus groups composed of a total of thirty-three Latino adults were conducted from September to November 2009. The focus groups were held in the home of a focus group participant and at the Hispanic Apostolate, a not-for-profit organization that provides social and emergency services to Latinos in the New Orleans area.[4] I recruited participants through the snowball sampling technique and with flyers provided at the main entrance of the community agency. When recruiting, I communicated to each interested individual that the study was about Latinos' attitudes toward blacks and whites, and that they would be compensated twenty dollars each for their time.[5] Each focus group session lasted approximately one hour.

The demographic characteristics of the focus group participants provide an interesting glimpse of the Latino population in New Orleans. Women made up 72 percent of the interviewees. The average reported age of the participants was forty-eight years. More than half of the respondents (70%) reported being employed and more than half of the respondents (approximately 64%) conveyed that they had an annual income of $25,000 or less. Furthermore, about 64 percent of the respondents reported having less than a college diploma. When it comes to nativity, the respondents identified as Argentine (12), Honduran (10), Cuban (3), El Salvadoran (2), Colombian (2), Brazilian (1), Belizean (1), Uruguayan (1), and Nicaraguan (1). Eighty-five percent of the respondents were foreign born.

Although this sample of Latino respondents may not be completely representative of the Latino population in the greater New Orleans area, there are several motives as to why this sample is adequate for this chapter's qualitative contribution. First, approximately half of my sample consists of Central Americans, who comprise more than half of the Latino population in Orleans and Jefferson parishes. In addition, similar to the Latino population in the New Orleans area from 2006–10, Hondurans are the largest national origin group from Central America in my sample. While a large number of Mexican migrants arrived in New Orleans after the hurricane, Mexicans comprised a small portion of the Latino population before the hurricane, and U.S. Census estimates for 2006–10 indicate that they comprised a smaller portion of the Latino population than Hondurans (U.S. Census Bureau 2006–10; Vargas 2009; Fussell 2007). The 2006 LNS reveals that Hondurans' attitudes toward

African Americans and whites are quite comparable to those of Mexicans. Further, it is important to emphasize that the results of these focus groups are primarily intended to delve further into complex, perplexing findings from the quantitative chapter.

Findings

The purpose of the following analysis is to examine closely Latinos' perceptions of whites and African Americans in New Orleans. Focus is placed on themes that emerge from answers to focus group questions that target Latinos' social networks and sense of commonality and rivalry with blacks and whites, in addition to the effects of social contact. The analysis will include actual quotes from the participants.[6]

Social Contact

One of the first questions asked in each focus group was how much contact the focus group participants (Latinos) have with blacks and whites. When it comes to contact with blacks, the majority of participants stated that they have some contact and most of it is in the workplace. Rosa said, "No, I don't have any black friends. I have coworkers."[7] When asked if he has had any contact such as friends, neighbors, or coworkers, one participant stated, "I have worked for blacks, but never any of those combinations."

On the other hand, Latinos in New Orleans seem to have a lot more contact with whites than with blacks. Social contact includes friends and neighbors as well as coworkers. Almost all of the participants seemed even more enthusiastic to talk about their contact with whites than their contact with blacks. For instance, some stated:

Lucy: I have contact with them [whites] regularly. Friends, neighbors, coworkers. . . .

Marco: Yes, yes. I work with them, I live among them. They care for me like family. I've had more relationships with whites than with blacks. . . .

Hence, Latinos in New Orleans may be more likely to have contact with whites than with blacks, and possibly view whites in a more positive light than blacks. These results greatly parallel those found using 2006 LNS data indicating that Latinos in the South (residents of Arkansas, Georgia, North Carolina, and Virginia) have greater interactions with whites than blacks, in comparison to Latinos in non-southern areas. Further, Latinos' social interactions with blacks may be more likely to occur in the workplace, while Latinos may have greater informal contacts with whites through friends and neighbors.

Perceptions of Commonality

In this section, I discuss Latinos' perceptions of commonality first with blacks then with whites. First, I describe the answers that focus group participants gave in a preliminary questionnaire regarding how close they feel to blacks/whites and then present the themes that emerged from Latinos' answers to focus group questions assessing how much commonality they perceive to have with blacks/whites.

COMMONALITY WITH AFRICAN AMERICANS

In a short questionnaire before the focus groups began, Latinos were asked to report their perceptions of commonality with blacks. Individuals were asked to portray how much in common they have with blacks on a scale from 0 (nothing) to 10 (a lot in common). The mean commonality with blacks score is 3.7, illustrating that the majority of Latinos perceive that they have little to some commonality with blacks.

When discussing perceptions of commonality with blacks in the focus group discussions, three main themes emerged: (1) blacks are minorities like us; (2) blacks have family values like us; and (3) participants do not consider race or skin color when thinking about whether they have commonality with a group. First, a resonant response to whether they perceive commonality with blacks is that Latinos think that they are like blacks since both are minorities. For instance,

Marisa: But these people are a minority, like we are. This is what we have in common. . . . We are a minority. Blacks and Latinos are the same thing.

Besides clearly stating that Latinos like blacks are a minority, some Latinos stated that they are victims of discrimination like blacks.[8]

Maria: I think that we have something in common. When it comes to being discriminated against.

Inez: I have a good bit in common with them. I have black friends and we have a lot in common and we have both experienced discrimination.

A second major idea that arose in participants' answers was the fact that blacks, like Latinos, have family values:

Lisa: I think that when it comes to emotional aspects, when it comes to identifying with a group that honors family, the responsibility that parents, grandparents and children have to each other, that is how I identify our Latino culture comparing with the black culture.

Alicia: We have, with the type of people that I know is the type of family, people who have a strong sense of family similar to ours, disciplining our children and family.

On the other hand, several participants stated that race or skin color do not affect whether one has something in common with one group or another, and cultural level shapes commonality:[9]

Marina: I don't feel that there is a difference, I feel a difference in behavior [how one acts] not in color. That is the problem. It's not that I find a difference between African Americans because that same difference I may find with whites.

Pablo: There are things in common with a certain sector of the community where there is no distinction whether they are black or white, and there is another sector of the population that I have nothing in common.

When I asked Pablo what he would have in common with a certain sector of the population, he answered:

Pablo: With one sector of the African American population, family, the desire to progress, the desire to work. And then there's another group where I don't share anything. But it doesn't matter whether they are African American or white.

COMMONALITY WITH WHITES

To determine Latinos' perceptions of closeness with whites, I analyzed data from a questionnaire and focus group discussions. The preliminary questionnaire asked Latinos to measure their perceptions of commonality with whites on a scale from 0 (nothing) to 10 (a lot in common). The mean commonality with whites scores is 6.8, revealing that the majority of Latinos interviewed sense some or a lot of commonality with whites. In comparison to perceptions of closeness with blacks, Latinos seem to feel that they have more in common with whites.

As to the focus group discussions, two main themes emerged: (1) Latinos have a lot of commonality with whites since they share similar values and goals, and (2) sensing commonality with whites does not necessarily involve race.

When it comes to how close Latinos feel to whites, many emphasized how much in common they had with whites and highlighted the fact that they share whites' values and goals, such as the desire to work, to educate themselves, and to be polite to strangers:

Linda: I think that we have a lot of things in common with workers and the ambition to work, to educate ourselves. They are friendly, respectful. . . .

Claudio: I have a lot of things in common with whites. . . . Well, let me tell you like this. When you see a white American, you say hello to him and they acknowledge you and when you see a black person, they don't acknowledge you. For me, respect, values.

Similar to responses regarding commonality with blacks, many Latinos also asserted that commonality does not involve race or skin color but certain beliefs and objectives:[10]

Maria: So do I have something in common because that person is white? No. I may not have anything in common. I may have more in common with Blacks than with Whites. It's about how they act/their behavior. . . . Someone who is open-minded, who has principles, values regarding family, job and wants to move forward.

Tony: With a certain sector of the white population, a lot in common. . . . Basically, what the others said. Someone who desires to progress, someone who wants to improve, one who values family. . . .

Overall, my focus group results reveal that some Latinos in New Orleans have more in common with whites than with African Americans, yet for many race and skin color do not determine whether they have commonality with an individual. Interestingly, my analyses of 2006 LNS data reveal that Latinos in the South sense greater commonality with whites than with African Americans. The fact that I find that a significant portion of Latinos think that behavior and values and not race explain their perceptions of commonality with whites and blacks may help to explain my conclusion in the previous chapter that Latinos who perceive commonality with whites/blacks also identify with blacks/whites. If there are certain beliefs and characteristics that Latinos require in order to feel close to someone, it may be that Latinos who perceive commonality with one racial group also feel close to another group if they perceive that members of both groups value family and hard work and have a desire to succeed.

Perceptions of Competition

Besides commonality, I explore Latinos' perceptions of competition with blacks and whites in New Orleans. I begin with an examination of Latinos' antagonism toward blacks based on responses to a preliminary questionnaire and focus group discussions, and then analyze Latinos' attitudes toward whites also with questionnaire and discussion answers.

COMPETITION WITH BLACKS

Questionnaire results illustrate that Latinos sense narrow competition with African Americans. Focus group participants were asked to indicate how much competition they perceived with blacks on a scale from 0 (none) to 10 (a lot of competition). The mean general competition score is 2.8, indicating that the majority of Latinos sense that they have no or little competition with blacks.

In the focus group discussions of Latinos' sense of rivalry with African Americans, some Latinos stated that they do not perceive competition with blacks though Latinos with a low socioeconomic status seemed to be more inclined to perceive competition and discrimination than those with a high socioeconomic status. Nonetheless, a theme that emerged continuously in Latinos' responses was that a significant amount of competition exists in the workplace between black and Latino blue-collar workers, especially in construction jobs. Further, Latinos' antagonism toward blacks is associated with discrimination between blacks and Latinos in the workplace.

Some stated that the discrimination was brought on by blacks toward Latinos:

Marisa: They [blacks] want to put us in the jobs that they don't like. Jobs like to clean bathrooms they want to send people, they don't like it so they want to send Latinos to this. . . . I worked with them at Kmart and I noticed some racism toward Latinos a good bit. They try to help each other and sometimes when one tries to do the best job that he/she can do, and it's like they don't like it when one does it. They were frustrated. . . . I noticed that they didn't like it because one is reliable, on time. When I was doing my job, they wanted me to do their job too.

Claudio: There is discrimination by the blacks, but yes there is competition because when you work with a black person. The [black] person will steal from me. . . . I feel more comfortable working for a Hispanic man who will pay me than for blacks.

Susi: I don't think so. On the outside [to get the job], no. When you are working, yes there is. . . . Not in the job day to day but more about not being able to speak the language very well or speaking a broken English and we work more quickly and they don't and they want us to do their job and there are problems with that. Because I work for a company and not for them and my boss notices this and there is competition with them and they think that they should have an advantage since they are Americans and they think that but the boss knows how we are and knows how they are. There is competition day by day.

Still others recognized that Latinos discriminate against blacks also:

Lisa: I have observed that among the lower classes and among poor laborers, I noticed a lot of competition between them [Latinos and blacks] and to a certain extent, I noticed some discrimination of one against the other and mostly Latinos against blacks in order to prove that they are at a higher level than blacks are and that they are not at the bottom, at the lowest level of the social ladder.

The last portion of Lisa's quotation illustrates the constant struggle that individuals with low levels of sociopolitical clout, such as African Americans and Latinos, experience as described by Lawrence D. Bobo and Vincent Hutchings's (1996) modified group position theory. Many minority groups sense that they have to distinguish themselves constantly from those of similar positions by responding negatively to them, even with discrimination, since they feel alienated and that a comparable group is encroaching on their status (see Blumer 1958; Bobo and Hutchings 1996).

Additionally, some Latinos addressed the idea circulating greatly throughout New Orleans months after hurricane Katrina that Latinos were taking jobs away from African Americans. They stated with confidence and frustration at times that Latinos are hard workers, doing work that is not highly sought after, and are better workers than blacks:

Monica: We came here to work and they [Latino laborers] were doing the work that no one else here wanted to do.

Marisa: They [blacks] tell us, "you came here to take our jobs. You come from the outside. We are here." [But] so why don't you do the job since you live here? If you would do the jobs with the capacity of people who are reasonable would do it, we wouldn't be here occupying space that you would be able to occupy.

COMPETITION WITH WHITES

Regarding perceptions of competition with whites, I find that Latinos' sense of rivalry with whites does not diverge greatly from those toward blacks, though Latinos sense slightly greater rivalry with whites than blacks as found using 2010 CCES data. Latinos' sense of competition with whites was assessed in the preliminary questionnaire. The mean score for competition with whites is 4.1. While a few Latinos sense a lot of competition with whites, most sense little to no rivalry.

In the focus groups, three major themes materialized. First, several participants stated that there is little or no competition with whites. For instance, Mario said, "No, I don't think competition exists at all." Second, similar to responses regarding competition with blacks, numerous Latinos took into account socioeconomic status when talking about their competition with whites. Several said that Latinos have a lot of competition with whites who have high income and education levels. On the other hand, a few participants said that Latinos compete with whites who have a low socioeconomic position. It is critical to mention that the education and household income levels of Latino participants who perceived competition greatly matches the socioeconomic status of whites whom they view as competitors. When individuals were asked whether they sensed competition with whites, some stated:

Monica: It also depends on the type of job and the level that you are in.
Linda: I also don't think that there is competition especially with educated Americans, so there is no competition. One offers everything he/she has so maybe a little competition, but this is with people who have no skills or don't want to work or something.
Maria: Yes, not necessarily having to do with race but of level of education of the people or in some cases like friends at work.

Third, and similar to perceptions of competition with blacks, some Latinos linked competition with discrimination:

Isabel: I feel that there is a good bit of competition with us. And we try to, well, in my opinion, we try to be equal to them [whites] in education, schools, where we live, work. But them toward us, they judge us based on the color of our skin or by our hair, physical things.
Marisa: It seems like we are bothering them. I notice it. I personally notice it. I live in an area that is majority white. I am the only Latino there. . . . They reject you.

Discrimination by whites can be due to adopting strictly negative or racist views toward Latinos. Or, whites' discriminatory behavior can be a response to feelings that Latinos are infringing on their positions. As Latinos enter their neighborhoods and places of work, whites begin to regard Latinos as competitors and thus respond with discrimination.

In general, the focus group discussions of Latinos' sense of rivalry with whites and blacks yield some interesting results. First, Latinos do not seem to perceive a meaningful amount of antagonism with whites and blacks overall. Second, socioeconomic status appears to structure Latinos' sense of competition with both groups. A third way that Latinos' antagonism toward blacks compares to their antagonism toward whites is that Latinos who perceive competition link that rivalry (with blacks and whites) with discrimination, increasing our understanding of the group position theory. Still, I find a few disparities in Latinos' perceptions of blacks and whites as competitors. Unlike discussions about competition between blacks and Latinos, the idea that Latinos discriminate against whites was not as prevalent in the conversations regarding competition between whites and Latinos. Further, the idea that Latinos were taking jobs away from whites in a post-Katrina world was never raised.

Effect of Contact on Attitudes toward Blacks

Besides inquiring about Latinos' social networks and perceptions of commonality and competition with whites and blacks, I guided my focus group discussions toward the effects of contact on racial attitudes, specifically perceptions of closeness and rivalry toward these two racial groups. I begin with an analysis of the relationship between social interaction and Latino views toward blacks.

One major theme that developed from Latinos' responses to the question regarding the influence of contact on their attitudes toward blacks was that social interactions with blacks positively influenced their views toward them.

Alicia: Oh yes, contact affects, of course. For me in a positive manner of course.

Monica: When you start talking to them, you start realizing that . . . they have the same type of lifestyle that we have. They think the same regarding political views and so I think that it's for the best to have contact. Not for the worst.

Still, some stated that contact does not shape their views toward blacks. Additionally, many who asserted that contact does not affect their views emphasized that African Americans' cultural level (i.e., education level, desire to work and succeed, family values) does. This finding may explain why I find in my quantitative analyses that all forms of social interaction do not play a key role in shaping Latinos' perceptions of commonality and competition with blacks. As some commented:

Rosa: It depends on the cultural level . . . of the person. That has a big influence. . . . It depends definitely on the cultural level. . . . But if it's a regular person that doesn't have probably, just elementary school degree, it's one thing.

Marco: It depends on the level that one is at and it [experiences with blacks] is not always positive, in my case, I don't know.

Effect of Contact on Attitudes toward Whites

The participants were also asked if contact affected their perceptions of whites. A few said that social interaction had a positive effect, in support of the social contact hypothesis, and many said that contact did not affect their views toward whites:

Victoria: Being close to them [whites] has made me recognize the values that they have and of course the values that we have, and it has been positive.

Bill: Positive, because if not I would have left.

Among those who stated that contact has no influence on racial attitudes, some stated that cultural level drives racial attitudes and not contact:

Pablo: No, it has no effect—contact.

Tony: No, contact does not affect at all. . . . No, just because I know many whites doesn't mean that I can talk about how it affects my views of whites.

Rosa: According to the cultural level, the competition will be different but it exists. And the contact is the same because I can talk with certain people whoever they are: white or whoever, African American. And it depends on the level because probably I can have many things in common with certain people but with others, I say hello, bye.

Thus, when comparing the effects of social interaction on Latinos' attitudes toward whites and blacks, I find several comparisons. For some Latinos, contact has a positive influence on their views toward blacks and whites as found in my quantitative analyses. Yet for others, contact does not shape their racial attitudes, possibly explaining why not all forms of social contact structure how Latinos regard blacks and whites as found in the previous chapter. Furthermore, some Latinos who think that contact does not structure their perceptions of racial groups argue that individuals' (blacks' and whites') cultural levels play a key role in structuring Latinos' attitudes.

Conclusion

In this chapter, I explore Latinos' feelings of closeness and competition with blacks and whites using focus group data from an emerging Latino city, New Orleans. The analyses and conclusions are meant to further explore

Latinos' racial attitudes and delve into the complexities of any previous quantitative findings.

This study makes several pivotal contributions to our awareness of Latinos' perceptions of commonality and competition with blacks and whites. First, this is the first study that examines Latinos' racial attitudes toward blacks and whites in New Orleans. Likewise, no other study takes a qualitative approach to exploring Latinos' perceptions of commonality and competition toward these two racial groups. Another major contribution is that I find that Latino, black, and white relations in the South may be distinct from those in the non-South (Morin et al. 2011). While my national survey results presented in the last chapter reveal that Latinos feel slightly closer to blacks than whites, and regard whites as greater rivals than blacks, this study finds that Latinos in New Orleans regard whites more favorably than African Americans. This finding is supported by Marrow's (2011) study of Latinos in another emerging Latino area in the South as well as my descriptive analyses of Latinos in the South using 2006 LNS data. Another primary finding is that individuals' cultural levels (i.e., education level, desire to succeed, and value of family) may influence Latinos' perceptions of whites and African Americans. A theme that emerged from my focus group discussions is that individuals' cultural levels and not race affect who Latinos believe they are close to. This finding may help to better explain why Latinos who identify with blacks/whites sense greater commonality with whites/blacks as found in my quantitative analyses. Additionally, while I find some support for the social contact hypothesis (the greater Latinos' contact with blacks and whites, the more they feel close to them), contact is not always expressed as a determinant of Latino racial attitudes yet cultural level is. Several participants throughout the focus group discussions emphasized that their attitudes toward whites and blacks were strongly influenced by their own cultural levels and the cultural levels of the person whom they contact. Hence, future studies should examine the relationship between Latinos' principles and goals on their attitudes toward non-Latinos in order to unearth the influence of an individual's "cultural level." The following chapter explores African Americans' perceptions of Latinos.

4

African Americans' Perceptions of Latinos and Whites

A QUANTITATIVE ANALYSIS

The emerging presence of Latinos in the Southwest, Northeast, and South has provided African Americans with the opportunity to interact and develop alliances with Latinos, even resulting in blacks' stronger identification with Latinos than with whites and Asian Americans (McClain and Stewart 2002, 182). Latinos compare to African Americans in several ways. Besides generally possessing limited socioeconomic clout with comparable education and income levels, Latinos, like blacks, experience discrimination in private and public settings such as neighborhoods, grocery stores, and schools (Pew Hispanic Center 2011; Kochhar 2012). Blacks and Latinos also tend to align themselves with the Democratic Party and adopt similar attitudes regarding gay rights, poverty, healthcare, affordable housing, prayer in public schools, discrimination, maintaining ethnic culture, and government support for the needy (McClain 1996; Mindiola et al. 2002). For instance, Latinos and African Americans in Houston, Texas, agree on several issues regarding immigration. Residents of both groups strongly support policies that reduce the number of immigrants entering the Houston area while similarly favoring undocumented children being allowed to become citizens if they graduate from college or serve in the military. Further, both blacks and Latinos endorse granting undocumented immigrants a path to citizenship if they speak English and have no criminal record (Rodriguez and Mindiola 2011). These analogous issue stances and experiences can pave the way for political coalition formations between both groups (Mindiola et al. 2002, 109). What is more, blacks and Latinos have formed political alliances in the past, including the election of Mayor Antonio Villaraigosa in Los Angeles in 2005 and the election of President Barack Obama in 2008 (Sawyer 2011).

These issues notwithstanding, there are several factors that prompt African Americans to regard Latinos as rivals. Latinos' growing presence in formerly black residential and business areas influence some blacks to resent newcomers and view them as competitors. Similarities in socioeconomic status can lead to an assumed hierarchy among minorities resulting in competition for limited political and economic resources (see Gay 2006). Additionally, the influx of Latinos into African American neighborhoods can compel blacks to feel a sense of entitlement to social and political institutions because of the significant struggles that they experienced in the past and throughout the civil rights movement. These feelings can then motivate blacks to believe that Latinos are taking advantage of blacks' achievements (Mindiola et al. 2002). Hence, it comes as no surprise that a large portion of blacks in new immigrant destinations (e.g., Durham, North Carolina; Little Rock, Arkansas; Memphis; New Orleans) as well as in traditional Latino areas (e.g., Houston) think that Latinos take jobs from blacks and feel threatened economically and politically by increased immigration (McClain et al. 2007; McClain et al. 2011; Rodriguez and Mindiola 2011). Further, in Los Angeles, a city with a well-established Latino presence, a substantial number of black residents have even joined and continue to join anti-immigrant groups (Sawyer 2011, 177).

While it is unclear as to whether African Americans will embrace Latinos as allies or rivals in the near future, current research has substantially ignored the disparities among the African American community, which can significantly affect black/Latino relations. Although blacks have a lower socioeconomic status than whites and Asian Americans generally, African Americans have recently gained financial and political clout, with a considerable number joining the middle class, residing in majority-minority districts, and being descriptively represented at the local, state, and even national levels (Dawson 1994; Tate 2010). Moreover, differences in immigration stances exist among blacks of distinct education and income levels. African Americans in Houston with lower income and education levels express stronger support for the notion that immigrants take jobs from blacks and adopt less favorable views toward Latino immigrants and the Spanish language than those with a higher socioeconomic status (Rodriguez and Mindiola 2011, 160).

In addition to blacks' disparities in socioeconomic and political power, blacks diverge in their levels of social interaction with the Latino population. Some blacks live in more traditional Latino areas with extended histories of social contact between blacks and Latinos in public schools and neighborhoods, often resulting in deep tensions and conflict between the two groups. Others reside in predominantly black areas in the South (e.g., Atlanta, Memphis, and New Orleans) with limited contact with Latinos and with established African American networks. Other blacks in many southern areas have only recently begun to share neighborhoods and work environments with Latinos. They are slowly feeling that the new population places them at a considerable socioeconomic disadvantage since whites, at the top of the racialized social structure, favor Latinos over African Americans (Mc-Clain et al. 2007; see also McClain et al. 2011). This sentiment may not be surprising given that race has historically defined blacks' daily experiences and life chances, and in the South, there remain disparities in opportunities for political and economic advancement between blacks and whites and in some areas between blacks and Latinos (McClain et al. 2007).

The developing differences among the African American population today, and Latinos' emerging presence throughout the United States, raise many unanswered questions. Do blacks perceive as much commonality with Latinos as they do with their racial counterparts? Do blacks regard Latinos like whites? In particular, do blacks perceive as much closeness and competition with Latinos as they do with whites? How can we reconcile the developing differences among African Americans today with their response to an emerging Latino population that has outnumbered them in size and clout in some areas? To what extent do social contact, context, and feelings of identification structure blacks' perceptions of closeness and competition with Latinos and whites? Unfortunately, recent research on blacks' sense of closeness and rivalry with Latinos and whites is not extensive (McClain et al. 2007; Telles et al. 2011; Hutchings et al. 2011; Thornton et al. 2012). This chapter takes a more contemporary and systematic approach to uncovering black/Latino relations by using more recent national survey data (2004 National Politics Survey [NPS], 2010 Cooperative Congressional Election Study [CCES]) to address the questions posed above. The subsequent chapter takes a qualitative approach using focus group data of blacks in New Orleans to delve deeper into the complexities of blacks' racial attitudes.

Social Contact, Context, and Blacks

Scholars have examined interracial attitudes and coalition building between Latinos and African Americans for some time. Although much of the recent literature in this area has centered on Latino attitudes toward blacks (Sanchez 2008; Jones-Correa 2011; Morin et al. 2011), we have some knowledge of African Americans' attitudes toward Latinos and immigration, and the extent to which social contact, racial context, and economic self-interest shape these perspectives.

Social contact can structure blacks' perceptions of Latinos and immigration. In a multicity study, J. Eric Oliver and Janelle Wong (2003) present indirect support for the social contact hypothesis (i.e., greater direct social interactions among individuals with distinct backgrounds result in more affinity among the groups) and conclude that African Americans who live in an integrated neighborhood are less likely to express racial resentment. On the other hand, Irwin Morris (2000) finds opposing support for the social contact hypothesis in a study of African Americans' support for Proposition 187, a restrictive immigration proposal.[1] He finds that as the number of Latinos living in close proximity to blacks grows, black support for the proposition heightens.

Racial context also predicts African Americans' racial dispositions. Most of the studies analyzing racial context test the racial threat hypothesis (i.e., a growing out-group population heightens the socioeconomic threat that the in-group senses, resulting in negative views toward the out-group). In a study of race relations in Los Angeles, James H. Johnson, Jr., and his colleagues (1997) analyze blacks' perceptions of Latinos' growing presence in the area and find that African Americans' limited power and considerable struggles prompt them to regard their new Latino neighbors as economic and political threats. Furthermore, a considerable number of blacks perceive that they would experience a loss in economic and sociopolitical clout if immigration continues at its current rate. In a more recent study, Paula D. McClain and her colleagues (2011) indirectly test the racial threat hypothesis in emerging Latino cities in the South. They find that African American residents of a largely black city (Memphis), a mixed white/black city (Durham), *and* a largely white city (Little Rock) believe that their economic opportunities are disadvantaged with a growing Latino population. Hence, regardless of the racial composition of blacks' surroundings, an influx of Latinos seems to pose a threat to black southerners. Marylee C. Taylor and Matthew B. Schroeder also examine the effects of an emerging Latino population on blacks' feelings toward Latinos. They conclude that blacks' dispositions toward Latinos were relatively warm in areas with a scarce population change yet cooler when there had been a large growth in the Latino population over a span of several years (2010, 501).

While racial and economic context can be correlated, some studies particularly focus on economic self-interest as a predictor of black attitudes. Johnson and his colleagues (1997) find that blacks in Los Angeles perceive themselves to be at an employment disadvantage in situations where Latinos were thought to have access to better jobs (1061–62). Relying on survey data from the city of Los Angeles, Claudine Gay finds that "where Latinos enjoy an economic advantage [greater education level and a lower poverty rate] relative to blacks, African Americans are more likely to express racial prejudice toward the group and to engage in defensive political behavior" (2006, 995). Additionally, the extent to which economic disparities structure blacks' attitudes toward Latinos is conditional on the size of the Latino population.

Gay finds that when Latinos are the majority of the population, an increase in Latinos' economic advantage over blacks heightens blacks' beliefs that Latinos' gains are at the expense of blacks (991). In a study of race relations in a southern city, McClain and her colleagues (2007) conclude that blacks who think that Latinos place them at an employment disadvantage are more concerned about the rapid growth of the Latino population. Similarly, using national survey data, Tatishe Nteta (2013) finds that economic advantage affects blacks' dispositions. He concludes that blacks who perceive that they have lost their jobs to immigrants express greater support for decreasing immigration than those who have not.[2]

The Triangular Theory of Contact, Context, and Identification for Blacks

While extant research develops our comprehension of blacks' attitudes toward Latinos, there are several deficiencies in prevailing studies' approaches to analyzing blacks' racial dispositions. First, current research considerably centers on African Americans' perceptions of Latinos only, seldom examining how blacks' attitudes toward Latinos compare to their views of whites and other African Americans. While we may discover that blacks perceive considerable competition and closeness with Latinos, this may not give us an accurate understanding as to how they truly feel about Latinos if we do not compare these attitudes with blacks' views of others. Another way that this study fills the gap in our knowledge of how blacks regard Latinos is by taking a comparative approach to studying black racial attitudes. In order to determine whether blacks regard Latinos as partners or competitors and regard Latinos like whites or not, I compare African Americans' views toward Latinos with their views toward whites and examine the degree to which the determinants of these attitudes parallel or diverge for Latinos and whites. Only by taking a comparative approach to analyzing African Americans' attitudes toward Latinos are we able to obtain a more complete understanding of race relations today.

Moreover, to explain blacks' racial attitudes, I develop power-based hypotheses and the Triangular Theory of Contact, Context, and Identification (TTCCI) to explain the effects of social networks, economic and political context, and feelings of identification on African Americans' attitudes toward whites and Latinos. African Americans generally parallel Latinos in low socioeconomic status and clout, heightening their awareness of the discrepancies in power that exist among individuals, yet this cognizance is shaped by their social networks, sense of power, and identification with other racial groups.

Social Contact

Few studies have tested the social contact hypothesis on African Americans' perceptions of closeness and competition with Latinos and whites. Testing this theory on these attitudes advances our understanding of the theory as well as of the extent to which desegregation and zoning laws can foster improved relations between Latinos and blacks. Further, current studies have failed to examine how social contact with one group shapes attitudes toward another. Analyzing the effects of direct social interaction with one group on blacks' attitudes toward that same group does not always give us an accurate sense of intergroup relations, and thus cannot give us a real representation of the viable options for alliance formations. Race relations are complex, now more than ever, and I contend that interactions with one racial or ethnic group can significantly affect blacks' perceptions of others. In particular, I argue that blacks' social interactions with Latinos decrease their sense of closeness with whites, and blacks' contacts with whites depress their competition with Latinos. Given the significant disparities in sociopolitical struggles and power between whites and minorities, blacks are influenced to feel that they have to either side with whites (the majority) or with other minorities. Social interaction with a certain racial/ethnic group structures this feeling. Additionally, prevailing research provides too narrow an approach to testing the social contact hypothesis. Given African Americans' greater interaction with Latinos in public and more intimate settings, we must explore the effects of social interaction in the forms of friendship, neighbors, and coworkers to obtain a more complete understanding of the context in which social interaction occurs.[3] Based on these assertions, I hypothesize:

Social contact hypothesis: The greater contact (i.e., with friends, neighbors, or coworkers) African Americans have with Latinos and whites, the more prone they are to sense closeness and less competition with these groups.

Divisive effects hypothesis: As blacks interact socially (i.e., with friends, neighbors, or coworkers) with Latinos, they are less likely to perceive commonality with whites. Blacks' social contacts with whites depress their sense of competition with Latinos.

Racial Context

In addition, while prevailing research has consistently analyzed the relationship between racial context and blacks' racial attitudes, it does not lack shortcomings. First, we know relatively little about the extent to which the racial threat hypothesis applies to blacks' perceptions of competition *and* closeness with the largest minority in the United States. Does being surrounded by Latinos deepen blacks' regard for Latinos as aggressors of their territory and status, therefore diminishing blacks' perceptions of closeness yet heightening their sense of competition with Latinos? A second limitation of previous research is that blacks' sense of power is rarely taken into account when their sense of closeness and competition with whites and Latinos. Since a predominantly Latino environment is more than likely a low socioeconomic setting often relative to a largely white environment, blacks who reside in a county with a significant number of Latinos are more likely to regard Latinos as rivals than those who do not. On the other hand, blacks in a largely white context may be more prone to feel close to their white counterparts yet still regard them as competitors given the deep disparities in socioeconomic clout and opportunities that exist between blacks and whites.[4] Hence, these theoretical discussions prompt me to propose:

Racial threat and Latinos hypothesis: African Americans who reside in a predominantly Latino county perceive less closeness yet greater competition with Latinos.

Racial threat and whites hypothesis: Blacks who are surrounded by whites are more prone to feel close to whites and regard them as a sociopolitical threat.

Economic Context

Similarly, I theorize that blacks' perceptions of influence through their economic context structure their sense of commonality and competition with whites and Latinos. Although numerous studies examine the effects of economic self-interest and context in explaining black/Latino racial dynamics, these studies have several weaknesses. We know relatively little about the extent to which blacks' economic contexts and opportunities for upward mobility structure their perceptions of closeness and competition with Latinos and whites. The group position theory can certainly enhance our comprehension of blacks' sense of closeness and rivalry with these groups. Residing in an economically powerless area can increase the likelihood that African Americans attribute their socioeconomic mobility to race. This perception then makes them more prone to regard other minorities, such as Latinos, as encroaching on their status (Telles et al. 2011, 7). Hence, when African Americans perceive that they are in a high-threat environment (i.e., residing in a county with high unemployment and poverty rates), they may feel more threatened by a new immigrant group and view Latinos negatively. The opposite effect would occur when blacks reside in a low-threat environment. As to the relationship between economic context and blacks' perceptions of whites, blacks who reside in a high- *and* low-threat economic setting may perceive commonality with whites and be more prone to regard them as economic threats. Since whites are generally more economically stable than African Americans, when blacks reside in counties with high unemployment and poverty, they may want to feel closer to whites yet view them as competitors for social mobility. On the other hand, blacks in an economically powerful setting may sense greater closeness with whites but still regard them as threats because of the generally deep disparities in power that exist between blacks and whites. Based on the aforementioned theoretical discussions, I argue:

Economic context and Latinos hypothesis: When blacks are in a high-threat economic context, they perceive lesser closeness yet greater competition with Latinos. When blacks are in a low-threat economic setting, they are more prone to perceive closeness and sense less competition with Latinos.

Economic context and whites hypothesis: Residing in a high- and low-threat economic context increases the likelihood that blacks feel close to and perceive competition with whites.

Institutional Context

Besides racial and economic contexts, this study analyzes the effects of institutional context on African Americans' racial attitudes. Current research provides us with a quite restricted view of the relationship between institutional context and blacks' perceptions of closeness and competition with Latinos and whites. Most of our knowledge of institutional context and African Americans has centered on blacks' political behavior and attitudes (Bobo and Gilliam 1990; Tate 1991; Hero and Tolbert 2004; Banducci et al. 2005). A prominent theory that circulates in this literature is the empowerment thesis. While modified through the years, this theory asserts that when minorities, particularly blacks, are descriptively represented, they are empowered materially and psychologically. Hence, blacks in empowered cities obtain material rewards (e.g., greater municipal employment and government contracts) as well as feeling included, resulting in heightened group pride, trust in government, and even political participation. Being represented by someone of the same race sends a cue to individuals that policy responsiveness is likely and voting actually matters (Bobo and Gilliam 1990; Tate 1991; Gilliam and Kaufmann 1998; Mansbridge 1999).

Besides the empowerment thesis, a power-based approach to explaining the effects of institutional context on blacks' attitudes has been relatively absent. Latinos and blacks are gaining political clout, inevitably affecting whether they regard each other as allies or rivals. This study responds to this changing political landscape by building on Lawrence D. Bobo and Vincent Hutchings's (1996) extension of the group position theory and positing that blacks' political clout and perceptions of their political opportunities shape their perceptions of Latinos and whites. With greater political prospects, blacks are less likely to perceive closeness with Latinos and whites but are more inclined to sense competition with these groups. Blacks' relatively new presence in politics does not necessarily make them feel that they are like other groups, and does not make them immune to believing that other groups are encroaching on their political status and achievements. Still, having a Latino legislator has distinct effects on African Americans' racial dispositions. As Latinos' presence in state and national politics gains momentum, more African American communities are represented by Latinos. While blacks with a Latino legislator may feel closer to Latinos based on greater exposure, blacks represented by a Latino are more likely to perceive that Latinos are infringing on their status based on the considerable sociopolitical competition that exists between two groups. These theoretical discussions lead me to hypothesize:

Threat and institutional context hypothesis: Blacks who reside in a politically powerful setting (i.e., residing in a largely Democratic district, living in a state that permits ballot initiatives and/or political referenda) are less likely to sense closeness with Latinos and whites, and are more likely to perceive competition with whites.

Latino representative hypothesis: Blacks represented by a Latino legislator are more inclined to perceive closeness with Latinos and sense greater competition with Latinos.

Black representative hypothesis: Blacks represented by a black legislator are less likely to perceive closeness yet more likely to perceive competition with whites.[5]

Feelings of Identification

Latinos' emerging presence in distinct racial, social, political, and economic settings can structure African Americans' opinions toward them. Indeed, a number of studies evaluate the relationship between Latinos' attitudes toward blacks with their affinity toward whites, and the effects of Latinos' identification with other Latinos on their closeness with blacks (Kaufmann 2003; Wallsten and Nteta 2011). Little attention, however, has been paid to the role that feelings of identification with one group may play in structuring African Americans' views of that same group and those of others. This project overcomes this limitation by addressing the following questions: Does identifying with Latinos/whites increase the likelihood that blacks perceive competition with Latinos/whites, respectively? Do African Americans who identify with Latinos perceive greater closeness with whites? Do blacks who feel close to whites also feel close to Latinos?

In analyzing the effects of identification on blacks' racial attitudes, I rely on Herbert Blumer's (1958) group position theory. A component of this theory asserts that individuals place their racial/ethnic group in one category and others into distinct classifications. I build on Blumer's classification assertion and argue that when blacks think about one group, they inevitably make indirect or direct comparisons to their group and others, which affect their views toward other racial groups. In comparison to their views of whites, African Americans' dispositions toward Latinos may not be as well established given Latinos' relatively new presence on blacks' radars. Still when blacks develop an opinion about Latinos and feel close to them, they may be more likely to regard them as allies and less as rivals. These assertions lead me to hypothesize:

Identification and competition hypothesis: African Americans who identify with Latinos/whites perceive less competition with Latinos/whites, respectively.

Identification hypothesis: Blacks' feelings of identification with whites shape their sense of closeness with Latinos, and blacks' sense of identification with Latinos structures their perceptions of closeness with whites.

Other Predictors of Black Racial Attitudes

In addition to social contact, context, and identification, racial alienation, prejudice, class, and region can affect African Americans' views toward Latinos and immigration. For instance, research on African Americans' perceptions of competitive racial threat largely focuses on the effects of racial alienation. In a study of race relations in Los Angeles, Bobo and Hutchings (1996) extend Blumer's (1958) group position theory and posit that the more minorities feel powerless and disenfranchised from society, the more they feel that other groups are a competitive racial threat to their own group's social position. These scholars find support for this theory in concluding that blacks who feel alienated perceive greater competition with Latinos. Yet, in a study relying on national survey data, Hutchings and colleagues (2011) find little support for the group position theory in its ability to explain blacks' perceptions of competition with Latinos. While blacks who perceive discrimination toward their racial group and feel that society has not treated blacks fairly perceive greater competition with whites, these measures did not structure African Americans' sense of zero-sum competition with Latinos (65). Nonetheless, in our analysis of blacks' stances on illegal immigration, Natasha Bingham and I (2013) find that blacks who feel that they have obtained less than they deserve express stronger support for controlling illegal immigration. Based on these findings, I hypothesize that blacks who feel that African Americans are discriminated against are less likely to feel close to yet are more likely to perceive competition with Latinos and whites.

Prejudice also seems to play a critical role in shaping African Americans' attitudes toward Latino immigrants. In a study of blacks' dispositions toward Latinos in a new immigrant destination, McClain and her colleagues find that blacks who adopt more negative stereotypes of Latinos are more likely to believe that continued immigration will depress blacks' economic opportunities (2007, 108). Hutchings and colleagues (2011) also suggest that prejudice heightens blacks' predisposition to regard Latinos as threats by finding that blacks who reject interracial marriage in principle perceive greater competition with Latinos. As to blacks' attitudes toward immigration, Mark Q. Sawyer (2011) finds comparable results in Los Angeles, a traditional immigrant destination. The greater blacks' negative stereotypes of Latinos, the stronger their support for the mass deportation of Latino immigrants (195). Given these findings, I assert that African Americans who adopt a negative stereotype of Latinos (i.e., Latinos are lazy) perceive less commonality with Latinos and greater competition with them.

Numerous studies have focused on the relationship between economic self-interest and blacks' attitudes toward immigration and immigrants though recent research has centered on the effects of class on black dispositions. Using national survey data of blacks, Nteta (2013) finds that working-class blacks are significantly less likely to favor immigration than their middle-class counterparts. Further, measures of economic self-interest more strongly account for the immigration stances of working-class blacks than middle-class blacks. Based on these findings, I suspect that working-class blacks are more likely to regard Latinos as competitors than middle-class blacks.

Due to the recent, significant influx of Latino immigrants to the South, several studies have focused on African Americans' attitudes toward Latinos in southern cities and towns. While most research does not specifically explore the effect of residing in the South on blacks' racial dispositions, they elaborate on the importance of analyzing African Americans' views toward immigration and Latinos in a region with an extensive history of racial tensions between blacks and whites, and where race has greatly characterized blacks' struggles and opportunities for social mobility. In a national study of blacks' attitudes toward Latinos, Taylor and Schroeder conclude that blacks' dispositions toward the new immigrant group were not as favorable when there was a recent, fast growth in the Latino population, such as in southern locations (2010, 206). Additionally, in an intergroup study of racial dynamics in emerging Latino areas in the South, McClain and her colleagues (2011) find that African Americans more than whites and Latinos in Memphis, Little Rock, and Durham believe that their economic opportunities would be restricted due to a growing Latino population. These findings prompt the scholars to assert that blacks may be impacted negatively by Latino immigration, and that African Americans regard the new residents in these southern cities as social and political but mostly economic threats to their status (219–21). In this study, I further assess the effects of region by controlling for the effects of living in the South in analyses of blacks' perceptions of closeness with Latinos and whites, and by analyzing blacks' perceptions of competition among those who live in the South and those in the non-South. It is critical to examine blacks' sense of rivalry with Latinos and whites by region since the South, unlike several other areas, has been recently impacted by a large influx of immigrants, and it is a region where black/Latino antagonism can be particularly high (see Morin et al. 2011). I contend that southern and non-southern blacks' distinct experiences influence the degree to which my TTCCI shapes their attitudes toward their Latino and white counterparts. While I do not present specific hypotheses as to how residing in the South influences blacks' sense of closeness with whites and Latinos, nor as to how southern and non-southern blacks diverge in their perceptions of competition, I suspect that contact, context, and feelings of identification have a more robust effect on southern blacks' attitudes than those of non-southern blacks.

Data

This chapter analyzes blacks' attitudes toward Latinos and whites using the 2004 NPS and the 2010 CCES. The 2004 NPS is an ideal data set for this project. Most studies discussed previously do not rely on national survey data but use data from one or a few cities eliciting concerns about the generalizability of their findings. Thus, reliance on national survey data increases our confidence in this study's findings in addition to capturing a broader understanding of race relations today given Latinos' diffused presence in cities and small towns throughout the nation. Further, unlike several surveys used in previous studies of perceptions of closeness and competition, the 2004 NPS is a national survey with large samples of whites (n = 919), blacks (n = 756), and Latinos (n = 598). Survey respondents from four major U.S. regions were interviewed, allowing me to examine the effect of residing in the South (1,324 respondents) on racial dispositions. Another benefit of using 2004 NPS data is that this survey explores a variety of topics that are central to predicting and analyzing the racial attitudes explored here: perceptions of discrimination toward one's own racial group; adopting negative stereotypes of Latinos; perceptions of closeness to whites, blacks, and Latinos; and employment and political competition with these three groups. The 2010 CCES provides a more contemporary understanding of the intricacies of black racial attitudes. The data consist of a total of 2,000 respondents with 239 who identify as black or African American, thus I weight the sample in all of my analyses to make it proportionate to the black population in the United States. While the 2010 CCES does not have as vast a sample as the NPS, the CCES is a more current survey that distinctively assesses blacks' perceptions of racial diversity in their counties, a relatively uncovered topic. A detailed description of the survey questions and coding of the NPS, CCES, and contextual variables are provided in the appendix.

The NPS data set includes several questions that explore blacks' perceptions of closeness and competition with Latinos and whites. This data set analyzes blacks' perceptions of closeness with Latinos, blacks, and whites with measures that range from 0 (no closeness) to 3 (strong closeness). As to perceptions of competition, I analyze blacks' perceptions of employment and political competition, and combine them to create a general index of blacks' competition with Latinos and another for blacks' competition with whites. There are several reasons for the creation of these additive indexes. First, African Americans' relations with whites and Latinos are often characterized not only by economic but also by political tensions. I find few disparities in blacks' responses to their employment and political competition with Latinos and whites. Further, the correlation coefficients and the Cronbach's alpha score for the variables that compose the general competition with Latinos measure and the general competition with whites measure reveal that it is appropriate to create an additive scale for blacks' perceptions of competition with Latinos and for whites with these variables.[6] Each of the additive indexes of blacks' perceptions of competition ranges from 0 (no employment or political competition) to 6 (a lot of competition). Unlike the NPS, the CCES only examines African Americans' perceptions of economic competition with Latinos and whites.

Descriptive Results: Perceptions of Closeness and Competition

I begin my investigation by attempting to answer two questions that address the central concern of whether blacks and Latinos are allies or rivals: Do blacks regard Latinos as being like them? Do blacks view Latinos as being like whites? To address these questions, I start by analyzing African Americans' perceptions of closeness with Latinos, whites, and other blacks. The results presented in figure 8 reveal that African Americans sense greater closeness with their racial counterparts than with Latinos (Thornton et al. 2012), yet blacks perceive somewhat more commonality with Latinos than with whites. On the other hand, I find conflicting results from analyses of 2010 CCES data where blacks perceive slightly greater economic commonality with whites than with Latinos. A possible explanation for this finding is that the NPS measure of closeness does not explore the same concept as the economic commonality one. Thus, while it may not be completely clear as to whether blacks sense more closeness with whites than with Latinos, they feel closer to other blacks than either Latinos or whites. These findings suggest that African Americans draw clear distinctions between Latinos/whites and their own racial counterparts with little difference in how they regard whites and Latinos.

FIG. 8. Blacks' perceptions of closeness with Latinos, whites, and other blacks

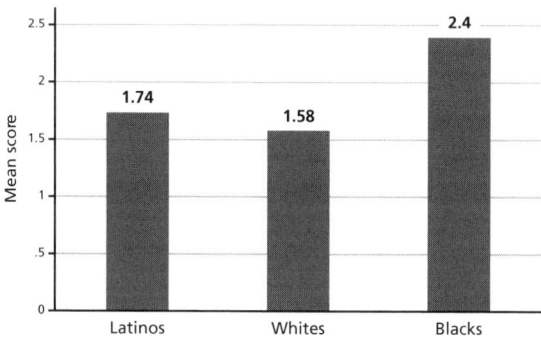

Source: Author's calculations using 2004 NPS data.

As to African Americans' perceptions of competition with Latinos and whites, I find more clear results. Figures 9 and 10 summarize African Americans' answers to questions addressing competition with Latinos and whites on a scale from 0 (no competition) to 6 (a lot of employment and political competition). The results shown in the figures illustrate that blacks sense greater competition with whites than with Latinos. These results are supported by the mean score of blacks' perceptions of competition with whites (3.25), which is greater than the mean score of African Americans' sense of rivalry with Latinos (2.29). My analyses of 2010 CCES data present similar findings. Thus, while blacks may perceive Latinos as economic and political threats, they perceive greater rivalry with whites (Thornton and Mizuno, 1999; Hutchings et al. 2011).

In general, the results in figures 8–10 do not provide convincing evidence that blacks perceive Latinos as a minority group like them or that blacks feel very close to or are threatened by Latinos. My analyses, however,

FIG. 9. Blacks' perceptions of competition with Latinos

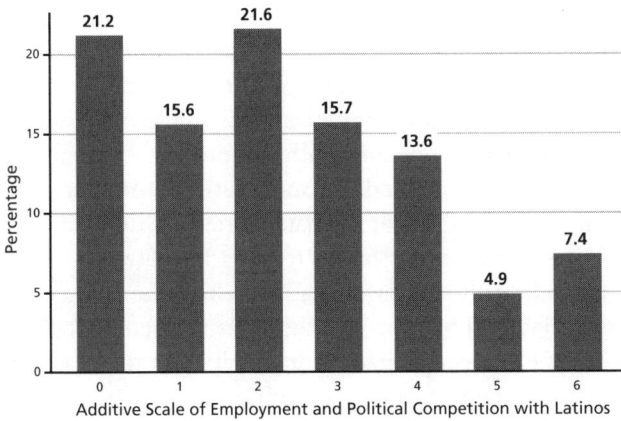

Source: Author's calculations using 2004 NPS data.

FIG. 10. Blacks' perceptions of competition with whites

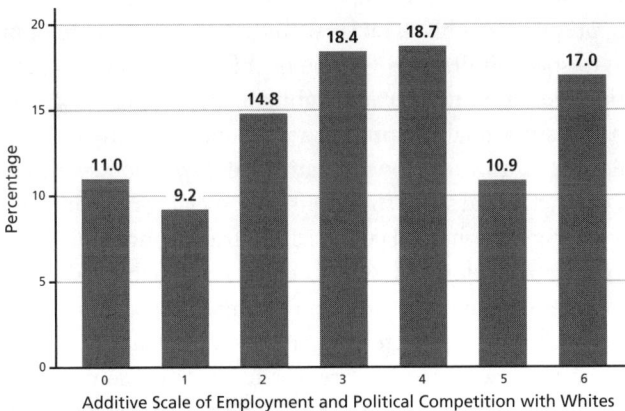

Source: Author's calculations using 2004 NPS data.

suggest that African Americans distinguish Latinos from other blacks but are not as certain of Latinos' identities and positions in society as those of whites.

Testing the Triangular Theory of Contact, Context, and Identification for Blacks

To what extent do social contact, context, and identification influence African Americans' perceptions of Latinos and whites? In this section, I test my TTCCI on blacks' sense of closeness and competition with whites and Latinos in several ways.[7] First, relying on 2004 NPS data, I juxtapose the effect of blacks' social networks, sociopolitical power, and feelings of identification with other groups or members of their own group on their sense of closeness with Latinos and whites. I also test my main theory on blacks' perceptions of competition with whites and Latinos with a focus on race relations in the South and in the non-South, since the South can provide a unique setting for race relations between Latinos and African Americans. After each of the closeness and competition analyses of NPS data, I provide a discussion of my analyses of 2010 CCES data centering on the relationship between subjective racial context and blacks' attitudes toward Latinos. Given the ordered nature of my dependent variables, I test my hypotheses using ordered logistic regression. I weight the black sample in all of my analyses so that it is proportionate to the black population in the United States.[8]

Perceptions of Closeness with Latinos and Whites

Table 9 presents ordered logistic regression results for blacks' perceptions of closeness with whites and Latinos. Analyses in this table include controls for leading predictors of black racial attitudes though they are omitted in the table due to space limitations.[9] In the next few paragraphs, I provide a summary of the findings in table 9 and highlight key findings in figures.

In general, the results in table 9 present some support for my TTCCI in its ability to explain blacks' attitudes toward Latinos and whites. Regarding the effects of social contact, I find some support for the social contact hypothesis and the divisive effects hypothesis. Having Latino friends increases the likelihood that blacks perceive closeness with Latinos. Further, blacks' social interactions with whites (by having mostly white friends) are positively related to feeling close to whites. As I expected, social contact can also have divisive effects: blacks who work with Latinos are less likely to perceive closeness with whites. Racial and economic context have some influence on African Americans' sense of closeness with Latinos and whites. While residing in a largely white county does not seem to play a critical role in structuring blacks' sense of closeness with whites, I do find some support for the racial threat and Latinos hypothesis, where blacks who reside in a predominantly Latino county are less likely to perceive closeness with Latinos.[10] The unemployment rate of a county does influence African Americans' racial attitudes. As expected, when blacks are in a high threat environment (as depicted by a high unemployment rate), they are less likely to perceive closeness with Latinos and more likely to feel close to whites. Illustrating these findings in further detail, figure 11 demonstrates that African Americans' sense of closeness with Latinos is lower in settings with a high unemployment rate

TABLE 9. Ordered logistic regression results for black perceptions of closeness with Latinos and whites

	Latinos		Whites	
SOCIAL CONTACT				
White friends	−0.51	(0.32)	0.68***	(0.26)
Latino friends	0.85***	(0.27)	0.04	(0.40)
White coworkers	−0.05	(0.12)	−0.21	(0.14)
Latino coworkers	0.34*	(0.21)	−0.61***	(0.20)
White neighbors	0.11	(0.16)	0.37	(0.22)
Latino neighbors	—		−0.16	(0.20)
RACIAL CONTEXT (COUNTY)				
Percentage Latino (2004 estimate)	−1.78**	(0.90)	—	
Percentage white (2004 estimate)	—		0.66	(0.97)
ECONOMIC CONTEXT (COUNTY)				
Percentage with high school degree (2000)	−0.03	(0.02)	0.01	(0.03)
Poverty rate (2007 estimate)	0.02	(0.02)	−0.04	(0.03)
Unemployment rate (2008 estimate)	−0.13**	(0.06)	0.17***	(0.06)
INSTITUTIONAL CONTEXT (COUNTY, 2004)				
Latino legislator	0.87**	(0.25)	—	
Black legislator	—		−0.23	(0.40)
Democratic candidate	−0.82	(0.88)	−1.28	(1.21)
State provisions for direct democracy	−0.43*	(0.23)	−0.32*	(0.24)
FEELINGS OF IDENTIFICATION				
Identification with whites	0.61***	(0.16)	—	
Identification with Latinos	—		0.77***	(0.17)
Identification with blacks	0.79***	(0.19)	0.17	(0.19)
N	507		528	
Pseudo-R^2	0.13		0.09	

Source: 2004 NPS.

Note: ***$p < 0.01$ level; ** $p < 0.05$ level; *$p < 0.10$ level. Entries not in parentheses are unstandardized b coefficients. Entries in parentheses denote the corresponding standard errors to the b coefficients and are clustered by county. Due to collinearity issues, I do not control for the effects of percentage white in models that assess blacks' perceptions of Latinos, and I do not control for the effect of percentage Latino in models that assess blacks' perceptions of whites. Models control for perceiving discrimination against blacks, adopting negative stereotypes of Latinos, being part of the working class, and residing in the South.

than in settings with a lower unemployment rate.[11] The opposite is true for whites. These findings provide support for Bobo and Hutchings's (1996) racial alienation hypothesis suggesting that blacks who feel disadvantaged by their economic context are less likely to identify with Latinos. Further, these results reinforce the idea that when blacks are not economically stable, they may choose to identify with a more powerful group like whites.

FIG. 11. Probability of blacks' closeness with Latinos and whites by county unemployment rate

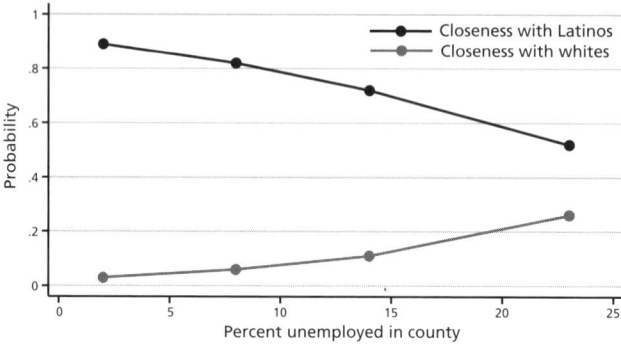

Source: Author's calculations using 2004 NPS data.

Although the institutional context measures in table 9 do not seem to structure blacks' attitudes toward whites, I find that political context does shape blacks' perceptions of closeness with Latinos. In support of my hypotheses, African Americans who are represented by a Latino legislator are more likely to perceive closeness with Latinos.

The results for the effects of identification yield compelling results. In line with my identification hypothesis, feelings of identification with whites influence blacks' sense of closeness with Latinos and vice versa. In line with my hypotheses, blacks' identification with whites is positively related to their perceptions of closeness with Latinos, and blacks' identification with Latinos is positively related to their feelings of closeness with whites. Interestingly, the more blacks identify with other blacks, the more likely they are to perceive closeness with Latinos. This finding is further supported by the results in figure 12, which demonstrate that perceptions of closeness with Latinos are much higher among blacks who identify greatly with other blacks than those who do not identify with them at all.

Thus, while previous findings suggest that blacks distinguish whites and Latinos from their racial counterparts, this last finding presents some hope for improved relations between blacks and Latinos. At the very least, this

FIG. 12. Probability of blacks' closeness with Latinos by identification with blacks

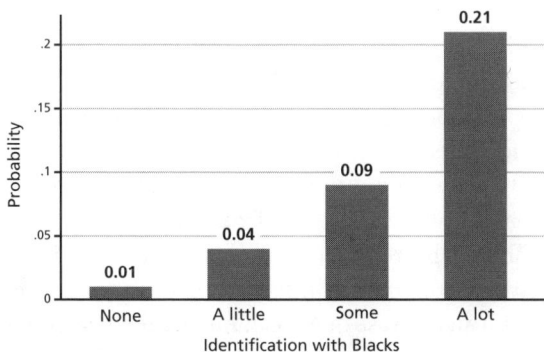

Source: Author's calculations using 2004 NPS data.

result illustrates that blacks may not always place themselves and Latinos in separate categories, or that many blacks do not consider race when thinking about whether they feel close to one group or another. This empirical puzzle is further examined in the subsequent chapter using focus group data of African Americans.

Leading predictors of black racial attitudes have some significant effect on blacks' dispositions toward Latinos and whites. Analyses not presented in table 9 reveal that, as expected, African Americans who reside in the South and who are part of the working class perceive less closeness with Latinos. What is more, perceiving that blacks are discriminated against is negatively related to blacks' sense of closeness with whites.

The 2010 CCES data allows me to take a more contemporary approach to testing my hypotheses in addition to examining the extent to which subjective racial contexts structure black attitudes. Most of the literature regarding the relationship between black racial attitudes and racial contexts centers on an objective context, and we have limited knowledge as to the effect of blacks' perceived racial contexts on their attitudes toward Latinos and whites. I find that the correlation between blacks' perceptions of the number of Latinos in their counties and the actual number of Latinos (based on 2011 U.S. Census estimates) is low (0.31), suggesting that African Americans' perceptions of who lives close to them and who actually lives close to them are not related. This finding greatly contributes to our understanding of the extent to which blacks' perceptions of how many Latinos surround them is an accurate representation of how many Latinos actually reside near them. Table 12 below presents analyses of blacks' sense of closeness with Latinos and whites. While several of the results in this table compare to those in table 9, I find several surprising results regarding the effects of racial context. Unlike what I expected in my racial threat and Latinos hypothesis, the more that blacks are surrounded by Latinos or *perceive* that they are surrounded by Latinos, the more they perceive closeness with them. In order to further delve into the surprising relationship between subjective Latino context and blacks' perceptions of closeness with Latinos, I examine the progression in the predicted probability of sensing economic commonality with Latinos when blacks perceive that they have no Latinos living in their county to having a lot of Latino neighbors. This relationship is demonstrated in figure 13. Contrary to what I hypothesized, a rise in the number of perceived Latinos in one's county coincides with an increase in African Americans' perceptions of economic closeness with Latinos. A plausible explanation for this finding is that Latinos' and blacks' generally limited economic status influences them to reside near each other, thus highlighting the commonalities that exist between the two groups.

FIG. 13. Probability of blacks' closeness with Latinos by perceived number of Latinos in county

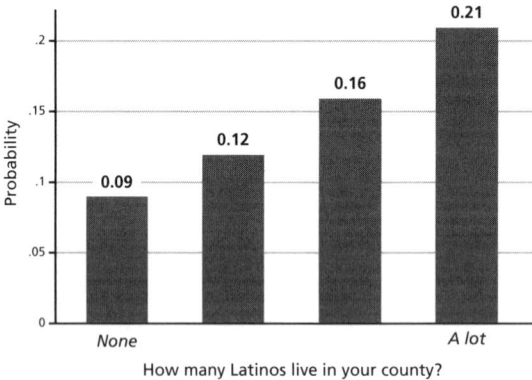

How many Latinos live in your county?

Source: Author's calculations using 2010 CCES data.

Perceptions of Competition with Latinos and Whites by Region

So far, I have found that some measures of contact, context, and identification influence African Americans' sense of closeness with whites and Latinos. Yet, to what extent does my TTCCI explain blacks' sense of competition with these groups?

Table 10 presents the ordered logistic regression results for blacks' perceptions of general competition with whites and Latinos by those who live

TABLE 10. Ordered logistic regression results for black perceptions of competition with Latinos and whites, by region

	Latinos		Whites	
	South	Non-South	South	Non-South
SOCIAL CONTACT				
White friends	0.07	0.61*	−0.30	0.58*
	(0.21)	(0.32)	(0.39)	(0.34)
Latino friends	0.08	−0.83**	−0.41	−0.98***
	(0.32)	(0.16)	(0.29)	(0.38)
White coworkers	0.44*	−0.14	0.17	−0.28**
	(0.24)	(0.16)	(0.17)	(0.14)
Latino coworkers	−0.14	0.15	−0.08	−0.20
	(0.32)	(0.27)	(0.30)	(0.26)
White neighbors	−0.47**	0.22	−0.13	−0.22
	(0.24)	(0.38)	(0.19)	(0.28)
Latino neighbors	−0.37*	0.48*	−0.28	0.15
	(0.26)	(0.27)	(0.22)	(0.19)
RACIAL CONTEXT (COUNTY, 2004)				
Percentage white	—	—	0.71	0.84
			(0.77)	(2.11)
Percentage Latino	0.34	2.39*	−0.64	1.97*
	(1.15)	(1.56)	(0.91)	(1.50)
ECONOMIC CONTEXT (COUNTY)				
Percentage with high school degree (2000 estimate)	−0.05*	0.08*	−0.04*	0.08*
	(0.03)	(0.05)	(0.03)	(0.04)
Poverty rate (2007 estimate)	−0.05	0.13***	−0.05	0.09**
	(0.05)	(0.04)	(0.04)	(0.04)
Unemployment rate (2008 estimate)	0.02	−0.05	0.04	−0.03
	(0.15)	(0.07)	(0.10)	(0.07)
INSTITUTIONAL CONTEXT (COUNTY, 2004)				
Latino legislator	1.81***	0.07	—	—
	(0.67)	(0.28)		
Black legislator	—	—	0.23	0.01
			(0.45)	(0.58)
Democratic candidate	−0.52	0.57	0.55	0.98
	(0.99)	(1.31)	(1.27)	(1.11)
State provisions for direct democracy	−0.04	0.64*	−0.10	−0.17
	(0.29)	(0.42)	(0.30)	(0.36)
FEELINGS OF IDENTIFICATION				
Identification with whites	—	—	−0.34**	−0.48**
			(0.19)	(0.22)
Identification with Latinos	−0.42**	0.14*	—	—
	(0.19)	(0.09)		

TABLE 10. (*continued*)

	Latinos		Whites	
	South	Non-South	South	Non-South
N	228	283	235	290
Pseudo-R²	0.05	0.05	0.02	0.05

Source: 2004 NPS.

Note: ***p < 0.01 level; **p < 0.05 level; *p < 0.10 level. Entries not in parentheses are unstandardized b coefficients. Entries in parentheses denote the corresponding standard errors to the b coefficients and are clustered by county.

in the South and in the non-South.[12] A general analysis of blacks' perceptions of competition with Latinos and whites is presented in table 11. At the outset, the results in the non-South and South models are quite distinct though the pseudo-R² values in all analyses reveal that I am not better able to explain black/Latino and black/white relations in the South than in the non-South.

Still, the results in the competition with Latinos and whites analyses (in the non-South and South) illustrate some support for my hypotheses. When it comes to the effects of social contact on blacks' sense of rivalry with Latinos and whites, I find some support for the social contact hypothesis. Non-southern blacks with mostly Latino friends are less likely to sense competition with Latinos, and blacks with mostly white coworkers are less inclined to regard whites as rivals outside of the South. Interestingly, I do not find support for the divisive effects hypothesis in the non-South; yet, as I expected, having mostly white neighbors is negatively related to perceiving competition with Latinos in the South.

While racial context does not seem to structure blacks' perceptions of competition with Latinos and whites, some economic and political context coefficients unveil intriguing results. In line with my economic context and Latinos hypothesis as well as my economic context and whites hypothesis, African Americans who reside in a high poverty area are more likely to regard Latinos and whites as competitors in the non-South. Illustrating these results in further detail, figure 14 shows the progression in the probability of perceiving competition with Latinos and whites by the amount of poverty that surrounds African Americans. Blacks who reside in high poverty settings are more likely to perceive competition with Latinos and whites than those in lower poverty settings. Interestingly, these findings do not apply to blacks' attitudes in the South. What is also quite surprising is that a county's

TABLE 11. Ordered logistic regression results for black perceptions of
competition with Latinos and whites

	Latinos		Whites	
SOCIAL CONTACT				
White friends	0.24	(0.21)	0.08	(0.27)
Latino friends	-0.38*	(0.24)	-0.78***	(0.26)
White coworkers	0.16	(0.17)	0.05	(0.13)
Latino coworkers	-0.14	(0.22)	-0.15	(0.17)
White neighbors	-0.07	(0.21)	-0.02	(0.16)
Latino neighbors	0.05	(0.19)	0.02	(0.15)
RACIAL CONTEXT (COUNTY, 2004)				
Percentage white	1.31	(0.85)	1.13**	(0.66)
Percentage Latino	1.65	(1.13)	0.14	(0.88)
ECONOMIC CONTEXT (COUNTY)				
Percentage with high school degree (2000 estimate)	-0.01	(0.03)	-0.01	(0.03)
Poverty rate (2007 estimate)	0.03	(0.04)	0.02	(0.03)
Unemployment rate (2008 estimate)	-0.03	(0.06)	-0.03	(0.05)
INSTITUTIONAL CONTEXT (COUNTY, 2004)				
Latino legislator	0.45*	(0.30)	—	
Black legislator	—		0.31	(0.36)
Democratic candidate	0.23	(0.81)	0.65	(0.97)
State provisions for direct	0.33	(0.26)	0.02	(0.23)
FEELINGS OF IDENTIFICATION				
Identification with Whites	—		-0.34***	(0.15)
Identification with Latinos	-0.17	(0.15)	—	
LEADING PREDICTORS OF BLACK RACIAL ATTITUDES				
Perceived discrimination against blacks	0.25*	(0.15)	0.68***	(0.20)
Negative stereotypes of Latinos	0.07	(0.08)	—	
Residing in the South	0.30	(0.29)	0.08	(0.28)
Member of the working class	0.38*	(0.22)	0.62***	(0.22)
N	490		521	
Pseudo-R^2	0.03		0.04	

Source: 2004 NPS.

Note: ***p < 0.01 level; **p < 0.05 level; *p < 0.10 level. Entries not in parentheses are unstandardized b coefficients. Entries in parentheses denote the corresponding standard errors to the b coefficients and are clustered by county.

unemployment rate does not play a critical role in structuring blacks' rivalry with Latinos in the South or in the non-South. These insignificant findings suggest that while threat (as created by a county's poverty rate) may have an effect on non-southern blacks' perceptions of Latinos, threat as determined by residing in a county with a high unemployment rate is not a central determinant of black/Latino relations throughout the United States.

FIG. 14. Probability of blacks' perceptions of competition with Latinos and whites in the non-South by county poverty rate

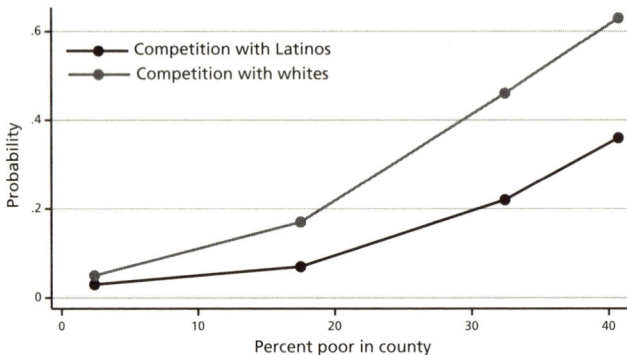

Source: Author's calculations using 2004 NPS data.

As to institutional context, most measures do not have statistically significant effects on blacks' attitudes, though the Latino legislator measure yields quite intriguing findings. In line with my Latino representative hypothesis, southern African Americans who are represented by a Latino legislator perceive greater competition with Latinos than those not represented by a Latino. This finding reinforces Bobo and Hutchings's (1996) modified group position theory, which conveys that blacks are more likely to feel threatened by Latinos with a growth in Latinos' clout given blacks' generally scant political influence in the South.

On the other hand, feelings of identification with Latinos and whites significantly shape blacks' attitudes toward both whites and Latinos. As presented in the identification and competition hypothesis, the more blacks identify with Latinos and whites, the less likely they are to regard them as competitors (with the exception of non-southern blacks' attitudes toward Latinos). Illustrating these findings in further detail, figures 15 and 16 portray comparable relationships. These results imply that, unlike Latinos (as illustrated in chapter 2), African Americans regard perceiving closeness and sensing competition with a group as mutually exclusive.

While my analyses of 2004 NPS data convey that racial context does not

FIG. 15. Probability of blacks' competition with Latinos
in the South by identification with Latinos

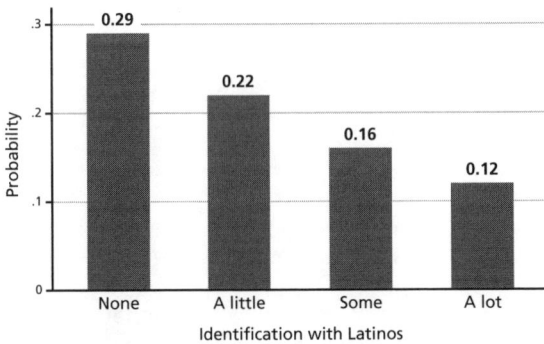

Source: Author's calculations using 2004 NPS data.

FIG. 16. Probability of blacks' competition with whites in the
South and non-South by identification with whites

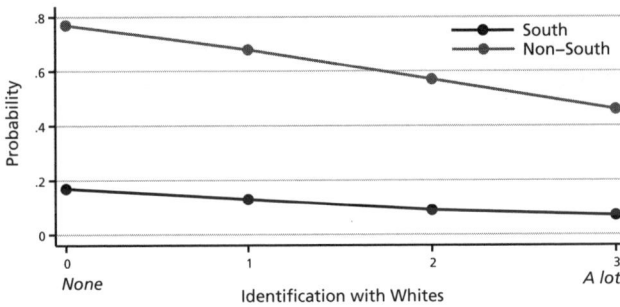

Source: Author's calculations using 2004 NPS data.

affect blacks' perceptions of competition with Latinos, do we obtain the same findings with more recent data? Also, do blacks' perceptions of who lives near them (indirectly addressed by prevailing studies) structure African Americans' sense of rivalry with Latinos and whites? Table 12 presents analyses of blacks' perceptions of employment competition with Latinos and whites controlling for the effects of objective and subjective racial context as well as other measures.[13] While some of the results regarding the effects of contact and perceptions in this table compare to those in table 10, the coefficients for perceived number of Latinos and whites in one's county yield interesting results. In accordance with my racial threat hypotheses, the more African Americans perceive that they are surrounded by Latinos/whites, the more likely it is that they regard them as economic threats.

TABLE 12. Ordered logistic regression results for blacks' perceptions of closeness and employment competition with Latinos and whites

	Closeness with		Competition with	
	Latinos	whites	Latinos	whites
SOCIAL CONTACT				
White friends	−0.25	0.67**	−0.36*	−0.35*
	(0.28)	(0.33)	(0.22)	(0.25)
Latino friends	0.47	0.37	−0.15	−0.46*
	(0.39)	(0.32)	(0.26)	(0.26)
White coworkers	0.14	0.20	−0.36**	−0.07
	(0.18)	(0.19)	(0.19)	(0.19)
Latino coworkers	0.71***	−0.51*	0.25	−0.20
	(0.26)	(0.30)	(0.26)	(0.25)
White neighbors	0.05	0.50**	0.37**	0.15
	(0.19)	(0.24)	(0.19)	(0.19)
Latino neighbors	0.42*	0.42*	−0.53*	0.004
	(0.32)	(0.26)	(0.32)	(0.31)
RACIAL CONTEXT (COUNTY)				
Percent Latino (2011 estimate)	0.04***	—	0.01	—
	(0.01)		(0.01)	
Perceived number of Latinos	0.37**	—	0.33**	−0.15
	(0.16)		(0.18)	(0.20)
Percent white (2011 estimate)	—	−0.02***	—	—
		(0.01)		
Perceived number of whites	—	0.16	—	0.37**
		(0.24)		(0.20)
ECONOMIC CONTEXT (COUNTY)				
Percent high school degree	0.03*	0.002	−0.04*	−0.04**
(2006–10 estimate)	(0.02)	(0.03)	(0.03)	(0.02)
Percent unemployment rate	0.05	−0.03	−0.03	0.01
(2008 estimate)	(0.06)	(0.07)	(0.06)	(0.07)
INSTITUTIONAL CONTEXT (COUNTY, 2010)				
Latino legislator	−1.83**	—	0.39	—
	(0.78)		(1.08)	
Black legislator	—	−0.43	—	−0.08
		(0.39)		(0.49)
Democratic candidate	−0.17	−0.54	1.02	−0.39
	(0.79)	(1.08)	(0.73)	(1.13)
State provisions for direct	−0.10	−0.01	−0.06	−0.28
democracy	(0.29)	(0.27)	(0.27)	(0.28)

TABLE 12. (*continued*)

	Closeness with		Competition with	
	Latinos	whites	Latinos	whites
FEELINGS OF IDENTIFICATION				
Identification with whites	0.65***	—	—	−0.56***
	(0.16)			(0.19)
Identification with Latinos	—	0.66***	−0.42**	—
		(0.17)	(0.18)	
N	212	209	203	206
Pseudo-R²	0.12	0.13	0.05	0.06

Source: 2010 CCES.

Note: ***p < 0.01 level; **p < 0.05 level; *p < 0.10 level. Entries not in parentheses are unstandardized b coefficients. Entries in parentheses denote the corresponding standard errors to the b coefficients and are clustered by county. These models do not control for the effects of the poverty rate of a county because this measure is highly correlated with a county's education level and it depresses the model's sample size to the point where the researcher is not able to conduct a thorough test of the TTCCI.

Conclusion

This chapter overcomes several limitations of past research on black racial attitudes. It is seminal in its comparative approach. By comparing African Americans' perceptions of closeness and competition with Latinos as
well as with whites, and by analyzing the degree to which the determinants
of these attitudes parallel or diverge for Latinos and whites, I am better able
to determine the extent to which blacks regard Latinos and whites similarly.
A second contribution of this study is that the hypotheses in this chapter
heighten our understanding of the ability of the social contact, racial threat,
and the group position theories to explain African Americans' perceptions
and relations with whites and Latinos. Results from multivariate analyses
of black attitudes reveal that my power-based hypotheses associated with
the effects of contact, context, and identification do help to explain African
Americans' sense of closeness and rivalry with Latinos and whites. What is
more, this study's reliance on national and more contemporary survey data
provides a unique and essential contribution to what we know about black
racial attitudes.

Relying on 2004 NPS and 2010 CCES survey data, my analyses unveil several intriguing findings that advance our understanding of black/Latino and
black/white relations today. African Americans do not clearly differentiate
Latinos from whites when it comes to perceptions of closeness, yet blacks

feel closer to other blacks than their white and Latino counterparts. Blacks regard whites as greater rivals than Latinos. As to the effects of social contact, context, and feelings of identification on blacks' attitudes, measures in these three categories structure blacks' racial dispositions, though as a whole, contact, context, and identification better account for blacks' perceptions of closeness with Latinos and whites than for blacks' sense of rivalry with these groups. Greater social interaction with Latinos and whites is positively related to blacks' perceptions of closeness with these groups. Further, increased social interaction with Latinos and whites decreases the likelihood that blacks regard these groups as competitors. Thus, greater social interaction across racial/ethnic groups has the potential to improve inter-race relations.

Context also yields some interesting results. I find that objective racial context has generally limited effects on blacks' racial attitudes, while blacks' perceptions of their racial surroundings significantly heighten their sense of closeness *and* competition with Latinos. These results contribute significantly to our knowledge of blacks' attitude formation and thus challenge future studies to seriously assess the effect of subjective contexts on blacks' racial dispositions. Economic contexts also seem to play a key role in shaping blacks' attitudes. When African Americans reside in high poverty settings (thus in less powerful settings), they are less inclined to perceive closeness with Latinos yet are more likely to regard Latinos and whites as rivals.

The effects of identification with blacks and others yield some intriguing results. The more blacks identify with whites, the more likely they are to feel close to Latinos. The more African Americans identify with Latinos, the more inclined blacks are to perceive commonality with whites. Yet, identifying with other blacks is positively related to perceiving closeness with Latinos but not with whites. Thus, do blacks actually regard Latinos and whites similarly? Are African Americans' perceptions of closeness and competition with Latinos and whites mutually exclusive? Can blacks identify with Latinos as well as regard them as competitors? These questions are further examined in the next chapter on African Americans in New Orleans.

5

African Americans Discuss
Race Relations in New Orleans

Besides analyzing national survey data to test the Triangular Theory of Contact, Context and Identification (TTCCI), I rely on focus group data to obtain a more comprehensive view of black/Latino and black/white relations. The number of prevalent qualitative analyses of black racial attitudes is quite limited. Focus group data of blacks not only allow me to examine the depth and intensity of blacks' racial dispositions but also provide a deeper understanding of what is at the core of black attitudes and the extent to which they regard whites and Latinos similarly. In this chapter, I rely on New Orleans focus group data of African Americans to assess their perceptions of commonality and competition with whites and Latinos, and to delve further into some key, perplexing findings from the previous chapter.

African Americans in New Orleans

New Orleans is known for being "the birthplace of jazz" and "the city that care forgot," but, simultaneously, it is a city with a long history of racism and of upholding a rigid social structure (Spain 1979; Wieder 1987). It was once one of the largest slave trading centers in the country. On one hand, slaves, free blacks, and whites intermingled throughout the city; on the other, "the purpose of this mix was . . . to keep an eye on blacks and prevent the growth of a cohesive black community" (Spain 1979, 86). With the introduction of Jim Crow laws in 1902 and the advent of public housing in 1937, segregation became more prevalent in New Orleans. In addition, the socioeconomic status of blacks remained poor throughout the twentieth century. In 1970, "forty-four percent of the city's blacks earned incomes below the poverty level, compared to 10 percent of the whites" (Spain 1979, 94). Today, African Americans represent the majority of residents at 59 percent in Orleans Parish (Mack and Ortiz 2013). Yet as census data compiled by the Greater New Orleans Community Data Center reveal, black residents in New Orleans trail whites and Latinos in various ways. The employment rate of black men in the New Orleans metro area is at 53 percent, considerably lower than the rate for white males (75%) and Latino males (78%). Further, the 2011 annual income of African American households in the New Orleans metro area ($28,265) is 50 percent less than the income for white households ($56,128) and is also lower than the annual income for Latino families ($43,647). As to educational attainments, African American males and females are obtaining bachelor's and graduate degrees at considerably lower rates than their white and Latino counterparts (Plyer et al. 2013). After hurricane Katrina, the New Orleans metro area's Latino population increased tremendously. Latinos in New Orleans heavily occupied the blue-collar employment sector, primarily obtaining jobs in the construction and service industries, positions often occupied by African Americans before the storm. Thus, Latinos' emerging presence elicited some tension between blacks and the newcomers.

Still, the shifting demographic landscape and racial tensions that exist between black and Latino residents in New Orleans are not unique to the city. Many cities throughout the United States, including both traditional and new immigrant destinations, have faced tensions between blacks and Latinos. Often these strains are due to deep concerns that African Americans have about Latinos' posing a threat to them in the workplace, in neighborhoods, in politics, and in society in general (Johnson et al. 1997; Susman 2010; Guidi 2012). Thus, the black/Latino racial dynamics that exist in New Orleans may not be substantially distinct from those in other parts of the country.

Data and Methods

The data reported in this qualitative project derive from focus group interviews directed by the author. The interviews were broadly conceived as an exploratory analysis of African Americans' perceptions of commonality and competition with Latinos and whites.[1] Given that this project is one of the first focus group studies that explores African Americans' sense of closeness and rivalry with Latinos and whites, I modeled my colloquial focus group questions on 2004 National Politics Survey questions. My questions concentrated on the levels of social interaction that blacks have with whites and Latinos, African Americans' sense of commonality and competition with these two groups, and the relationship between social contact and blacks' dispositions toward whites and Latinos. The questions for these focus groups are found in the appendix.[2]

The methods that I employed to obtain and analyze the focus group data of blacks were very similar to those employed for the focus groups of Latino residents in New Orleans. The discussions were tape recorded and topically structured, allowing for participants to feel unconstrained in their ability to discuss the topics addressed by the questions. The data were collected in a data display format. To guarantee that the findings were accurate, two researchers transcribed all of the focus group responses individually and extracted the themes from each focus group individually. The commonality in the themes between the two researchers was approximately 80 percent, illustrating that both researchers found the same themes while reading each transcribed focus group with the exception of a few themes.

From May to June 2012 in a classroom at Loyola University New Orleans, we conducted four focus groups comprising a total of thirty-one black adults.[3] I recruited participants randomly by placing an advertisement on the Craigslist website and in the local New Orleans newspaper, the *Times Picayune*. When recruiting, I communicated to each interested individual that the study examined blacks' attitudes toward other racial groups and that they would be compensated twenty dollars for their time.[4] Each focus group session lasted approximately one hour.

The demographic characteristics of the focus group participants and the overall population in Orleans Parish (based on 2006–10 U.S. Census, American Community Survey estimates) are somewhat comparable. Women comprised 48 percent of those interviewed, and the census estimates indicate that Orleans Parish is 54 percent women. The average age of participants was forty-three years old, and the census indicates that the average age of blacks in this parish is thirty-three years old. Fifty-two percent of respondents reported being employed, compared to the estimated 82 percent in Orleans Parish.[5] Eighty-three percent of respondents reported having an annual income of $25,000 or less, and the 2006–10 census estimates for Orleans Parish reveal that the median household income was $27,107. As to education, 18 percent of respondents reported having a college degree or higher, close to the estimated 14.8 percent of individuals who earned a college degree or higher (U.S. Census Bureau 2006–10).

Findings

The goal of the following analysis is to explore African Americans' perceptions of closeness and competition with Latinos and whites. Focus is placed on themes that emerge from answers regarding blacks' social interaction, sense of closeness, and competition with these groups.

Social Contact

The focus group interviews began with a discussion of respondents' social contact with whites and Latinos.[6] As to blacks' interactions with whites, most stated that they have a lot of contact in the neighborhood and workplace, and a few mentioned that they have white friends:

Carol: A lot of contacts, my church is probably 95 percent white so we interact with them all the time. I think all of my neighbors in my neighborhood are just about white. And then we have two parents that are actually with kids here that are white, so we do have some contact.

Alex: I have a lot of white friends. I work with a lot of white people and we all associate so I work with white people every day. As far as living around my house, I don't see white people ever but I am in contact with white people every day. My profession is a waiter so I associate with white people every day, so a lot.

Lester: I work with a lot of construction workers, I work with white guys. I don't have a problem with them. I don't judge people by their color. I don't have a problem with them.[7]

When discussing their social networks, a few African Americans stated that they were bothered by the differences in socioeconomic opportunities for blacks and whites:

Lisa: Every day now and I find that for me, I work at the convention center, and so I find that most of the whites are in superior roles in now. . . . When I first started working in January. You know I just didn't have a job then, I just kept searching and searching, you know. But as I observed and sit back and you find a lot of minorities, whether they are African Americans or Latinos, in the back and they are not in that role of higher up like white people. And, um, and that really started to bother me, the fact that the minorities for whatever reason had not obtained, except maybe like one or two. You know what I'm saying, or and it just bothers me in that way, you know. But, you know, life goes on you know. Not to say that it won't happen, I guess there is a process, a transition that is happening. But maybe right now, you know, it's just not in that scope yet.

Regarding blacks' social contact with Latinos, some had limited contact with them and others had a significant amount. Contact was described as being mostly in public places and neighborhoods, though in general, blacks seemed to have more interaction with whites than with Latinos:

Mark: I don't have too much contact with them, besides bumping into them in the store, but nothing else.

Katy: I have contacts with them daily.

When discussing their social interactions with Latinos, a few mentioned that they do not have problems with Latinos while a few fervently argued that Latinos are not like blacks:

Greg: I have quite a bit of contact with Hispanics. I have quite a bit of contact with Hispanics in working. Like now in New Orleans, that's where you know they got Hispanic people, they opened the Mexican consulate here. They opened the Mexican consulate here right after Katrina so they can legally import those construction workers for their companies. . . . Hispanics are our family here. Black people have always had an association with Hispanics so we ain't got problems with Hispanics.

Kevin: Oh, I have no problem with them. I work with them a lot in construction. Because they are all around my work . . . I see them at work.

Some contended that Latinos are given preferential treatment by the immigration and criminal justice systems and that African Americans are disadvantaged:

Leroy: With Hispanics and Latinos? . . . I used to teach them how to cook. I teach them how to cook corn because they didn't know how to cook it. I taught them how to roast it and how to soak it in water. I also used to cook more. . . . They [Latinos] ask to come from Mexico and they can get a check from the government and you know and I can speak English and they can get deported and go back to Mexico, a free ride, and they go back freely. Or they do commit a crime and go back, come back under a new name. And it's so much shit man that goes on in this world. . . . We came from Africa, and we are here in America. We call ourselves African American. But Africa don't want you. Africans here they think that they are better here than we are. We are lost people in here. Whites don't like us, Africans don't like us. We don't speak one language with them. They don't belong with us. . . . You know what I am saying? If you really think about it, it just makes you so fucking mad. . . . That doesn't mean that I don't love these people, it just means that I can't deal with the hatred that is going on, I cannot deal with it.

These findings illustrate that African Americans in New Orleans have greater interactions with whites than Latinos. Analyses of 2004 NPS data (of blacks in the South and in the non-South) provide support for these findings and reveal that blacks in the non-South and South have more white social networks than Latino ones. Further, blacks have greater contact with Latinos in the non-South than in the South.

Perceptions of Commonality

In this section, I examine African Americans' sense of commonality with whites and then with Latinos. I begin with a description of participants' answers to a preliminary questionnaire and then present the themes that emerged from the focus group discussions.

COMMONALITY WITH WHITES

Before the focus groups began, participants were asked to fill out questionnaires that assessed their sense of commonality with whites. Individuals were asked to convey how much in common (on a scale from 0 [none] to 10 [a lot]) they have with whites. The mean commonality score for all of the focus groups is 7.02, suggesting that blacks sense that they have a considerable amount of commonality with their white counterparts.

Throughout the focus group discussions, four themes emerged: (1) blacks have a lot in common with whites, and skin color is the only distinguishing factor between the two races; (2) individuals do not consider skin color or race when examining whether they have something in common with someone; (3) blacks have limited commonality with whites; and (4) blacks have significant commonality with whites but they feel that discrimination creates disparities in power. A resonant theme in the conversations was that several African Americans feel considerable closeness with whites and that skin tone is the only factor that distinguishes the two groups:

Betty: No difference, I mean they can't dance like us can, they are white. But it's basically no difference, only the color. I think it pretty much evens out at the end of the day, if you are around them, they kinda pretty much adapt to your atmosphere just like you can adapt to theirs. I think it's pretty much the same.

Wilma: I think we have a lot in common. . . . It's just in color, we just look different than the white people that's all.

Besides asserting that skin color is the only thing that differentiates blacks from whites, some African Americans stated that they do not consider skin color or race when thinking about how much in common they have with whites:

Greg: We have, I have a lot in common with white people. You know, I need a place to eat, they need a place to eat. I raise children, they raise children. Ah, I need the economy, they need the economy. But that's stuff that's built in the situation. It's not about me. I have a lot in common with any human being living in the planet earth. I need bread and water, they need bread and water, you know. That we all have the same things in common when it comes down to being people. I have a lot in common with white people but if you ask me the question, I have a lot in common with anything. Anyone on the earth, black, white, brown, yellow. We all have those things in common. We have desires, we have needs, we have wants. Those things are required for your basic existence. We all have those things in common. Just coping to exist.

Cathy: It depends. . . . Like I said, I can be your best friend or I can be your worst enemy. My white next door neighbor comes to talk to me every day . . . so like I said it depends.

Leroy: I look at them just like you and me. Like looking in the mirror. That's what I think about when it comes to having in common.

Roy: As far as what I think that I have in common, I would think that it would be, you know, a decent amount of things but it seems to me that especially recently as I have gotten older . . . I would say that I have more in common with people in general whether black, white, Indian or Hispanic.

Another major idea that surfaced in the discussions is that blacks have little to no commonality with whites:

Leroy: We put our pants on the same way. But other than that, the way we talk, the way we are, I mean we just are totally different. Their skins get red, but other than that, I don't see much things in common. We don't have much in common. We can talk, but other than that, not much in common.

Tyler: Not too much you know. I feel like we have zero, they just seem to be on a different wavelength.

On the other hand, many participants asserted that African Americans have a lot in common with whites yet blacks are discriminated against and are thus not able to attain the same status and opportunities as whites. For some, these disparities can then heighten their sense of competition with and even resentment toward whites.

Roy: I go to the same school, I go to the same things, hangouts as some of them and being in the same groups. But it's like, you know, when it comes to certain things we are different and it's because of the color of our skin individually. It is racism. And when you ask me how much we have in common, it makes me think of hate.

Lydia: Well, when you ask that question, I try to think that as black people we do want the same thing. We do want our kids to get an education. We want to live in a good neighborhood. We want to make the type of money that we think we should earn. Um, in my case, I think that even though you get the education and all that, you're still oppressed. . . . Society says go and get an education. Yeah you will get more money than someone who doesn't have an education but it's not the same as the whites. I'm thinking that your white counterparts, in some cases, there are some people who work in our office and whites have the high positions. They are not going to pay us what they pay them. So I don't think that that's fair but I do know that we want the same things. We want to have a good income, be in a good neighborhood, you know. Have the luxury items. And it doesn't even have to be luxury items, it can just be nice clothes, nice cars to ride in, you know. It doesn't have to be a Mercedes or like that but just a decent car to get back and forth. In that sense, we don't have a lot in common, but we do have that in common with white folks. We all want the same thing but sometimes we are still oppressed. Because of that, even with the education we get, we still can't be the same.

Katy: Whites are on top of blacks. It just makes me strive to work harder, at my craft, to do better at what I'm doing. Um, that's just also a mental thing because I assure you that you can be intimidated to be better and all that but that doesn't get you anywhere. Um, so I just have to set my priorities you know and, um, sometimes it's a struggle. Because I am African American, you know, we may have one job but that one job does not suffice the income of a white person so we may have to work one or two jobs or a side job just to make ends meet. Whereas a white person can have one job and it takes care of, you know, whatever they need. I think that's just wrong. Do I think it's comparable? Oh absolutely not, not at all. It's not the same if you have a college degree or like something like that for people like me. It's still very hard and it's not even to say that we want anything exorbitant, it's just day to day needs. You know having to find some rainy day money if you got some big emergency that comes up. You know what I'm saying? It's just a struggle. It's still a struggle.

Tyler: Especially after Katrina, there is a whole lot of difference in treatment between blacks and whites. You know, I can relate to them but there is this underlying racism, there's still racism you know. There is this competition between individuals of different economic and educational levels.

COMMONALITY WITH LATINOS

To assess African Americans' sense of commonality with Latinos, I collected data from preliminary questionnaires and focus group discussions. On the questionnaires, focus group participants were asked how much in common they have with Latinos on a scale from 0 (none) to 10 (a lot). The mean commonality with Latinos score is 6.22, suggesting that blacks sense that they have some commonality with their Latino counterparts. Relative to blacks' identification with whites, African Americans seem to sense slightly more commonality with whites than Latinos.

The same information was expressed in the focus groups. African American participants generally expressed more in common with whites than Latinos. Furthermore, three main themes emerged from blacks' discussions of their closeness with Latinos: (1) commonality exists because Latinos are like us; (2) we do not have a lot in common with Latinos; and (3) since competition with Latinos exists, there is no commonality.

First, some African Americans expressed that they have a lot in common with Latinos since both groups work hard, have comparable values, and experience similar struggles:

Penny: They will get down and work and we will get down and work. They don't look at us no different, and we don't look at them no different cause we both are the same. We all just go and work. I mean you can't even say that. It be fifty people in one house, we do that too.

Carol: I feel the same, African American and Hispanics are in the same boat and we all strive for the same things and we are the minority which I know they are beginning to be the minority also. I think that they pretty much have the same upbringing and values as we do but just a different skin tone. I think that they are trying to do the same things that we are trying to do and they are unfortunately struggling in the same way we are because sometimes they end up with the sharp end of the stick just like black people. I think that we are much like Hispanics.

Similar to blacks' perceptions of whites, a few participants asserted that they had very little in common with Latinos, emphasizing differences in language between Latinos and blacks:

Katy: I don't necessarily have a problem. The only problem I have is when they are speaking their native language. They act like they don't know that much English, but a lot of times they do. I mean they can speak their language, they came a long way from where they used to be. I don't think they are just like the African American population. . . . I would say we really don't have too much in common. I would say they mostly watch the soap operas and stuff.

Still, as found in blacks' discussions of their commonality with whites, commonality with Latinos is associated with feelings of resentment and rivalry toward this group. Several emphasized that since competition exists between blacks and Latinos, blacks do not have a lot in common with them:

Christy: Well, that's the grey area for me because I don't think we have much in common in my opinion. Because like she said for jobs, we go in for a job me versus a Hispanic, the Hispanic will get the job. So I think they [whites] consider us the minority.

When the interviewer asked Christy why Latinos think that blacks are the minority, she answered,

Christy: Just because we are at the bottom of the totem pole. Even though they [whites] look at them [Latinos], they [whites] look down on them [Hispanics] but they look down on us more. And our skin color makes a difference. Look at us like a different class of people. We are still being stereotyped either way you look at it. In the same direction, but they still look at us and give us the short end of the stick.

Kevin: We have, ah, very little in common and there are competitions for jobs like they say, you know.

In general, my focus group findings regarding blacks' commonality with Latinos and whites reveal several intriguing results. Blacks feel that they have slightly more closeness with whites than with Latinos. These results are analogous to those obtained using 2004 NPS data in which I find that southern and nonsouthern blacks feel marginally closer to whites than Latinos. Further, like the themes that emerged from blacks' sense of commonality with whites, some blacks perceive significant commonality with Latinos and others do not. Still, African Americans' sense of closeness with whites and Latinos may be related to their perceptions of rivalry with each group. While greater commonality with whites may increase blacks' sense of competition with them, since shared values and goals do not always translate to comparable opportunities for blacks and whites, the relationship between black perceptions of commonality and competition with Latinos may be quite distinct. African Americans who sense competition with Latinos may be less likely to believe that they have significant commonality with Latinos since they are not viewed like blacks in the eyes of whites.

Perceptions of Competition

Besides commonality, I analyze African Americans' sense of rivalry with Latinos and whites in New Orleans. First, I examine blacks' perceptions of competition with whites and then assess their attitudes toward Latinos with each section briefly summarizing questionnaire results.

COMPETITION WITH WHITES

The preliminary questionnaire results reveal that blacks perceive considerable economic and general competition with whites. Individuals were asked to indicate how much economic and general competition they perceive with blacks on a scale from 0 (none) to 10 (a lot). The mean general competition score is 8.3, and the mean economic competition score is 8.1, suggesting that the majority of focus group participants regard whites as competitors.

Throughout focus group discussions, most participants stressed that there is significant competition between blacks and whites. One theme that emerged was that a lot of competition with whites exists because blacks are not provided with the same opportunities as whites. Another theme is that considerable rivalry exists because whites feel threatened by African Americans.

Some stated that rivalry between blacks and whites is high since those in power discriminate against blacks and thus place blacks at a disadvantage:

Christy: I think it's probably everything because black kids growing up we don't grow up with the white kids. But as they get older, they start going to school with whites and they [whites] get cars and the black kids don't. So in their minds they are saying I want what they have so they gonna do things to get what they have whether they do it the illegal way or the right way. But they will never be looked at in the same way a white person is looked at. So, I think it's pretty much everything, same thing on jobs. They may have good jobs, a white person may have a good job, a black person may get that good job the honest way. But because people don't look at blacks in the same way and they wouldn't give them the same credit. They think ok they work their way up to get this job whereas some white person they may have the same job but it is because of who they know they got that job. So I think it's pretty much they are competing with everything not just jobs and education but everything that comes with life.

Renee: Competition? [nods head] We'd be in a situation working and I think that they treat white people more superior than blacks because I know my supervisor does that. . . . At work, this girl she is supposed to know Microsoft word and she makes more than me and then she lied and said that she knew how to do it. There is a lot of competition I think towards whites.

Alex: Kind of like what Christy was saying. I mean there is an underlying theme within the black world about how you know there is competition between blacks and whites. You know a lot of black children when they are born, it's like inside of them. You know, constantly, they don't, they don't measure up to white kids. And so they have to put forth the effort, you know, to get things and for the white side, you know, it's a lot of it is kept up inside. It's just there, they think that they deserve it. And as for black kids, you know, they have to go out of their way to show that we don't mess up.

Lydia: I think a lot of people are finding that it's difficult and a lot of times when they check the credit . . . I mean to me, we have to work harder. We have to work harder and I think that a lot of us are smarter but because they're white, then, you know, they all tend to get at the top.

Tyler: Especially after Katrina, there is a whole lot of difference in treatment between blacks and whites. You know, I can relate to them but there is this underlying racism, there's still racism you know. There is this competition between economic and educational levels.

Another common theme was that competition is high and it is due to whites' feeling threatened by African Americans and thus responding negatively toward them:

Roy: I think there is competition. One of the things that I think we need to distinguish is that we look at it from the perspective of a black person. I always feel that at no matter what point there is competition. There may not be competition . . . a white person doesn't think that you are worth anything but the minute that they feel that you might threaten them, if you are educated, if you have any sort of advantage over them, thinking how does this black person have this? How is this black person better than me? You know, there's something that they go through and that's when you feel accomplished. I go to college, I am 23 years old, just ah finishing up. And most of the students in the business school who are part of the program and so there are some who have more work experience but . . . for the most part, still, the first couple weeks of school in that part of the program when you don't know anybody, you know assignments will come up. It was all fine and dandy but for I guess it was easy for people to overlook me at first, but then when I started to get better grades, when I started to do well on assignments, it was like, man, oh we are going to have to do everything to stop this kid because we have to make sure that he works alone so that we can all pull together, you know. Some may think that that's what I'm doing [working alone] but that's the reality.

Greg: I guess historically it has always been there, I would have to say about 60–70 percent. We were the first black family in an all-white neighborhood in 69. We were the first black team in an all-white neighborhood. I played football. . . . I was at practice at the start of, you know, basketball season and they told us all the guys on the basketball team who were on the football team were not able to play because we didn't have the grades to play . . . most schools have a system for practice and if you were an athlete and a student then you didn't have the college preparatory courses that maybe somebody who . . . but the point is that they ended up disqualifying all the blacks on the basketball team and . . . so they didn't want us to win the championship and that was it. When we played, we were the only black team among all the white teams. They went out of their way to make sure that we had penalties, personal fouls, the little things that they made sure to do so that we wouldn't succeed. I really gave a lot of white guys some competition because I was a threat to them.

Kevin: We have to strategize because we compete with jobs with them but with everything else, they compete with us. Lacrosse, basketball, football.

COMPETITION WITH LATINOS

When examining African Americans' sense of competition with Latinos, I find that blacks perceive less competition with Latinos than with whites. Questionnaire results reveal that the mean economic competition with Latinos score is 6.3, and the mean general competition score for Latinos is even lower at 5.8. As with the commonality and white competition measures, competition with Latinos is measured on a scale from 0 to 10.

Regarding the focus group findings, three main themes emerged. The first theme is that blacks do not regard Latinos as threatening and can view them, like blacks, as an oppressed minority group:

Carol: We just don't feel like each other is a threat.

Greg: I would say that white people create laws to be against Hispanic people and use them for their labor and use them for their taxes just like they do black people. I don't have any problems because white people do to Hispanics to what they've done to me. Took my life just like what they did to us during the civil war and then it took another 100 years for us to get our rights back. So what they do to Hispanic people and like my children who are suffering and not graduating from schools right now and just like my children are populating prisons for the last fifty years and now even incarcerating my females, I don't have any problems with Hispanic people.

The second theme is that blacks expressed how strong Latinos' work ethic is, some even conveying admiration for them:

Kevin: They are going to bed tired. They work hard. They are all over the place. They do a good job. They work a long time. Most people leave around 5 or 6. They stay and keep working. If you get the right one, they will work.

Mark: They are not bad people. They just do cheaper labor. They get away a lot of jobs. They work seven days a week. They don't spend any money. Every week, they are sending money back home, to buy food and stuff.

Kim: You got all these Mexicans and they'll be around by the block and when they get out they have 9 people living in a 2 bedroom house. And then when they get sick, they will bring in money. . . . You got all these Mexicans and they'll do a job, they do a job.

Third, and as discussed regarding how much they identify with Latinos, blacks perceive little commonality and high competition with Latinos since white employers appear to favor Latino workers over blacks, and thus blacks often lose jobs to Latinos:

Johnnie: We have little in common. There is competition in the jobs. Also, I feel like they do hate black men. We accept the minimum wage but then when we learn that we are worth more than what we get paid for then they have to come up with something . . . they [Latinos] work for less and we are moved to the side . . . they are going to work for anything. You say you are gonna get a job at seven dollars an hour and then they give a Mexican five or four, below minimum wage. And then you won't get it.

Keith: We have, ah, very little in common and there are competitions for jobs like they say, you know.

Christy: Because like she said for jobs, we go in for a job me versus a Hispanic, the Hispanic will get the job.

African Americans' discussions of their rivalry with Latinos and whites illustrate several interesting findings. First, blacks do not seem to perceive as much antagonism with Latinos as with whites. They believe that whites are at an advantaged position and discriminate against them, thus forcing blacks to compete with whites and Latinos. This finding develops our understanding of the group position theory as it applies to African Americans. Furthermore, the results above address several questions posed in the previous chapter. While blacks' perceptions of commonality and competition with Latinos seem to be mutually exclusive (blacks who sense high competition with Latinos perceive low commonality with this group), African Americans' perceptions of whites are not. Most blacks associate significant commonality with whites with high competition with them because they think that though blacks can be like whites, whites victimize blacks in order to distinguish themselves from African Americans, thus resulting in rivalry. Therefore, whites' behavior toward blacks influences blacks' perceptions of whites and Latinos.

Effect of Contact on Attitudes toward Whites

In addition to examining African Americans' perceptions of whites and Latinos, I inquired about the extent to which blacks' social interactions with whites and Latinos affect their perceptions of commonality and competition toward them.

One major theme that emerged from focus group discussions was that social contact with whites does shape blacks' attitudes toward whites. Increased social interactions with whites illustrate how distinct blacks are from whites, as well as how much of an economic threat whites pose to blacks:

Betty: Yah, a lot of things. It's just certain things, things you do a certain way when it comes to things in common. Like I am not going to jump off nobody's building and walk a tight rope off of the Niagara fall. That's just not something, to me that's just not something that black people do. So if they are willing to go out there and do things like that, certain things they are willing to die for that we are just not going to do. Like if they go after an alligator, we are not about to be eaten by an alligator. It's just certain things you know, I think it's a part of the upbringing. Like I wasn't raised to go bungee jumping and do all of that stuff. I was raised on a budget, what is normal. What I think is normal, but to them it may not be normal. I guess they view it as normal because they have the resources to do that and so we were limited because we do not have those resources. But when it comes to common themes, as we get a little older and you have a daughter, maybe one day I will think of those things, maybe we'll think of a ski trip or something like that. But I guess as you get older and you have the resources then we can do those things. Because when we were young we were just limited, I can't tell my mom to take me to the same things.

Katy: Um, yah it does influence how I perceive and interact with them. I think that like I said before, we want the same things but I think that it's so unequal. It's just not fair to black people as a whole. Right, there are things that I do for my job that I don't get recognized for. I am not the only black person that feels the way I feel. Like the competition and for applying to different jobs.

Still, some stated that contact does not structure their attitudes toward whites. A few stated that competition with whites is not related to how much interaction they have with this group:

John: No, I think it remains the same.
Kevin: No.
Leroy: Based on the contact, it doesn't make a difference.
Greg: Just based on that contact? No, because to me it's broader than that, it's a broader context about competition, not just about my people but it can affect anybody else I guess. We may have a social relationship with them and we may not have a social relationship with them and whether we have competition with them may not change. It's a broader context question than that.

Effect of Contact on Attitudes toward Latinos

Focus group participants were also asked if social interactions with Latinos influenced their perceptions of commonality and competition with them. Many did not answer the question and just reiterated how much commonality or competition they perceived that they had with them. A few, however, stated that contact does affect their attitudes, possibly increasing their sense of rivalry toward Latinos:

Tyler: Yeah.
Jared: Yeah, I see that they are taking jobs away.
Lydia: [in response to Jared's comment] I think that I see it that way too. I mean yeah.

Hence, these results reveal that the relationship between social contact and blacks' perceptions may not be the same for whites as it is for Latinos. While social interaction with whites and Latinos may develop blacks' beliefs that these groups pose an economic threat to them, if social contact structures blacks' racial attitudes, it seems to have a more robust effect on African Americans' dispositions toward whites than toward Latinos. A plausible explanation for this is that blacks in the South have a greater history of relations with whites than Latinos, and that the racialized social structure in the South continuously reminds blacks that their status is not comparable to the one for whites.

Conclusion

In this chapter, I explore blacks' sense of commonality and competition with Latinos and whites relying on focus group data from the city of New

Orleans. Conclusions made in this chapter are meant to enhance our comprehension of blacks' relations with Latinos and whites in the South, and to address some unresolved questions from previous survey data analyses.

I make several critical conclusions. First, black/Latino and black/white relations in the South may be distinct from relations in the non-South. Blacks in New Orleans perceive greater commonality and competition with whites than Latinos as found in my descriptive analyses of 2004 NPS data of blacks in the South. As to social interactions, my qualitative and quantitative findings reveal that southern blacks on average have more contact with whites than with Latinos. These results are not always true for blacks' relations with others outside of the South. I also find that the social contact hypothesis may not explain blacks' attitudes toward Latinos in the South. Social contact with Latinos does not seem to improve African Americans' perceptions of them, and for some blacks, increasing social contact with Latinos can actually augment their sense of antagonism toward this group.

Another primary contribution of this study is to demonstrate that blacks may not consider race or skin tone when thinking about whether they feel close to a group. When examining whether blacks regard Latinos and whites similarly, some respondents emphasized that they do not consider race or skin tone when thinking about whether they identify with one group or not. Thus, it makes sense that some blacks who feel close to whites also feel close to Latinos, since these individuals may not consider race or ethnicity when thinking about whether they perceive commonality with a person. It is critical to point out, however, that I find that many African Americans do not regard Latinos and whites similarly since some believe that Latinos are like blacks in that Latinos are a minority group with struggles and experiences with discrimination comparable to that for blacks. Still, a predominant finding in every focus group is that blacks believe that whites are the most powerful racial group and that whites use their positions of power to disadvantage African Americans even to the point where they create competition between blacks and Latinos. How do whites regard Latinos and African Americans? The following two chapters provide comprehensive analyses of whites' perceptions of commonality and competition with these groups.

6

Whites' Perceptions of Latinos and African Americans

A QUANTITATIVE ANALYSIS

Similar to African Americans, whites have noticed the growing presence of Latinos throughout the United States and responded to them in distinct ways. When whites feel threatened socioeconomically and racially, they are more prone to regard Latino immigrants as rivals. Whites in areas with rising undocumented immigrant populations adopt more negative immigration attitudes (Hood and Morris 1998). When whites perceive that immigrants threaten national cultural identity, they are less likely to favor immigration (Citrin et al. 1990; Hood and Morris 1997). Further, when communities experience large influxes of immigrants, and "when salient national rhetoric politicizes the demographic change," individuals adopt anti-immigrants views and local anti-immigrant ordinances are more likely to emerge (Hopkins 2010, 55–56). Arizona's S.B. 1070 and Alabama's H.B. 56 can be deemed some of the most aggressive anti-immigrant laws enacted in traditional and emerging Latino areas. These laws are a response to nativism and growing concerns of Latinos' threatening natives' socioeconomic and political standing. A key provision of the laws is that officers can make a reasonable attempt to determine the immigration status of an individual if they have reasonable suspicion that the individual is undocumented (Liptak 2012). In accord with some whites' hostile responses to an emerging Latino immigrant population, it does not come as a surprise to find that whites feel closer to African Americans than to Spanish-speaking individuals (Thornton et al. 2012). Notwithstanding this, whites are the majority group in the United States, with substantially greater sociopolitical power than blacks and Latinos, influencing Latinos and African Americans to perceive each other as natural allies.[1] Still, all whites do not regard Latinos with hostility, and some actually do not feel threatened (particularly economically) by Latinos (McClain et al. 2011, 233). Actually, some research suggests that whites in the South and throughout the United States may be more likely to identify with Latinos and favor them as coalition partners than to identify with African Americans (Meier and Stewart 1991; Mindiola et al. 2002; McClain et al. 2011; Marrow 2011).

While it is uncertain as to whether whites will embrace Latinos as allies or rivals in the near future, it is important to recognize that disparities exist among the white population, and these divergences can structure white/Latino relations. Some whites throughout the country live in segregated white neighborhoods with limited contact with nonwhites and with few concerns that other minorities such as Latinos pose a threat to them. Yet others reside in traditional Latino areas (e.g., Houston, Miami, and Los Angeles) and new immigrant destinations (e.g., eastern North Carolina) with significant opportunities for interaction with Latinos in grocery stores, schools, parks, and neighborhoods (Marrow 2011). Although relations between whites and Latinos may be better than those between Latinos and blacks in new immigrant destinations in the South (Marrow 2011), nativism among whites does exist, and tensions between whites and Latinos are prevalent, especially in areas with unfriendly immigration legislation (e.g., Arizona, Alabama). Similar to racial context, whites differ in economic clout. Some reside in economically vibrant counties with fixed education levels and low poverty and unemployment rates. Still, others' employment opportunities and general prospects for upward mobility have declined due to the emerging immigrant population as well as the recent economic downturn, placing whites at a fiscal disadvantage relative to the newcomers. Additionally, whites in the South have considerably higher levels of poverty, lower median incomes, and are less likely to have health insurance than whites in other regions (DeNavas-Walt et al. 2011).

Besides differences in socioeconomic status and economic context, whites' political clout varies with the growth of the Latino electorate and number of Latino legislators. While whites as a whole have greater political leverage in Congress and across state legislatures, the 2012 election illustrated the unfaltering growth and power of Latino legislators and voters nationwide. In 2012, more whites found themselves residing in majority-minority districts, which often shaped election results. In Texas, Senator Kay Hutchinson was replaced by Republican Ted Cruz, who became the first Latino U.S. senator in this state (Dunham 2013). In Colorado, a significant number of Latino legislators were elected resulting in a record thirty-one Latinos serving in the Colorado General Assembly (Preuhs 2012). Altogether across the United States, Latinos were elected to state legislatures in thirty-six states. Not only were Latinos elected in majority Latino areas but they were also elected in largely white states like Oregon, Minnesota, Connecticut, and even Maine, which has a Latino population of only 1.4 percent (Carrero 2012). What is more, Latino voters' overwhelming support of President Obama in 2012 (75%) has the predominantly white Republican Party considerably modifying its agenda and possibly its stance on immigration so as to not lose the Latino vote as it did in the last election (Latino Decisions 2012a; Barreto 2013).

The developing presence and influence of the Latino population, in addition to the disparities among whites today, raise many questions. Do whites regard Latinos as a minority group like African Americans or do whites feel closer to Latinos than blacks? Conversely, are whites more inclined to regard their racial counterparts as allies and competitors relative to Latinos and blacks? To what extent do social contact, sense of power (as established by context), and feelings of identification with other whites and nonwhites structure whites' perceptions of closeness and competition with Latinos and blacks? While studies on white immigration attitudes are abundant, research on whites' sense of closeness and rivalry with Latinos is quite limited (McClain et al. 2011; Hutchings et al. 2011; Thornton et al. 2012). This chapter takes a comprehensive approach to uncovering white/Latino and white/black relations by relying on national survey data (2004 National Politics Survey [NPS], 2010 Cooperative Congressional Election Study [CCES]) to examine whites' perceptions of Latinos and blacks as well as to analyze the effects of social contact, context, and identification on whites' attitudes.

Social Contact, Context, and Whites

Research on the precursors of coalition formation and actual coalition building has centered greatly on Latinos and African Americans. Although most research on whites' attitudes toward Latinos has concentrated on their dispositions toward immigrants and immigration, some studies have analyzed whites' attitudes toward Latinos through the lens of perceptions of competition and stereotypes. Extant research has focused on the effects of social contact, racial context, and economic self-interest on whites' racial attitudes.

The first set of research findings examines the effects of social contact on whites' perceptions of Latinos. In a multicity study, J. Eric Oliver and Janelle Wong (2003) present indirect support for the social contact hypothesis and conclude that whites who live in integrated neighborhoods are less likely to adopt negative stereotypes and perceive less competition with out-groups, including Latinos, blacks, and Asian Americans. Vincent L. Hutchings and his colleagues (2011) also examine the effects of social contact on white attitudes and do not find that social contact shapes whites' perceptions of zero-sum competition with Latinos. Further, in a study of blacks and whites in Durham, a city in North Carolina with an emergent Latino population, Paula D. McClain and her colleagues (2007) find that contact with Latinos is not a statistically significant predictor of whites' concerns about a rapidly growing Latino population.

A second group of research analyzes the extent to which racial context plays a key role in structuring whites' racial dispositions. Oliver and Wong find support for the racial threat hypothesis in that whites in cities with a significant Latino population like Los Angeles exhibit greater hostility toward Latinos than those who live in cities like Atlanta with a much smaller share of Latinos (2003, 575). While their findings provide support for the social contact and the racial threat hypotheses, which some deem opposing theories, they argue that the differences in context (neighborhood versus metropolitan levels) help to explain their support for these two hypotheses (580). Interestingly, Oliver and Wong's findings also suggest that whites in largely white neighborhoods adopt greater negative stereotypes of minorities and perceive a greater threat from immigration than those who do not live in such neighborhoods. Still, in a later study of race relations in southern cities with emergent Latino populations, McClain and her colleagues (2011) find that regardless of city context (particularly the size of the white and black populations), whites do not perceive that new Latino residents pose an economic threat to them. Additionally, whites in Little Rock (a majority white city) believe that relations between Latinos and their racial group are generally positive (233).

A third set of studies focus on the relationship among economic context, self-interest, and whites' racial dispositions. Although economic context and self-interest are prominent predictors of black attitudes toward Latinos, these factors also structure whites' dispositions. Oliver and Tali Mendelberg (2000) find that whites in low-education contexts are more likely to express out-group hostility and adopt negative racial attitudes than those in higher socioeconomic environments. Similarly, Oliver and Wong (2003) conclude that whites in neighborhoods with high education levels sense less competition with Latinos, blacks, and Asian Americans, and feel less threatened by immigrants. Interestingly, Regina P. Branton and Bradford Jones (2005) posit that the influence of racial context on white attitudes toward racial policies is conditioned by the socioeconomic context of the environment. Using national survey data of whites, they conclude that racially diverse and highly educated environments are associated with favorable attitudes toward minorities and high support for racial social policies. Moreover, they find that racially diverse counties with lower rates of education are associated with lesser support for these policies. Instead of relying on national survey data, McClain and her colleagues (2007) explore more recent survey data from a southern city and find that whites who felt economically threatened by Latino immigrants expressed significantly greater concerns about Latinos' rapid influx to their city. Furthermore, in support of economic self-interest theories, the scholars find that whites with lower income and education levels expressed a stronger concern for the rapid growth of the Latino population.

Theory and Hypotheses

Despite the insights these studies provide, our comprehension of whites' perceptions of their Latino counterparts is quite limited. First, current research greatly centers on white attitudes toward Latinos and African Americans separately, failing to compare systematically white perceptions of Latinos with those of blacks. Finding that whites perceive Latinos as allies and/or competitors does not provide us with an accurate understanding of what whites think of Latinos, since we do not know whether whites regard Latinos as a minority group like blacks or whether they favor Latinos over African Americans. Hence, only by taking a comparative approach to studying whites' perceptions of closeness and competition with Latinos am I able to disentangle and address these topics.[2]

Further, in order to uncover whites' attitudes toward Latinos, I develop power-based hypotheses and adopt the Triangular Theory of Contact, Context and Identification (TTCCI) to explain whites' attitudes toward Latinos and African Americans. Although whites have a generally higher sociopolitical status than other racial groups, their distinct economic, political, and racial settings influence their perceptions of power, which structure their attitudes toward Latinos and blacks.[3]

Social Contact

Besides limitations in measurement and approach to uncovering whites' dispositions, there are several deficiencies in extant studies' approaches to testing the effects of social contact. First, our knowledge of the extent to which the social contact hypothesis can explain white perceptions of competition and closeness with Latinos is quite restricted. Thus, testing this hypothesis on white attitudes will advance our comprehension of the theory as well as the implications of laws that foster proximity among groups who differ by race and ethnicity. In addition, current research is limited in the forms of social contact that it explores. Since whites today are interacting with Latinos and blacks in various ways and intensities, I explore the effects of social interaction in the form of friendship, neighbors, and coworkers to obtain a more complete grasp of the context in which contact occurs.[4] Lastly, our understanding of the effects of social contact with one group on whites' attitudes toward another is insufficient. Not only does analyzing the effects of social contact with whites on whites' attitudes toward a minority group give us a sense of intergroup power dynamics, but it also gives us a better grasp of the viable options for alliance formations. I contend that interactions with other whites depresses whites' affinity with Latinos and African Americans since whites' social proximity to other whites decreases whites' opportunities to feel close to nonwhites and can actually heighten the likelihood that whites adopt negative stereotypes of Latinos and blacks.[5] Hence, this study responds to several of the aforementioned weaknesses with the following hypotheses:

Social contact hypothesis: The greater contact (i.e., with friends, neighbors, or coworkers) whites have with Latinos and blacks, the more prone they are to sense closeness yet less likely to sense competition with these groups.

Divisive effects hypothesis: As whites interact socially (i.e., with friends, neighbors, or coworkers) with other whites, they are less likely to feel close and are more likely to sense competition with Latinos and blacks.

Racial Context

In addition, while prevailing research has analyzed the effects of racial context on whites' racial attitudes, it certainly does not lack limitations. First, we have limited knowledge of the effects of residing in a predominantly white context on whites' perceptions of closeness and competition with Latinos and blacks. Further, current studies fail to address thoroughly the extent to which residing in a majority white environment invokes whites' sense of power, thus shaping their perceptions of nonwhites. I posit that when whites reside in a white context, often quite socioeconomically higher from those of nonwhites, they are less likely to perceive closeness with Latinos and regard them as rivals.[6]

A second limitation to our knowledge of racial context on white racial attitudes is that we do not know the extent to which the racial threat hypothesis applies to whites' perceptions of competition *and* closeness with Latinos. Recent studies have not reached a consensus on the relationship between the growth of an out-group and whites' attitudes toward that out-group since they have found support for both the social contact hypothesis and the racial threat hypothesis. In order to address what some would deem incompatible results, I build on Branton and Jones's (2005) study examining the relationship between racial and socioeconomic context and whites' racial policy attitudes. I posit that the influence of the Latino/black composition of a county on white attitudes toward Latinos is conditioned by whites' socioeconomic environment. When whites reside in an environment that poses a maximum threat to them (racially and socioeconomically), they are less prone to regard Latinos and blacks in a positive light.

Thus, these theoretical discussions prompt me to propose:

White county effects hypothesis: Whites who reside in a predominantly white county perceive less closeness and competition with Latinos.

Racial and economic threat hypothesis: High education and low diversity contexts are associated with greater perceptions of closeness and lesser perceptions of competition with blacks and Latinos. Alternatively, low education and high diversity contexts are associated with lower perceptions of closeness and higher perceptions of competition with blacks and Latinos.

Economic Context

Similarly, I theorize that whites' perceptions of influence as formed through their economic contexts structure their sense of closeness and competition with Latinos and blacks. Although numerous studies examine the effects of economic self-interest and context to explain white/black/Latino relations, these studies do not lack weaknesses. We know relatively little about the extent to which whites' economic contexts and opportunities for upward mobility shape their perceptions of closeness with Latinos and blacks. Further, prevailing research (with the exception of Bobo and Hutchings [1996] and Hutchings et al. [2011]) greatly fails to consider the extent to which the group position theory can enhance our comprehension of whites' racial attitudes. Herbert Blumer (1958) attempts to explain whites' (the ingroup) attitudes toward African Americans (the out-group) by asserting that as whites feel that blacks are encroaching on their status and clout, they regard blacks as competitors and adversaries. I apply Blumer's group position theory to explain whites' perceptions of Latinos and blacks, and argue that when whites are in a high-threat economic setting, they are more prone to perceive that minorities are infringing on their status and thus regard them with hostility. Based on the aforementioned theoretical discussions, I argue:

Threat and economic context hypothesis: When whites are in a low-threat environment (i.e., high percentage of residents who have graduated from high school), they perceive greater closeness and less rivalry with Latinos and blacks. When whites are in a high-threat environment (i.e., high unemployment and poverty rates), they are less likely to perceive closeness with Latinos and blacks and are more inclined to perceive competition with them.

Institutional Context

Besides racial and economic contexts, this study analyzes the effects of institutional contexts on whites' racial attitudes. Extant research barely scratches the surface on the impact of institutional contexts on whites' perceptions of Latinos and blacks. Most of our knowledge of the effects of political context and minorities has centered on whites' political behavior and attitudes (Bobo and Gilliam 1990; Gay 2001; Hero and Tolbert 2004). This study addresses this critical weakness and analyzes institutional contexts in various ways. Besides exploring institutional contexts through residence in a state with provisions for direct democracy and in a majority-minority district, I analyze institutional contexts through considering the ideological climate of a congressional district and being represented by a nonwhite legislator. Further, in order to obtain a more accurate understanding of political context and white racial attitudes, I adopt a power-based approach to explain the relationship between institutional contexts and whites' attitudes. This study builds on Blumer's (1958) group position theory and posits that whites who perceive that they are in a politically vulnerable environment are more likely to perceive that Latinos and blacks are encroaching on their clout and thus regard them as antagonists. Notwithstanding this argument, when whites reside in a low-threat environment, they should perceive less closeness with blacks and Latinos and not view them as threatening since their political status is not in peril. Still, when it comes to residing in a largely Democratic district, nonwhites may not pose a political threat to whites since residing in a district that favors Democrats can develop whites' affinity with Latinos and African Americans, groups commonly aligned with the Democratic Party. These considerations lead me to hypothesize:

Threat and institutional context hypothesis: When whites perceive that they are in a politically weak setting (i.e., represented by a Latino or black legislator, residing in a majority-minority district), they perceive less closeness and sense greater competition with blacks and Latinos. Further, when whites are in a low-threat environment (i.e., a state with ballot initiatives and/or political referenda), they are less likely to perceive closeness and competition with these groups.

Democratic district hypothesis: Whites who reside in a largely Democratic district are more likely to sense closeness and are less likely to perceive competition with Latinos and African Americans.

Feelings of Identification

Latinos' emerging presence in distinct settings can structure whites' opinions toward them. Indeed, a number of studies evaluate the relationship between Latinos' attitudes toward blacks and their affinity toward whites as well as the relation between Latinos' commonality with other Latinos and their closeness with blacks (Kaufmann 2003; Wallsten and Nteta 2011). Yet, we know relatively little about the role that feelings of identification with one group may play in structuring whites' views of that same group and those of others. This project addresses this weakness by addressing the following questions: Does identifying with Latinos/blacks decrease the likelihood that whites regard Latinos/blacks (respectively) as rivals? Do whites who identify with Latinos also feel close to African Americans and vice versa? Are whites who identify with other whites more likely to regard Latinos and blacks as rivals?

In analyzing the effects of perceptions of closeness on whites' racial attitudes, I rely on Blumer's (1958) group position theory. A component of this theory is that individuals place their racial group and others into distinct classifications. I build on Blumer's assertion and argue that when whites think about one group, they inevitably make indirect or direct comparisons to their group and others, affecting their views toward other racial groups. These comparisons illustrate situations when individuals take an "us versus them" mentality. More specifically, I assert that whites draw distinctions between their racial counterparts and nonwhites given the sharp differences in status and clout between these two groups. When whites identify with one minority group, they are more likely to feel close to another minority. Then again, the greater whites' identification with other whites, the more prone they are to regard nonwhites as rivals (Blumer 1958; Bobo 1999; Nteta 2006, 199). Based on these theoretical discussions, I hypothesize:

Identification and competition hypothesis: Whites who identify with Latinos/blacks are less inclined to regard Latinos/blacks as competitors.

Identification with minorities hypothesis: Whites who identify with blacks/Latinos sense greater closeness with Latinos/blacks, respectively.

Identification with whites hypothesis: The more whites identify with other whites, the more likely they are to regard Latinos and blacks as rivals.

Data

This chapter analyzes whites' attitudes toward Latinos and blacks using the 2004 NPS and the 2010 CCES. The 2004 NPS is a national survey that explores numerous topics central to white/Latino/black race relations. The survey has a large sample of whites (N = 919) and respondents from four major U.S. regions, allowing me to examine the effect of residence in the South on racial dispositions. The 2010 CCES also provides a contemporary understanding of white racial attitudes. With a sample of 1,503 white respondents, I am able to examine a wide array of factors that structure white dispositions including whites' perceptions of racial diversity in their neighborhoods. A detailed description of the survey questions, coding of the NPS and CCES variables, and other predictors are provided in the appendix.

The dependent variables measure perceptions of closeness and competition using several survey questions posed in the 2004 NPS and the 2010 CCES. The NPS data set includes questions that individually explore whites' perceptions of closeness and competition with Latinos and blacks. The perceptions of closeness with Latinos measure ranges from 0 to 3 where 0 represents no closeness to Latinos and 3 represents strong closeness with this group. The closeness with blacks measure is operationalized in the same way. To assess how much competition whites sense with Latinos and blacks, I examine whites' perceptions of employment and political competition with minorities. I create general indexes of competition with Latinos and with blacks for several reasons. Given Latinos' and blacks' developing sociopolitical clout, white/Latino and white/black relations have recently been characterized by economic *and* political tensions. Additionally, my empirical analyses reveal that there are few disparities in whites' responses to their employment and political competition with Latinos and blacks. Further, the correlation coefficients between employment and political competition with Latinos and blacks are strong, and the Cronbach's alpha scores for the variables that compose the general competition with Latinos measure and the competition with blacks measure reveal that it is appropriate to create additive scales.[7] Thus, I create an additive index of whites' sense of competition with Latinos that ranges from 0 (no employment and political competition with Latinos) to 6 (a lot of competition). The additive index for whites' rivalry with African Americans is measured in the same way.

I also create relative measures of Latino/black closeness and competition to further assess the extent to which whites regard Latinos like blacks. Perceptions of closeness with Latinos and blacks are examined by the 2004 NPS and the 2010 CCES. Using NPS questions that explore whites' perceptions of closeness with Latinos and blacks, I create a relative scale of Latino/black closeness by combining the closeness with Latinos index with the closeness with blacks index.[8] This index ranges from −3 to 3 where −3 represents strong closeness with African Americans and little closeness with Latinos and a value of 3 denotes strong closeness with Latinos and limited closeness with blacks. A value of zero represents no difference in the values that white respondents provided in the amount of closeness that exists between these two minority groups. The relative scale of perceptions of Latino/black commonality using 2010 CCES data was created in the same way.[9]

As to whites' sense of general competition with Latinos and blacks, I rely on several competition measures to create relative scales of competition with these two groups. For the NPS Latino/black competition measure, I combine the additive Latino competition index with the black competition index to form a relative measure of Latino/black competition.[10] This index ranges from −6 to 6 where −6 represents strong general competition with blacks and little competition with Latinos and a value of 6 denotes great rivalry with Latinos and little competition with blacks. A value of zero denotes no difference in the values that whites provide concerning their sense of competition between blacks and Latinos. Unlike the NPS, the CCES only examines whites' perceptions of economic rivalry with Latinos and blacks. These measures range from 0 (strongly disagree that job competition exists) to 4 (strongly agree). I combine the economic rivalry with Latinos measure with the one for blacks. The CCES relative scale of Latino/black competition ranges from −3 to 4.[11]

Descriptive Results: Perceptions of Closeness and Competition

I begin my investigation by analyzing the descriptive frequencies of relative Latino/black closeness and competition measures. While analyzing the nonrelative measures of closeness and competition can be useful to assess whites' perceptions of Latinos and blacks, the relative measures of closeness and competition more accurately assess whether whites regard Latinos like African Americans. Figure 17 presents whites' perceptions of closeness with Latinos in relation to those of African Americans. The results presented in this figure reveal that whites perceive slightly more closeness with blacks than with Latinos (Thornton et al. 2012), yet most whites (65.8%) do not perceive differences in their sense of commonality with Latinos and blacks. Other analyses using the same data illustrate that whites feel much closer to other whites than Latinos and African Americans.[12] I find analogous results from my analyses of 2010 CCES data.[13]

FIG. 17. Relative scale of Latino/black closeness among whites

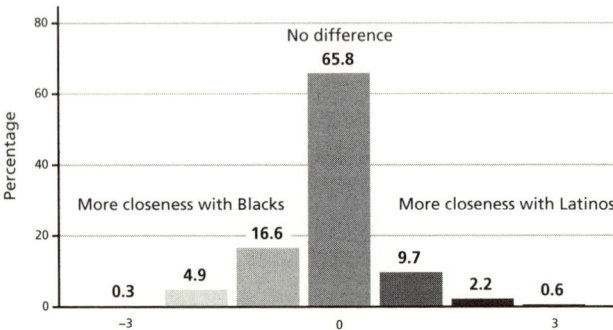

Source: Author's calculations using 2004 NPS data.

When analyzing whites' perceptions of competition with Latinos and blacks, I find comparable outcomes. The results shown in figure 18 reveal that the majority of whites perceive no difference in economic and political competition with Latinos and blacks. Still, I do find that whites sense slightly greater competition with Latinos than with African Americans (Hutchings et al. 2011, 60).[14] I found analogous results using 2010 CCES data. On the whole, the results in figures 17–18 suggest that whites regard Latinos and African Americans quite similarly. Whites do not draw sharp distinctions between the two minority groups yet they regard their racial counterparts quite differently than Latinos and blacks.

FIG. 18. Relative scale of Latino/black competition among whites

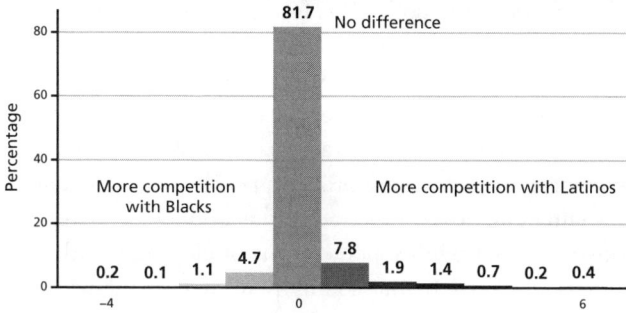

Source: Author's calculations using 2004 NPS data.

Testing the TTCCI on Whites' Perceptions of Closeness with Latinos and Blacks

To what extent do social contact, context, and identification account for whites' perceptions of closeness with Latinos and blacks? Relying on 2004 NPS data, table 13 presents two sets of analyses: one simply tests the TTCCI on whites' sense of closeness with Latinos and blacks, and another tests this theory while analyzing the extent to which the socioeconomic environment conditions the influence of racial/ethnic diversity on white racial attitudes. I do not conduct analyses of whites' perceptions of closeness with Latinos relative to blacks since I would not be able to test several of my hypotheses with this measure. Still, most of the results in this table are analogous to those obtained when testing the effects of contact, context, and identification on whites' perceptions of Latino/black closeness. To assess whites' perceptions of closeness with Latinos and blacks, I test my hypotheses using ordered logistic regression given the ordered nature of my measures of closeness.[15]

Further, I weight the sample in all of my models so that it is proportionate to the white population in the United States.[16]

Model 1 in table 13 reports the ordered logistic regression results for whites' perceptions of closeness with Latinos and blacks controlling for the effects of demographic characteristics and common predictors of white racial attitudes. The results in model 1 for whites' closeness with Latinos and blacks illustrate some support for my TTCCI in its ability to explain whites' perceptions of closeness with these groups. As to the effects of social contact, I find strong support for the social contact hypothesis. The more contact whites have with Latinos through friendship and in the workplace, the more likely they are to perceive closeness with Latinos. The results in the closeness with blacks models reveal comparable results. It is critical to note that support for the social contact hypothesis is found in distinct forms of social interactions. This illustrates that social contact does not necessarily have to be direct and consistent in order to result in positive relations (Welch et al. 2001; Oliver and Wong 2003). Context also has some effect on whites' perceptions of Latinos and blacks. As to racial context, I find that whites in a largely Latino environment are more prone to perceive commonality with Latinos (see McClain et al. 2011). Illustrating this finding in further detail, figure 19 demonstrates that whites' perceptions of closeness with Latinos are higher in a predominantly Latino county than in a setting with a minimal Latino presence.[17] On the other hand, in support of the racial threat hypothesis, whites who reside in a predominantly black county are less likely to perceive closeness with blacks. Interestingly, whites in a growing Latino

FIG. 19. Probability of whites' closeness with Latinos by percent Latino in county

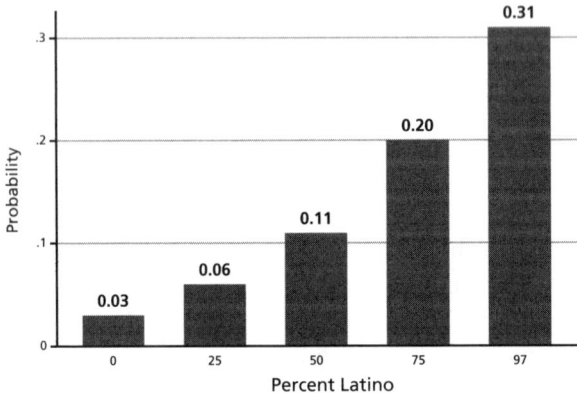

Source: Author's calculations using 2004 NPS data.

TABLE 13. Ordered logistic regression results for whites' perceptions of closeness with Latinos and blacks

	Latinos		Blacks	
	Model 1	Model 2	Model 1	Model 2
SOCIAL CONTACT				
Latino friends	0.88**	0.89**	—	—
	(0.39)	(0.40)		
White friends	−0.05	−0.03	0.36	0.36
	(0.27)	(0.27)	(0.29)	(0.29)
Black friends	—	—	1.38***	1.39***
			(0.30)	(0.30)
Latino coworkers	0.42*	0.42**	—	—
	(0.23)	(0.23)		
White coworkers	−0.04	−0.03	0.36	0.35
	(0.16)	(0.16)	(0.28)	(0.27)
Black coworkers	—	—	0.79***	0.79***
			(0.31)	(0.30)
Latino neighbors	−0.27	−0.26	—	—
	(0.24)	(0.24)		
White neighbors	−0.28*	−0.26*	0.02	0.02
	(0.20)	(0.19)	(0.26)	(0.27)
Black neighbors	—	—	0.28	0.27
			(0.29)	(0.29)
RACIAL CONTEXT (COUNTY, 2004 ESTIMATE)				
Percentage Latino	2.63**	11.08**	−2.68**	−2.59**
	(1.05)	(4.43)	(1.19)	(1.25)
Percentage white	0.04	−0.55	—	—
	(0.94)	(1.01)		
Percentage black	—	—	−2.03*	1.58
			(1.30)	(7.95)
ECONOMIC CONTEXT (COUNTY)				
Percentage with high school degree (2000 estimate)	0.06**	0.07**	−0.07***	−0.06*
	(0.03)	(0.03)	(0.03)	(0.04)
Poverty rate (2007 estimate)	0.08**	0.06*	−0.05*	−0.05*
	(0.03)	(0.03)	(0.03)	(0.03)
Unemployment rate (2008 estimate)	0.06	0.05	−0.03	−0.03
	(0.03)	(0.08)	(0.11)	(0.11)
Percentage Latino × Percentage with high school degree	—	−0.12*	—	—
		(0.06)		
Percentage black × Percentage with high school degree	—	—	—	−0.05
				(0.10)

TABLE 13. (*continued*)

	Latinos		Blacks	
	Model 1	Model 2	Model 1	Model 2
INSTITUTIONAL CONTEXT (COUNTY, 2004)				
Latino legislator	0.05	−0.15	—	—
	(0.39)	(0.39)		
Black legislator	—	—	−0.14	−0.15
			(0.47)	(0.47)
Democratic candidate	−0.39	−0.53	1.52*	1.54*
	(0.88)	(0.87)	(1.10)	(1.10)
Provisions for direct democracy	−0.16	−0.11	−0.44*	−0.45*
	(0.25)	(0.25)	(0.27)	(0.27)
Majority-minority district	0.06	0.04	−0.39*	−0.41*
	(0.29)	(0.29)	(0.29)	(0.29)
FEELINGS OF IDENTIFICATION				
Identification with Latinos	—	—	1.51***	1.51***
			(0.23)	(0.23)
Identification with whites	0.33*	0.32*	0.96***	0.96***
	(0.19)	(0.18)	(0.21)	(0.21)
Identification with blacks	1.51***	1.53***	—	—
	(0.24)	(0.24)		
N	533	533	531	531
Pseudo-R^2	0.21	0.21	0.29	0.29
Log pseudolikelihood	−484.15	−482.87	−404.73	−404.62

Source: 2004 NPS.

Note: ***$p < 0.01$ level; **$p < 0.05$ level; *$p < 0.10$ level. Entries not in parentheses are unstandardized b coefficients; entries in parentheses denote the corresponding standard errors to the b coefficients and are clustered by county. Due to collinearity issues, I do not control for the effects of percentage white in models that assess whites' perceptions of blacks. Other control variables were perceptions of discrimination, negative stereotypes of Latinos, negative stereotypes of blacks, residing in the South, age, gender, education, household income, and partisan identification.

county are less likely to feel close to African Americans.[18] These findings suggest that whites do not regard Latinos and blacks in the same way. I also find contradictory results when it comes to the relationship between economic context and whites' closeness with Latinos and blacks. In line with the threat and economic context hypothesis, residing in a high education environment is positively related to whites' perceptions of commonality with Latinos (see Oliver and Mendelberg 2000; Oliver and Wong 2003), though I find the opposite for whites' attitudes toward blacks. Whites who reside in a high education setting are less likely to feel close to African Americans. Still, contrary to what I expected, whites who live in a county with a high poverty rate are more likely to perceive closeness with Latinos than those who live in low poverty areas. Regarding the effects of institutional context, I find that political context does not structure whites' sense of closeness with Latinos, and it has minimal effects on their views of blacks.

Conversely, feelings of identification with other whites and others play a more prominent role in shaping whites' views of Latinos and African Americans. In accordance with the identification with minorities hypothesis, identifying with blacks is positively related to whites' closeness with Latinos and vice versa. Strikingly, and somewhat in contrast to the identification with whites hypothesis, whites who feel close to other whites are more likely to perceive closeness with blacks. These findings are further supported by the results presented in figures 20 and 21. Figure 20 displays the effects of whites' identification with whites and Latinos on their perceptions of closeness with African Americans. This figure shows that the probability of perceiving closeness with blacks is greater when whites identify greatly with Latinos than when they do not identify with them. Additionally, figure 20 reveals that the probability of perceiving closeness with blacks is greater when whites identify with other whites than when they do not identify with their racial counterparts. Figure 21 further illustrates the relationship between identification with blacks and whites' sense of closeness with Latinos. This figure demonstrates that a rise in whites' identification with blacks coincides with an increase in whites' perception of closeness with Latinos.

In general, the coefficients in model 1 of table 13 for Latinos and blacks present some provocative results. First, social contact, context, and identification structure whites' perceptions of closeness with Latinos and blacks

FIG. 20. Probability of whites' closeness with blacks by identification with Latinos and whites

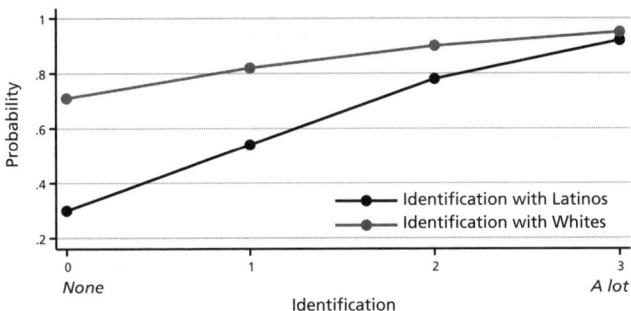

Source: Author's calculations using 2004 NPS data.

FIG. 21. Probability of whites' closeness with Latinos by
identification with blacks

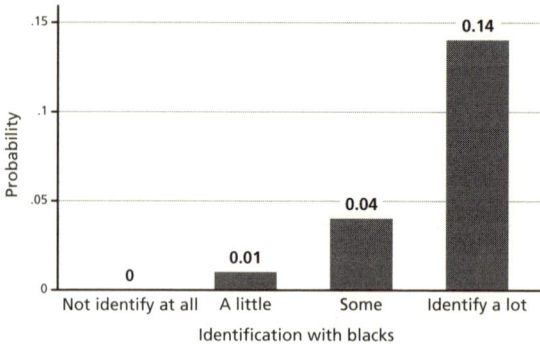

Source: Author's calculations using 2004 NPS data.

while controlling for the effects of leading predictors of white racial attitudes. Besides finding robust support for several of my hypotheses, the results in these models provide some support for the fact that whites regard
Latinos and blacks differently and that they may actually favor Latinos over
African Americans. Residing near blacks heightens whites' hostile attitudes
toward blacks, yet whites' perceptions of closeness with Latinos increase if
they live in an emerging Latino environment. Still, by contrast but in support
of my hypotheses, the more whites identify with blacks, the more they are
likely to feel close to Latinos and vice versa. Analyses of white focus group
data in the following chapter may shed light on the extent to which whites
regard blacks and Latinos in the same way.

In addition to testing the influence of social contact, context, and perceptions on whites' attitudes toward Latinos and blacks, I hypothesize that
the socioeconomic environment conditions the effects of racial diversity on
whites' sense of closeness with these groups. Model 2 of table 13 assesses
whites' closeness with Latinos and blacks and tests a component of the racial
and economic threat hypothesis: high education and low diversity contexts
are associated with greater perceptions of closeness with blacks and Latinos,
yet low education and high diversity contexts are associated with lower perceptions of closeness with these two groups.

The results in model 2 for whites' closeness with Latinos provide mixed
support for my hypothesis. For instance, when examining the coefficient for
percent high school degree (a constitutive term for the interaction of percent
Latino and education context), I find that there is a positive relationship between high education context and perceptions of closeness with Latinos in a

largely non-Latino context (i.e., when the percentage of Latinos in a county is 0).[19] On the other hand, the coefficient for percent Latino (the other constitutive term for the interaction) reveals that a largely Latino setting is positively related to whites' closeness with Latinos in a low education context (i.e., when the percentage of individuals with a high school degree is 0).[20] These results suggest that a high education and low diversity context poses less of a threat to whites, thus increasing their affinity with Latinos, yet the opposite (a high diversity and low education context) does not yield opposing results. Whites may not regard Latinos as threatening in a predominantly Latino and low education context.

In order to obtain a better understanding of the interaction coefficients of racial and education contexts, I examine how racial and education contexts influence the predicted dependent variables, perceptions of closeness with Latinos and blacks. I find that in low and high education contexts, a rise in the size of the Latino population in a county coincides with an increase in whites' perceptions of closeness with Latinos. Similarly, I find that in low and high education contexts, a rise in the size of the black population in a county coincides with a rise in closeness with blacks. These results suggest that education context does not actually condition the relationship between the racial context (percent black, percent Latino) and perceptions of closeness with African Americans and Latinos.[21]

The 2010 CCES allows me to test my TTCCI using more contemporary data in addition to examining the effects of subjective racial context on whites' perceptions of economic commonality with Latinos.[22] Given that research exploring whites' racial attitudes has greatly overlooked the effect of subjective racial context, I center my analyses below on the extent to which whites' perceptions of who lives near them explains their sense of closeness with Latinos. The first two analyses in table 14 presents the ordered logistical regression results for whites' perceptions of economic commonality (i.e., job opportunities, education, and income) with Latinos and blacks.[23] In general, the results in this table reveal that racial and political contexts and perceptions are better able to explain whites' perceptions of commonality with Latinos and blacks than social contact. As found in table 13 using 2004 NPS data, perceiving a significant number of Latinos in one's county is positively related to whites' sense of closeness with them. Thus, sensing that they are in a predominantly Latino county may improve whites' affinity toward them. Interestingly, whites who sense that they reside in a predominantly black county are less likely to feel close to Latinos. Since I also find that residing in a majority Latino context is negatively related to identifying with blacks in my analyses of 2004 NPS data, these results suggest that residing near

TABLE 14. Ordered logistic regression results for whites' perceptions of economic commonality and competition with Latinos and blacks

	Commonality with		Competition with	
	Latinos	blacks	Latinos	blacks
SOCIAL CONTACT				
White friends	0.33	−0.12	0.04	0.18
	(0.39)	(0.38)	(0.35)	(0.41)
Latino friends	0.65*	0.29	−0.16	0.002
	(0.42)	(0.41)	(0.37)	(0.43)
White coworkers	−0.001	0.08	0.04	0.08
	(0.08)	(0.08)	(0.18)	(0.07)
Latino coworkers	0.25	0.11	0.40**	0.18
	(0.20)	(0.22)	(0.18)	(0.17)
Black coworkers	−0.08	0.30*	−0.26	−0.01
	(0.22)	(0.23)	(0.19)	(0.18)
White neighbors	−0.03	0.52**	0.12	0.09
	(0.23)	(0.25)	(0.21)	(0.21)
Latino neighbors	0.30*	0.01	−0.07	−0.11
	(0.23)	(0.22)	(0.17)	(0.17)
Black neighbors	−0.16	0.56***	−0.05	0.13
	(0.22)	(0.24)	(0.19)	(0.20)
SUBJECTIVE RACIAL CONTEXT (COUNTY)				
Perceived number of Latinos	0.20***	−0.23**	0.22***	0.08
	(0.08)	(0.10)	(0.08)	(0.09)
Perceived number of blacks	—	0.36***	—	0.12*
		(0.10)		(0.08)
Perceived number of whites	0.48***	—	−0.78***	—
	(0.18)		(0.16)	
ECONOMIC CONTEXT (COUNTY)				
Percentage with high school degree (2006–10 estimate)	−0.01	0.02*	0.01	0.001
	(0.01)	(0.01)	(0.01)	(0.01)
Unemployment rate (2008 estimate)	−0.01	−0.001	0.002	−0.0002
	(0.03)	(0.03)	(0.03)	(0.03)
INSTITUTIONAL CONTEXT (COUNTY, 2010)				
Latino legislator	0.80**	—	0.45	—
	(0.46)		(0.39)	
Black legislator	—	1.19***	—	−0.10
		(0.35)		(0.29)
Democratic candidate	−0.57	−0.72	−1.08**	−0.94*
	(0.58)	(0.59)	(0.51)	(0.53)
State provisions for direct democracy	0.26**	−0.14	−0.01	0.04
	(0.12)	(0.12)	(0.11)	(0.11)
Majority-minority district	0.16	−0.60**	0.05	0.15
	(0.25)	(0.25)	(0.23)	(0.21)

TABLE 14. (continued)

	Commonality with		Competition with	
	Latinos	blacks	Latinos	blacks
FEELINGS OF IDENTIFICATION				
Identification with blacks	2.55***	—	−0.02	−0.24***
	(0.13)		(0.09)	(0.09)
Identification with Latinos	—	2.65***	−0.48***	−0.27***
		(0.13)	(0.09)	(0.09)
Age	−0.01*	0.004	0.004	0.002
	(0.004)	(0.004)	(0.004)	(0.004)
Gender	−0.35***	0.30**	−0.02	0.0004
	(0.12)	(0.12)	(0.11)	(0.11)
Education	0.15***	−0.05	−0.31***	−0.30***
	(0.04)	(0.04)	(0.04)	(0.04)
Household income	0.02	−0.02	−0.08***	−0.05***
	(0.02)	(0.02)	(0.01)	(0.01)
N	1,314	1,317	1,266	1,270
Pseudo-R^2	0.34	0.34	0.07	0.05

Source: 2010 CCES.

Note: ***$p < 0.01$ level; **$p < 0.05$ level; *$p < 0.10$ level. Entries not in parentheses are unstandardized b coefficients. Entries in parentheses denote the corresponding standard errors to the b coefficients and are clustered by county. These models do not control for the effects of a poverty rate of a county because this measure is highly correlated with a county's education level and it depresses the model's sample size to the point where the researcher is not able to conduct a thorough test of the Triangular Theory of Contact, Context, and Identification.

Latinos or blacks has divisive effects on whites' attitudes toward the alternate group. As predicted and found in my 2004 NPS analyses, sensing commonality with blacks is positively related to perceiving closeness with Latinos and vice versa. Surprisingly, whites who sense that they reside in a largely white county are more likely to perceive commonality with Latinos. Given this unexpected finding, I further explore the relationship between subjective racial context (particularly sensing a large white population in one's county) and perceiving economic commonality with Latinos with predicted probabilities. I find that a rise in the number of perceived whites in the county coincides with an increase in whites' perceptions that they are close to Latinos regarding education, income, and job opportunities. A potential explanation for this finding is that when whites believe that they are surrounded by other whites, their sense of threat is not invoked and thus they are more likely to feel that they can relate to those of a distinct ethnic background.

Testing the TTCCI on Whites' Perceptions of Competition with Latinos and Blacks

So far I have found that social proximity, context, and feelings of identification with other whites and nonwhites shape whites' sense of closeness with Latinos and blacks. To what extent, however, do these factors shape whites' perceptions of competition with both groups? Also, to what extent does education context moderate the relationship between racial context and competition with Latinos and blacks? Table 15 reports ordered logistic regression results for models of whites' perceptions of competition with minorities.[24] In model 1, I test hypotheses associated with the effects of social proximity, context, and perceptions of closeness on whites' sense of competition with Latinos and blacks while controlling for the effects of leading predictors of white attitudes. In model 2, I also test the conditioning effect of education environment on the relationship between racial diversity and perceptions of competition with Latinos and blacks.

The results in model 1 illustrate some support for my TTCCI in its ability to explain whites' perceptions of competition. As to the effects of social contact, I do not find support for the social contact hypothesis but find considerable support for the divisive effects hypothesis as it relates to whites' views of Latinos. Whites' social interactions with other whites through friendship and in the workplace are positively related to perceptions of competition with Latinos. When it comes to competition with blacks, this hypothesis is not greatly supported. While I find that whites with mostly white friends are more likely to regard blacks as rivals, the coefficient for this measure is only significant at the 0.10 significance level. Moreover, I find that whites with white neighbors are less likely to perceive competition with blacks. While racial and institutional context do not seem to structure whites' sense of competition with Latinos and blacks, economic context does to an extent. In support of the threat and economic context hypothesis, whites who reside in a high education context are less likely to perceive competition with Latinos and blacks.

Still, identification with other whites and nonwhites plays a prominent role in shaping whites' sense of competition with Latinos and African Americans. In line with the identification and competition hypothesis, whites who identify with Latinos are less likely to perceive competition with Latinos. Illustrating this finding in further detail, the results shown in figure 22 demonstrate that identifying with Latinos is negatively related to whites' perceptions of competition with this group. The probability of whites' sense of rivalry with Latinos is lesser when they identify with Latinos (0.36) than

TABLE 15. Ordered logistic regression results for whites' perceptions of competition with Latinos and blacks

	Latinos		Blacks	
	Model 1	Model 2	Model 1	Model 2
SOCIAL CONTACT				
Latino friends	0.09	0.09	—	—
	(0.30)	(0.30)		
White friends	0.46**	0.47**	0.39*	0.39*
	(0.25)	(0.25)	(0.27)	(0.27)
Black friends	—	—	−0.02	−0.03
			(0.36)	(0.37)
Latino coworkers	0.62**	0.62**	—	—
	(0.29)	(0.29)		
White coworkers	0.53**	0.55**	0.10	0.11
	(0.27)	(0.27)	(0.22)	(0.22)
Black coworkers	—	—	−0.03	−0.02
			(0.28)	(0.28)
Latino neighbors	0.11	0.12	—	—
	(0.27)	(0.28)		
White neighbors	−0.27	−0.25	−0.44**	−0.44**
	(0.20)	(0.21)	(0.19)	(0.19)
Black neighbors	—	—	−0.26	−0.25
			(0.23)	(0.23)
RACIAL CONTEXT (COUNTY, 2004 ESTIMATE)				
Percentage Latino	−1.27	7.69	−0.69	−0.79
	(1.09)	(7.96)	(1.01)	(1.01)
Percentage white	0.49	−0.20	—	—
	(1.12)	(1.05)		
Percentage black	—	—	0.04	−3.54
			(1.24)	(6.95)
ECONOMIC CONTEXT (COUNTY)				
Percentage with high school degree (2000 estimate)	−0.05**	−0.05**	−0.04*	−0.05*
	(0.03)	(0.03)	(0.02)	(0.03)
Poverty rate (2007 estimate)	−0.04	−0.07	−0.06*	−0.05*
	(0.04)	(0.04)	(0.03)	(0.03)
Unemployment rate	−0.07	−0.07	−0.01	−0.01
	(0.08)	(0.08)	(0.09)	(0.08)
Percentage Latino × Percentage with high school degree	—	−0.12	—	—
		(0.11)		
Percentage black × Percentage with high school degree	—	—	—	0.05
				(0.09)

TABLE 15. (*continued*)

	Latinos		Blacks	
	Model 1	Model 2	Model 1	Model 2
INSTITUTIONAL CONTEXT (COUNTY, 2004)				
Latino legislator	0.13	−0.09	—	—
	(0.64)	(0.74)		
Black legislator	—	—	0.02	0.02
			(0.55)	(0.55)
Democratic candidate	−0.66	−0.88	−1.13	−1.18
	(1.15)	(1.18)	(1.01)	(1.01)
Provisions for direct democracy	0.17	0.23	0.08	0.09
	(0.26)	(0.27)	(0.25)	(0.25)
Majority-minority district	0.21	0.21	0.08	0.09
	(0.56)	(0.56)	(0.46)	(0.46)
FEELINGS OF IDENTIFICATION				
Identification with Latinos	−0.65***	−0.66***	−0.41***	−0.41***
	(0.16)	(0.15)	(0.15)	(0.15)
Identification with whites	0.31*	0.29*	0.13	0.13
	(0.18)	(0.19)	(0.20)	(0.20)
Identification with blacks	−0.23*	−0.22	−0.06	—
	(0.16)	(0.16)	(0.18)	
N	521	521	519	519
Pseudo-R^2	0.12	0.12	0.12	0.12
Log pseudolikelihood	−641.65	−640.07	−601.69	−601.56

Source: 2004 NPS.

Note: ***$p < 0.01$ level; **$p < 0.05$ level; *$p < 0.10$ level. Entries not in parentheses are unstandardized b coefficients; entries in parentheses denote the corresponding standard errors to the b coefficients and are clustered by county. Due to collinearity issues, I do not control for the effects of percentage white in models that assess whites' perceptions of blacks. Other control variables were perceptions of discrimination, negative stereotypes of Latinos, negative stereotypes of blacks, residing in the South, age, gender, education, household income, and partisan identification.

when they do not identify with them (0.64). As to the relationship between identifying with Latinos and whites' sense of rivalry with blacks, I find that whites who identify with Latinos are less likely to regard blacks as competitors. I also find fair support for the identification with whites hypothesis in that identifying with whites is positively related to whites' perceptions of competition with Latinos.

While contact, context, and identification are not able to explain whites' sense of competition with blacks and Latinos as well as they are able to explain whites' closeness with these two groups, the results in table 15 reveal

FIG. 22. Probability of whites' competition with Latinos
by identification with Latinos

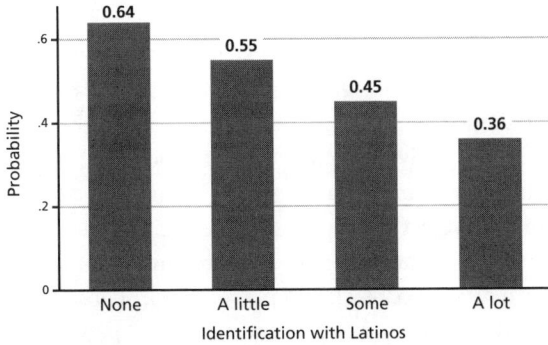

Source: Author's calculations using 2004 NPS data.

some interesting findings. Social contact with other whites may deter whites from regarding Latinos as allies, though the same factors may not necessarily influence whites' attitudes toward blacks similarly. I do not find support for the social contact hypothesis nor the racial threat hypothesis when it comes to whites' perceptions of competition with minorities. Although racial and institutional contexts do not seem to shape whites' sense of rivalry, their feelings of identification with Latinos does. Not only does whites' identification with Latinos decrease their competition with them but whites' identification with Latinos can also decrease the likelihood that whites regard blacks as threats. These results provide hope for improved relations between whites and Latinos, and whites and blacks, and suggest that whites do not draw deep distinctions between Latinos and blacks when it comes to perceptions of rivalry.

Thus far I have presented evidence that education context shapes whites' perceptions of blacks and Latinos, and fair evidence that an interaction between racial diversity and education context structure white perceptions of closeness with Latinos and blacks. What about the effect of racial diversity and education context on whites' perceptions of competition with people of color? Model 2 of table 15 assesses whites' sense of competition with Latinos and blacks and tests a component of the racial and economic threat hypothesis, that high education and low diversity contexts are associated with lower perceptions of competition with blacks and Latinos yet low education and high diversity contexts are associated with higher perceptions of competition with these two groups.

The results in model 2 for whites' competition with Latinos and blacks provide limited support for my hypothesis. In line with what I hypothesized, the coefficient for percent high school degree illustrates that there is a negative relationship between high education context and perceptions of competition with Latinos in a largely non-Latino context.[25] Yet, the coefficient for percent Latino (the other constitutive term for the interaction) reveals that racial context does not shape whites' attitudes in a low education context (i.e., when the percentage of individuals with a high school degree is 0).[26] Furthermore, the coefficients in model 2 for whites' sense of competition with blacks provide relatively little support for my racial and economic threat hypothesis. In order to obtain a better comprehension of the interaction coefficient of percent Latino/black and percent high school degree, I analyze how racial and education contexts structure whites' perceptions of competition with Latinos and African Americans. I find that in low and high education contexts, a rise in the size of the Latino population in a county coincides with an increase in whites' sense of rivalry with Latinos. What is more, in low *and* high education contexts, a rise in the size of the black population in a county coincides with a surge and a fall in whites' perceptions of competition with blacks. Hence, education context does not seem to condition the relationship between racial context and competition with Latinos and blacks.[27]

To address several of the perplexing findings above, I turn to analyses of 2010 CCES data. My analyses center on the effects of whites' subjective racial context since the effects of perceived county diversity on whites' antagonism toward Latinos and blacks has been relatively untapped. The last two analyses in table 14 examine whites' perceptions of employment competition with Latinos and blacks. Comparable to my results using 2004 NPS data, social contact and economic and political contexts do not play key roles in shaping whites' competition with Latinos and blacks. Yet, analogous to my analyses of 2004 NPS data, identification with Latinos/blacks are negatively related to whites' sense of rivalry with Latinos/blacks, respectively. While I do not find that objective racial context structures whites' perceptions of competition with nonwhites, my analyses of 2010 CCES data reveal that subjective racial context does. In accordance with the racial threat hypothesis, whites who perceive that they reside in a largely Latino county are more likely to perceive employment competition with them. Thus, though objective racial context may not influence whites' sense of competition with Latinos, whites' perception that many Latinos live near them can heighten their antagonism toward Latinos. I also find that whites who believe that many whites surround them are less inclined to regard Latinos as job competitors, as expected. To further explore this intriguing result, I rely on predicted probabilities displayed in figure 23. In line with my hypothesis and analogous to the results in table 14, perceiving that many whites live near them coincides with a consistent decrease in whites' sense of competition with Latinos.[28] Hence, sensing that they reside in a predominantly white context can depress whites' hostility toward Latinos. When whites do not feel racially threatened, they may be less likely to respond with hostility toward their new neighbors.

FIG. 23. Probability of whites' employment competition with Latinos by perceived number of whites in county

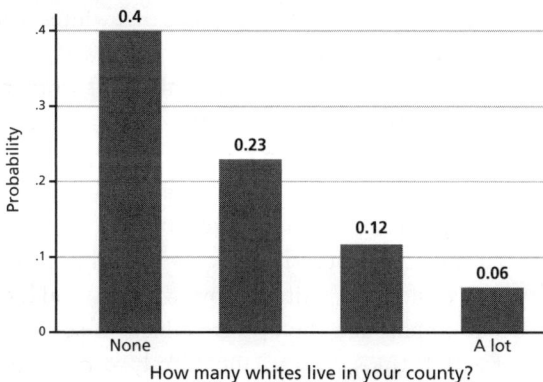

Source: Author's calculations using 2010 CCES data.

Conclusion

The focus of this chapter is to obtain a comprehensive understanding of whites' perceptions of Latinos by comparing their views toward Latinos with those of African Americans. My analyses center on three questions: Do whites regard Latinos like blacks? Are whites more inclined to regard other whites as allies and competitors relative to Latinos and blacks? To what extent do contact, context, and feelings of identification shape whites' sense of closeness and competition with Latinos and African Americans?

First, I begin by addressing whether whites view Latinos and blacks similarly. Preliminary analyses illustrate that whites' perceptions of Latinos and blacks are related, and most whites do not perceive that the two groups are distinct. I do find, however, that whites perceive more closeness with blacks than with Latinos and perceive marginally greater competition with Latinos than with their black counterparts. When determining the relationship between identification with one minority group on whites' attitudes toward another, I find that the more whites identify with one group, the more likely they perceive closeness with another, thus providing some support for the notion that whites regard both groups in the same way. On the other hand, I find that residing in a largely Latino context is negatively related to whites' sense of closeness with African Americans, revealing the divisive effects of context and suggesting that whites do not regard both groups similarly under all circumstances.

A critical contribution of this chapter is its examination not only of whites' perceptions of Latinos and blacks but of other whites as well. As to whether whites' views of their racial counterparts compare to their views of blacks and Latinos, I find that whites feel much closer to other whites than African Americans and Latinos. This finding suggests that whites regard their racial counterparts quite distinctly from nonwhites.

Results from contemporary national survey data analyses of white attitudes illustrate that several of my power-based hypotheses associated with the effects of contact, context, and identification explain whites' perceptions of Latinos and blacks. In general, whites' social interactions with other whites and other racial groups play key roles in shaping white racial attitudes. I find robust support for the social contact hypothesis (increased social interaction with another group has positive effects on attitudes toward them) and for my power-based hypothesis that emphasizes the divisive effects of social contact. When whites interact with Latinos, they are more likely to have affinity toward them, yet when whites have increased contact with other whites, they are less likely to feel close to Latinos. Interestingly, the social contact hypothesis is supported by various measures of social interaction suggesting that friendship is not the only type of contact that results in improved interracial relations. My findings also reveal that whites' sense of power as created by the racial context that surrounds them significantly structures their perceptions of Latinos and blacks. Whites who perceive that they reside in a largely white neighborhood are less likely to regard Latinos as economic rivals. Further, while whites in a predominantly black environment are less inclined to regard African Americans positively, I find the opposite for Latinos—residing in a largely Latinos environment is positively related to whites' sense of closeness with Latinos. Finally, as to the influence of identifying with other whites and nonwhites, I find that the more whites identify with Latinos, the less likely they are to view Latinos as a threat, suggesting that feelings of identification and rivalry with a group are mutually exclusive. I also find that identifying with Latinos/blacks is positively related to perceiving closeness with blacks/Latinos, respectively. These results provide hope for improved relations between whites and Latinos, and whites and blacks, and suggest that whites do not draw deep distinctions between Latinos and blacks under all circumstances.

Thus, while this chapter addresses several limitations of extant research, it raises a few more questions. Under what circumstances do whites not regard Latinos and blacks in the same way? Are whites' feelings of identification and competition with Latinos mutually exclusive? These questions will be further addressed in the next chapter relying on focus group data of whites in New Orleans.

7

Whites Discuss Race Relations
in New Orleans

This chapter relies on focus group data to further explore whites' perceptions of closeness and competition with Latinos in comparison to those of blacks. What distinguishes this chapter from the previous one is that I rely on focus group data of whites in an emerging Latino area in the South to delve deeply into the depth and complexities of whites' sense of closeness and rivalry with Latinos and African Americans. Further, I focus a significant portion of my analyses to address the unanswered questions from quantitative analyses of white racial attitudes. I begin this chapter with a discussion of whites in New Orleans and the data and methods employed to conduct the focus groups. Then, I analyze the themes that emerged from the focus group discussions to answer my research questions.

Whites' Response to Their New Neighbors

Whites have noticed the developing presence of Latinos in New Orleans. Although African Americans make up the majority of the residents of New Orleans, whites have always maintained a steady presence in New Orleans. Before hurricane Katrina in 2000, they made up 26.6 percent of the Orleans Parish population, and the latest estimated census data reveals that they compose 35 percent of the population (Plyer and Ortiz 2009; U.S. Census Bureau 2013).[1] While there is limited information on whites' actual response to the prevailing presence of Latinos, the conversation about whether food trucks are permitted on city streets has guided most of the media's discussion of the changes brought about by the new population. A surge in the Latino worker population after hurricane Katrina resulted in the growing presence of taqueria food trucks throughout the city and in the greater New Orleans area. Some welcomed the new food vendors and options while others did not. Several months after the trucks' emerging presence, the council of Jefferson Parish (right outside of the city of New Orleans with a majority white population) barred food trucks from selling food along major streets and required them to provide permanent restrooms. Concerns regarding these trucks involved their posing safety and health risks and cluttering streets as well as trucks not maintaining a permanent commitment to the area (Waller 2007). Recently, mayor of New Orleans Mitch Landrieu has vetoed a city council ordinance that would reduce some of the restrictions that food trucks in New Orleans have to follow. He suggested that the primary reason for his action was to protect "brick-and-mortar" restaurants from losing business to food trucks. On the other hand, right outside of New Orleans in Metairie, Louisiana, food truck rallies and celebrations with food trucks (including La Cocinita and Empanada Intifada) have recently been held in efforts to revive an area that was the hub of nightlife for several decades (Rainey 2013; Quinlan 2013).

Data and Methods

Data for this study come from focus groups conducted by the author in the city of New Orleans in early spring 2010. For as intense a topic as whites' attitudes toward blacks and Latinos, focus group research is critical since it permits me to track respondents' thought patterns as well as the intensity of their responses. Although focus group interviews were conceived as an explanatory analysis of whites' perceptions of commonality and competition with Latinos and blacks, I guided discussions with questions regarding whites' social interactions with nonwhites, perceptions of closeness and competition with Latinos and blacks, and the relationship between whites' social contacts and their racial attitudes.[2] The questions asked during the focus groups were modeled from national survey questions addressing similar topics. These are found in the appendix.

In this study, I employed comparable methods as those from focus group analyses of blacks and Latinos to obtain and examine focus group data. Each hour-long focus group session was tape recorded and then transcribed individually by two researchers. The data were collected in a data display format. The commonality in the themes extracted from the focus groups was 90 percent, indicating that the two researchers found the same themes while reading each transcribed focus group with the exception of a few themes.

Recruitment of participants was conducted in various ways. In order to obtain as random a sample as I could, I placed flyers on cars in grocery store parking lots in New Orleans and surrounding areas. I placed a newspaper advertisement in the classified section of the *Times Picayune*, the local newspaper of the greater New Orleans area. I recruited Louisiana State University undergraduate students from the New Orleans area who identify as white by visiting university classrooms and informing students about my study and leaving flyers with the presiding professors so that any interested students could obtain my contact information. In addition, I placed several ads in the New Orleans section of the Craigslist website. I also relied on the snowball sampling technique to recruit a few individuals. I recruited in these various ways given that recruitment of participants for these focus groups, unlike those for blacks and Latinos, was quite challenging. A possible explanation for this is that some whites, unlike blacks and Latinos, are more skeptical of discussing topics regarding race than others. When recruiting, I communicated on the ads, flyers, and in person that I was recruiting white residents of the greater New Orleans area and that this study was part of a multiracial study on race relations in New Orleans. Also, potential participants were informed that each participant would be compensated twenty dollars for an hour of their time.

After recruitment, I conducted six focus groups with a total of twenty-one whites from the city of New Orleans and its surrounding areas.[3] Most of the focus groups were conducted in a public library in Metairie, a suburb of New Orleans, as well as in a classroom at the Baton Rouge main campus of Louisiana State University.[4] The demographic characteristics of the focus group participants provide an interesting glimpse of the white population in New Orleans. The percentage of interviewees who were men was 76 percent. Also, the average reported age of the participants was thirty years old. More than half of the respondents (62%) reported being employed, and more than half of the respondents (approximately 52%) reported having an annual income of $25,000 or less. As to education, about 67 percent of the respondents reported having less than a college diploma. I recognize that my sample of white respondents may not completely represent the white population in the greater New Orleans area, yet it is critical to note a few observations. Previous experiences recruiting black and Latino focus group participants reveal that the unemployed and individuals of a lower socioeconomic status may be more interested in participating in a focus group since they may have more time to participate in a focus group study and the twenty-dollar compensatory reward may appeal to them more than others. Further, a certain type of person may be more willing to participate in a study of race relations than others. Whites in general may be more hesitant to discuss race relations than others for fear of sounding insensitive or racist. Additionally, a significant number of white focus group participants were young men. This did not occur with the focus groups for blacks and Latinos. (Actually, Latinas greatly outnumbered Latinos, and the number of black men was marginally higher than that of black women in the focus group samples.) So, why did so many white men decide to participate? It may be possible that white men are more willing to talk about their attitudes toward race and interrace relations than white women.

Findings

In this section, I present data on whites' perceptions of Latinos and blacks in New Orleans.[5] I place emphasis on themes that emerged regarding whites' social networks, perceptions of commonality and competition with Latinos and blacks, and the relation between contact and whites' attitudes toward these two groups.[6]

Contact

One of the first questions asked in each focus group was how much contact whites have with blacks and Latinos. When it comes to contact with blacks, the majority of participants stated that they have a good bit of contact with blacks and most have black coworkers and neighbors:[7]

Gary: Several neighbors, and my last job was about half black workers.

Frank: That's funny, actually. Um, every job I've had in New Orleans I've been surrounded by black coworkers. Um, I'm often the only white guy around all the jobs I've held. Been a teacher, you know, all the students were black, mostly black faculty. I was a union organizer most of the members of the union were black. Most of the union staff were black. Ah, tutored for a little while with a tutoring company. A little of my fellow tutors were all white but the students were black in that program. Now I'm a census numerator right now and about to move back and go back to grad school. Um, mostly black folks doing that.

In addition, a few mentioned that they had black friends: "I have a few black friends and some on my block." On the other hand, whites have some contact with Latinos but not as much on a regular basis as blacks. Some have Latino friends and have worked with them and live close to them:

Kyle: I do have some [Latino friends] but I just don't see them . . . yeah, not every day.

Joe: Um, we didn't have all that many Hispanics living around us. Like when I used to, like when I did construction, we had a lot of Hispanic workers.

Jim: Yeah, I work with them, some live in my apartment. You know, when you live in an apartment, you don't really talk to your neighbors. You say hello when they pass by but you don't really know them.

Hence, whites in New Orleans have more frequent contact with blacks in the workplace and neighborhood than Latinos, yet contact with Latinos exists.

Perceptions of Commonality

This section focuses on whites' perceptions of commonality with Latinos and blacks. I begin with a description of whites' answers to a preliminary questionnaire and then present themes that emerged from focus group discussions.

COMMONALITY WITH LATINOS

Before the focus groups began, participants were asked to complete a questionnaire assessing their racial attitudes. One of the survey questions examined their sense of commonality with Latinos on a scale from 0 (none) to 10 (a lot). The mean commonality score for all of the focus groups was 5.6, revealing that whites sense some commonality with Latinos.

In the focus group discussions, four main themes emerged regarding commonality with Latinos. The themes centered on: (1) whites like the same food as Latinos; (2) Latinos are more family-oriented and have deeper traditions than whites; (3) the Spanish language can be a barrier to sensing commonality with Latinos; and (4) perceiving commonality with an individual is not related to race or ethnicity.

A response that appeared throughout many focus groups is that whites like the same food that Latinos like, particularly Mexican food:

Gary: As far as food goes, I love Mexican food. They are one of my favorite types of food. But culture aspects such as music and clothes, probably very little.
Troy: I like the same food that they do.

Moreover, a few participants recognized that Latinos are very family-oriented and probably more family- and community-oriented than most whites:

Kevin: I believe that Hispanics have more of a solid family unit than whites do and especially in America, Hispanics seem to ask their mother and grandmother to live with them instead of putting them in a nursing home. Um, they also seem to have more of a community. It's more of a unity in the community.
Michael: They have always been very warm, really family-oriented and very, ah, just good. . . . I'm not as family-oriented . . . it seems like they keep in contact with their people and make sure that they're taken care of.

In several focus groups, individuals mentioned that there are few differences between whites and Latinos though the Spanish language does distinguish Latinos from whites:[8]

Troy: Every Hispanic person that I have come across is like, they're all like really nice people. It's like the language barrier is the only difference.

Joe: I haven't really met a Hispanic that I would necessarily dislike or hate. I mean there are people where there is a language barrier like the only difference. . . . And they are like, they're striving to like mix our cultures and there's really not that much difference.

Another prominent theme that emerged in the focus groups is that race or ethnicity is not a determining factor for deciding whether one has something in common with an individual. Many respondents indicated that Latinos just want the same basic things as whites:

Leroy: So I don't think it's a black/white/Hispanic thing whether I have something in common with them. . . . It's not about race, definitely more about the person . . . we all more or less strive for the same things, you know: family, job, food on the table, roof over your head. You know, a nice life or as nice as you can have.

Sean: I think we are all, we are all people. You know, family, we want a comfortable bed. You know, there's so many things we have in common if you put language and a couple other things [aside].

COMMONALITY WITH BLACKS

To assess whites' sense of commonality with African Americans, I collected data from preliminary questionnaires and focus group discussions. On the questionnaire, participants were asked to measure their perceptions of commonality with blacks on a scale from 0 (none) to 10 (a lot). The mean commonality with blacks score is 5.6, suggesting that whites sense some commonality with their African American counterparts.

Throughout the focus groups, most participants expressed the view that there are few differences between blacks and whites overall. Still, four specific themes emerged from white participants' answers: (1) they like the same music that blacks like; (2) they have something in common with them if they share the same financial situation as blacks; (3) race does not play a factor in determining commonality; and (4) not all blacks are the same.

Music taste (particularly rap and hip-hop) seems to be something that many whites share with African Americans:

Troy: I like to listen to music that is considered black.

Jay: I listen to a lot of the same music black people listen to.

When it comes to specific music tastes that whites share, one individual stated, "I like jazz, I like funk. I like hip hop."

Moreover, several focus group participants regard blacks as individuals who are part of the working class or a lower middle class. Therefore, if they were part of the working class, then the participants felt that they had something in common with African Americans:

Jack: I have to say it's more of a poor thing. My neighborhood in Chalmette wasn't that rich or anything. . . . My parents are on food stamps right now so they had the same problems that people in the city had and that kind of stuff.

Michael: I think that my differences are not as much black and white but rich and poor. . . . I guess I do have a stereotype of blacks being a little underprivileged but, you know, and not having that much money so in that regard I feel in common.

Jim: So at that point I could kinda relate to blacks because I was in the same kind of situation—we were both lower working class, lower middle class white. Now, I make a heck of a lot more money because I'm a permanent park ranger and maybe I can't relate with blacks anymore.

Similar to whites' perceptions of commonality with Latinos, a few focus group participants stated that they have many things in common with blacks regardless of race:[9]

Leroy: I found out in general that everyone likes to get the same thing out of life. In general, everyone is more or less, you know, likes more or less the same things and has hopes, same hopes and dreams more or less.

Nonetheless, throughout whites' discussion of their sense of closeness with blacks, several emphasized the differences that exist among blacks. For instance, some state that blacks on college campuses are not the same as those in the inner city:

Jack: I guess it depends on how much you hang around those type, like if you hang around a lot of African Americans on college campuses like you will have a better view. But if it's like city African Americans who have not had much education, you might have a more negative view.

Moreover, some whites perceived blacks from the North differently than blacks from the South, suggesting that they regard southern blacks as less hardworking, responsible, and strong-willed than blacks outside of the South:[10]

Sally: I just feel like there's a difference between blacks from the north and blacks from here. A different attitude, a different mindset . . . just their attitude about work and education and about just community involvement and how much responsibility, they are willing to take for their own life, community and well-being.

In addition, some whites indicate that young blacks act differently than older ones:

Sally: And I think that I have more in common with the older black people than young people . . . my experience with younger black people is that they feel like either violence or being threatening or anger, that's the way to handle a problem. Not to think it out or talk it out or be reasonable.

It is critical to mention that throughout whites' discussions as to whether they perceived commonality with blacks and the differences that they noted among blacks, several expressed negative stereotypes toward African Americans. Many of the negative stereotypes conveyed are that blacks tend to be lazy, uneducated, and opportunistic:

Sean: You know what, I know what I get with a black contractor, I want a white contractor. That's what it is. We know what we get. Four years of having black politicians, we want a white one.

Tom: I feel like for black folks they got a whole lot of bad especially if you go down to lockup and you'll go visit somebody there's a large black population, some Spanish and not too many white guys . . . I got in common with the guys that's working for a living. I got nothing in common for the guys out there hustling, selling and doing dope which I see a lot when I drive down my street.

Further, several participants recognized that they can have racist tendencies against blacks, yet they try to resist them. The majority of those who stated this were part of the younger generations, individuals younger than thirty years of age:

Sean: Yeah, they [blacks] broke into my car three or four times. They stole tools. . . . So but there's this, you wait for something to happen like you're, you're not disappointed or surprised when it does. You're not disappointed. You're like, well, I kind of half-way expected it. And I hate to think that. . . . I know but I specifically thought that I don't want to be perceived as a racist.

Rod: Let me tell you what goes through my head when I'm walking down the street. If I see a black dude or a black person from afar I'm like, hmm, it will only be a thought and it will only be something I acknowledge. No, just acknowledging that racist thing. I mean, yeah, I'm not trying to sit here and be like . . . say no I don't think about race at all. . . . I have racist tendencies. I have racist thoughts and it gets weird like Sean said to like acknowledge them and don't and fall back in shame that I have them.

Jack: With race, you always want to jump to like a stereotype or something . . . if I'm on the street somewhere trying to walk, carrying something in my house and a black guy is standing in my way. It's like, wow, why is that guy being so rude? And like in my head, I will jump to a conclusion to like, wow, black people are rude but then I'll have to try to keep that out of my head and say like that's just that one person.

As a whole, my focus group findings of whites' perceptions of commonality with Latinos and blacks reveal several interesting findings. First, whites perceive comparable levels of commonality with blacks and Latinos as found by my analyses of 2004 National Politics Survey (NPS) data. Nonetheless, the focus group discussions illustrate that whites generally adopt more positive views of Latinos than African Americans. When mentioning the differences that exist between whites and Latinos, whites stress that the differences between whites and Latinos are minimal unlike their discussions of how much they identify with African Americans. Furthermore, several whites (predominantly older ones) adopt negative stereotypes of blacks conveying that some whites regard blacks as lazy, uneducated, and opportunistic. Latinos were not associated with these stereotypes. Another major conclusion from this section is that whites may not consider race or ethnicity when thinking about whether they perceive commonality with blacks and Latinos. This finding may help to explain why I find in previous analyses that sensing closeness with Latinos/blacks is positively related to feeling close to blacks/Latinos, respectively.

Perceptions of Competition

Besides perceptions of commonality, I explore whites' perceptions of competition with blacks and Latinos in New Orleans. First, I examine whites' perceptions of competition with Latinos and then their attitudes toward African Americans with each section briefly summarizing questionnaire results.

COMPETITION WITH LATINOS

The preliminary questionnaire results reveal that whites perceive limited competition with Latinos. Individuals were asked to indicate how much general competition they perceive with Latinos on a scale from 0 (none) to 10 (a lot). The mean general competition score is 2.0, suggesting that whites do not generally regard Latinos as threats.

Throughout the focus groups, the responses regarding competition with

Latinos were divided. Some participants stated explicitly that they do not perceive competition with Latinos:

Kyle: Personally, no competition.
Kevin: And Hispanics, I believe, they have, I pretty much don't think that I have competition with Hispanics at all or like illegal immigrants.

On the other hand, others stated that there was a good bit of job competition:

Joe: For competition, it would be jobs cause in the Westbank where I'm from, you see, a lot of Hispanic people like on the side of the road are like looking for work and like and just like labor competition. Like I guess just for work, there's competition.

Among those who noted job competition with Latinos, several stated that job competition was specifically with undocumented immigrants who can charge less and with Latinos who are bilingual. Moreover, the majority of those who perceived job competition with Latinos were whites who were involved in manual labor in one way or another:

Tom: There's some job competition but with Hispanics . . . it's a lot of illegals that are causing a problem . . . they're working for so much less. Everybody's wage is falling by maybe as much as thirty percent.
Pam: I think the one competition that, you know, that I have with Hispanics would be, especially if they speak English well enough. To be bilingual. I think that it's an asset to be able to speak more than one language and that's admirable especially in a workplace so in that, competition-wise.
Michael: Honestly, I have more competition with Hispanics because there are Hispanic contractors there now and they have crossed the language barrier better than I do and they can negotiate cheaper labor prices than I can and so.

COMPETITION WITH BLACKS

When examining whites' sense of rivalry with blacks, I find that whites perceive marginally greater competition with African Americans than Latinos. Questionnaire results illustrate that the mean general competition with blacks score is 3.3. Like the competition with Latinos measure, this measure ranges from 0 (no competition) to 10 (a lot of competition).

In the focus groups, two major themes emerged from participants' answers. One theme is that competition does not exist between whites and blacks:

Pam: I don't feel like I have this competition between me and blacks. I don't feel that I have to compete with blacks for my happiness or my job or, you know, that kind of measure or anything like that.

Sean: I don't have any competition with blacks.

Similar to the results for whites' sense of rivalry with Latinos, some whites perceive that employment competition exists between whites and African Americans. Further, among those that say competition exists, several bring up the fact that whites have an unfair advantage over blacks due to employers' discriminatory treatment of blacks. Since blacks perceive competition with whites, competition exists:[11]

Kevin: Actually, I think there's competition between me and African Americans because African Americans actually have it harder, you know, in getting jobs and um than whites do. . . . I notice that a lot of times when . . . an African American is more qualified than a white for a position, the white person gets the job rather than an African American.

Joe: In one of my jobs in the past . . . like me and my boss were pretty tight and like he told me that one day on the job they hire white people if they can. Just, the only reason they said that is because they are statistically more reliable and ah, other than that, there's not that much competition.

Michael: I seem to think that it's a lot harder for a black person to be a CEO position in a company or to get to that point where they can get the CEO position.

Amy: Yes, competition exists.

When asked why she would think that competition exists between blacks and whites, Amy responded:

Amy: Because if they [blacks] were raised in particularly a bad neighborhood, they would have to fight extra hard to get what they needed and if they, you know, see me and assume that I was just going to get it just because, even if, it's not the case. That's again, in certain situations.

These focus group themes reveal numerous significant findings. Whites perceive slightly more competition with blacks than Latinos, unlike what 2004 NPS analyses suggest.[12] Further, whites either believe that there is considerable competition between whites and Latinos, and whites and blacks, or they perceive that rivalry does not exist. A key difference between how whites think about economic competition with Latinos and blacks, however, is that several whites perceive competition with blacks because they believe that blacks have an unfair advantage in the employment sector. Thus, competition with blacks exists because blacks have competition with whites. On the other hand, whites who do regard Latinos as economic threats believe that whites have competition with Latinos. In particular, whites perceive that Latinos actually have an advantage over whites (e.g., being bilingual, willing to work for lower wages, able to negotiate lower contract deals). One unresolved question in the previous chapter on whites is whether whites' perceptions of commonality and competition with Latinos and blacks are mutually exclusive. Unlike the focus group analyses of blacks in New Orleans, my focus group data of whites do not seem to consider whether Latinos and blacks are threats when thinking about whether they identify with them or not. While this may suggest that perceiving closeness and competition with Latinos and blacks are mutually exclusive, the results presented above do not permit me to make this claim.

Effects of Contact on Attitudes

Besides asking questions regarding perceptions of commonality and competition, I guided the discussion toward examining the effects of contact on whites' perceptions of commonality and competition with Latinos and blacks. This question was not addressed in the questionnaire but it was mentioned in the focus groups.

Whites' responses to the effects of contact on their attitudes toward Latinos consisted of one common theme: contact has a positive effect on attitudes toward Latinos. When speaking of the effects of contact on attitudes, many spoke very highly of Latinos:

Carol: Oh, definitely. I would definitely say so because getting very close to someone, you know, and getting to know their family and just hearing their story and what they have had to overcome to get here. . . . I really admire them, you know.

Pam: The contact that I have is positive and actually I think that when we talk about New Orleans and Katrina, I think they really saved the city in a lot of ways. I respect them. . . . They came in and did the job that no one else wanted to do.

Sean: It's positive. . . . I don't think that I've had any negative experiences. . . . Yeah, I enjoy them as a culture. I enjoy the food. I enjoy their company as a friend.

I also asked individuals in the focus groups about the effects that contact has on their views toward blacks. Similar to the effects of contact on whites' views toward Latinos, many participants perceive that contact has a positive effect on their attitudes toward blacks:

Tom: Because you're working with somebody and you're spending all this time with them, you're going to get to know them whether they are black or not. You can't help it, you're going to be friends with this person, you know . . . has a positive effect.

Among the younger generations, several said that contact with blacks had a positive effect on their views toward blacks and helped them to reject the negative stereotypes conveyed by their older relatives:

Ashley: Yeah, I would say positive. Like he said, everything is different and people try to tell you certain things. Um, if you have contact with black people, it really helps you make your own opinion than what the stereotypes and older generations want you to believe.

Jay: I guess you hear different people's opinions. My grandmother grew up seventy years ago and that was the common theme. Racism has always affected what she said but I know black people. They [older generations} are just mistaken. They were in a different time than we did.

Unlike what was mentioned regarding Latinos, however, several whites stated that contact affects their views positively on a case-by-case basis:

Joe: Like everyone has their own personality, it depends on like. Like if you run into a good person, you think that they're good people. But if you run into a rude person or someone that's like inconsiderate . . . it's different. It depends on the situation.

Leroy: Contact with blacks specifically doesn't really ah transfer to blacks in general because contact that I have had with blacks in my life, I have treated them on an individual basis. I mean if the contact was good, then I kept up the contact. If the contact was negative, well then I wanted to have as little contact as possible.

These findings illustrate that increased social contact with blacks and Latinos has a positive effect on whites' attitudes toward these two groups. Still, contact may generally have a more positive effect on views toward Latinos than views toward blacks as found in my quantitative analyses in the previous chapter. Unlike Latinos, whites do not have (or perceive to have) similar experiences with all blacks, and thus increased interaction with blacks does not always translate into positive views about the entire black population.

Conclusion

This chapter takes a qualitative approach to exploring whites' perceptions of closeness and competition with blacks and Latinos, relying on focus group data in New Orleans. Its focus is to develop our understanding of whites' racial attitudes and address some unresolved questions from the preceding chapter using survey data of whites.

This study makes several key improvements to existing research. It is one of the first studies to analyze whites' perceptions of blacks and Latinos in New Orleans. By using focus group data to answer my research questions, I am able to delve deeper into the intensity of whites' racial attitudes. Further, the flexible interview structure of focus groups allows me to track the thought patterns of individuals and develop my understanding of relationships among variables that I would have not examined or been aware of previously. For instance, one unexpected finding in this study is that whites may not consider race or ethnicity when thinking whether they perceive closeness or competition with another group. Thus, this finding may help to explain my finding (using quantitative data) that perceptions of commonality with one group is positively related to commonality with another group. Another contribution of this study is that I find that whites regard Latinos more favorably than African Americans. Hence, whites in the South may adopt more negative stereotypes and less affinity toward blacks than Latinos. Further, whites view competition with Latinos and blacks divergently. White/black competition is often regarded by whites as *blacks'* competition with whites, yet whites seem to regard white/Latino competition as *whites'* competition with Latinos. This finding affirms that whites do not perceive blacks and Latinos in the same way, and suggests that whites sense that Latinos are higher on the social hierarchy than African Americans. While my focus group findings do not allow me to determine whether whites regard perceptions of commonality and competition with blacks and Latinos as attitudes that are mutually exclusive, I find strong support for the social contact hypothesis. Increased social interactions with Latinos and blacks heighten whites' favorability toward these groups. Social contact, however, can have divergent effects on whites' attitudes toward Latinos and blacks. Social contact with blacks in the workplace can increase whites' perceptions that blacks feel threatened by whites while increased interactions with Latinos can develop whites' perceptions that Latinos pose an employment threat to whites. I also find that age may affect whites' attitudes toward blacks in that older whites are more likely to adopt less affinity and more negative stereotypes of blacks than younger whites.

So what do these results really mean for future inter-race relations? Greater proximity with Latinos and blacks can develop whites' affinity toward both groups, yet it can also increase groups' awareness of the racial hierarchy that exists when it comes to opportunities for upward economic mobility. Further, white/black relations may improve since younger generations are more aware of their racial biases and adopt less negative stereotypes than older generations.

Conclusion

While several altercations between blacks and white authority figures have recently taken place, the shooting and killing of Trayvon Martin reveals the complexity of interracial relations today. After George Zimmerman, a neighborhood watchman of Latino descent, killed African American Trayvon Martin, Zimmerman's white father sought to disassociate his son from the perception that George Zimmerman killed Martin out of hate by publicly emphasizing that his son came from a multiracial family who would not discriminate against blacks (Stutzman 2012). Not only did this incident revive conversations about Stand Your Ground laws but also of the emerging, diverse Latino population and the current state of black/Latino relations.

In order to obtain a present-day, complete view of race relations and to determine what Latinos, blacks, and whites really think of each other, this book analyzes these three groups' perceptions of commonality and competition with each other. These perceptions, commonly known as precursors of coalition formation, assess the complex racial dynamics that exist among blacks, whites, and Latinos. Exploring these perceptions is vital to uncovering racial attitudes since they are able to expose intricate, intense attitudes about one's own racial/ethnic group and other groups. Further, analyses of perceptions of closeness, commonality, and competition address one of the main questions of this book: Do Latinos, African Americans, and whites regard each other as allies or rivals? This study relies on these attitudes to uncover the extent to which (1) Latinos (a growing, influential minority group) have more affinity with blacks than whites; (2) blacks regard Latinos as partners and not rivals; and (3) whites view Latinos like African Americans. While existing studies have increased our understanding of how similar and yet distinct Latinos are from whites and blacks (Sanchez 2008; Abrajano and Alvarez 2010; Hutchings et al. 2011; McClain and Stewart 2013), they have not sufficiently analyzed Latinos', whites', and blacks' sense of closeness and competition with each other. Similarities between blacks and Latinos may not automatically prompt them to regard each other as partners, and it is still not clear whether whites and Latinos feel closer to each other than to blacks. In order to unearth these complexities and gaps, this project takes a comparative approach and examines "the triangle of perceptions" among Latinos, blacks, and whites: Latinos' perceptions of whites and blacks relative to those of other Latinos; African Americans' perceptions of Latinos, whites, and other blacks; and whites' perceptions of blacks, Latinos, and other whites. Thus, this study challenges the conventional practice of examining a racial or ethnic group's attitudes toward another, comparing individuals' views toward one group with those of another and comparing individuals' views toward one group with those of their own race or ethnicity. Reliance on quantitative and qualitative research methods with contemporary national survey data and New Orleans focus group data places this study at the forefront of innovative methods to study Latino, black, and white perceptions of closeness, commonality, and competition.

I dedicate the next few paragraphs to elaborating on the contributions of this study as well as to discuss current and future interracial coalitions. After summarizing the Triangular Theory of Contact, Context, and Identification (TCCI), I expand on the substantive and theoretical improvements that this study has made in the racial and ethnic politics literature. Then, I discuss the policy implications of my findings and end with a brief discussion of recent and potential future alliances among these three groups.

Theoretical and Substantive Contributions of This Study

To uncover when Latinos, blacks, and whites perceive closeness, commonality, and competition with each other, I develop the TTCCI. While we know that sociopolitical power is not congruent across all racial and ethnic groups, the changing demographics of this country and the various environments, attitudes, and opportunities that blacks, Latinos, and whites have do not clearly establish how these three groups distinguish from each other and how they relate. Hence, this book attempts to take a more current, comprehensive approach to uncovering inter-race dynamics by arguing that unequal levels of power exist across and among Latinos, blacks, and whites, thereby fostering an "us versus them" mentality, yet this mentality is moderated by these groups' social networks; sense of clout established by their racial, political, and economic environments; and sense of identification with members of their own group and others. Increased social contact with one group has positive effects on individuals' attitudes toward that group. Social interactions with one group, however, can have negative effects (i.e., divisive effects) on one's attitudes toward another. Being surrounded or perceiving to be surrounded by another group of a comparable socioeconomic status can heighten one's sense of threat and result in greater antagonism toward the neighboring group. Further, when individuals find themselves in vulnerable economic and political contexts, they are less likely to perceive closeness and more likely to sense competition with another group of a similar status. As to feelings of identification, the more individuals identify with one group, the less inclined they are to regard them as a threat. Moreover, identifying with one group shapes one's sense of closeness with another. Thus, my TTCCI overcomes the limitations of previous studies by being able to apply to the perceptions of commonality and competition of not just one but *three* racial groups (blacks, whites, and Latinos) who differ in sociopolitical clout.

My TTCCI is seminal for several more reasons. While this project tests and builds on prominent, well-established theories (i.e., social contact, racial threat, and group position theories), it extends the capabilities of these theories by testing the interactive effects of social contact and racial context. It examines and tests hypotheses about the effects of social interaction with one group on the attitudes toward another, and the effects of being objectively and subjectively surrounded by one racial group on the attitudes toward another group. This project is one of the first studies to adopt power-based hypotheses regarding the effects of contact and racial, economic, and political contexts on white, black, *and* Latino racial attitudes. Further, this study is innovative for its incorporation of hypotheses that build on the group position theory and explain the relationship between perceptions of commonality and perceptions of competition for Latinos, blacks, and whites.

Before discussing my findings as they relate to my TTCCI, I report the extent to which whites, blacks, and Latinos regard each other as allies or rivals. Analyses of national survey data reveal that Latinos sense a little more commonality with blacks than whites and marginally greater economic competition with whites than blacks. While these results suggest that Latinos have more affinity with blacks than whites, they do not clearly indicate that Latinos regard blacks as allies. Instead, I find that Latinos perceive considerably more commonality and competition with other Latinos than whites and African Americans, illustrating that Latinos draw clear distinctions between blacks/whites and their ethnic counterparts. My New Orleans focus group results illustrate that Latinos interact more, identify more, and are more favorable toward whites than African Americans. Thus, Latinos' relations with whites and blacks in the South may be distinct from those in the non-South (Morin et al. 2011).

In terms of my findings regarding African Americans, there are several critical and intriguing results. My survey data results illustrate that blacks do not differ in their perceptions of closeness with Latinos and whites though they perceive more competition with whites than Latinos. Still, my focus group results reveal that African Americans in New Orleans sense greater commonality and competition with whites than with Latinos. A plausible explanation for this finding is that blacks' views toward Latinos are not as fixed as those toward whites, since Latinos are slowly establishing a presence in New Orleans and blacks are gradually interacting and determining whether Latinos are their allies or rivals. Given that many southern cities and towns are becoming emerging Latino areas, these findings may only be relevant to the South.

My analyses of whites' perceptions of closeness and competition also yield some interesting results. Using national survey data, I find that whites' views toward blacks and Latinos are related, yet whites feel slightly closer to blacks than to Latinos and sense marginally greater competition with Latinos than with African Americans. On the other hand, my focus group data of whites in New Orleans reveal that whites view Latinos in a much more positive light than African Americans by adopting less negative stereotypes of Latinos and portraying more affinity toward Latinos. Based on the racial hierarchy and the long history of racial discrimination by whites against blacks in the South, these findings may be particular to this region and not hold true at the national level.

As to what explains perceptions of commonality and competition among Latinos, African Americans, and whites, I find strong evidence for my TTCCI. Tables 16–18 summarize the major findings from my national survey data analyses of black, Latino, and white racial attitudes. There are various findings that must be highlighted. First, unlike Vincent L. Hutchings and colleagues (2011), I find robust support for the social contact hypothesis—the more social interaction whites, blacks, and Latinos have with another group, the more likely they are to regard that group in a positive manner. Still, social contact can have divisive effects. When minorities have largely black or Latino social networks, they are less likely to perceive closeness with whites. Whites with significant contact with whites are more prone to regard Latinos as competitors and less inclined to view blacks as rivals. These findings bolster the notion that Latinos and blacks view the world in terms of siding with whites (those with clout) or with minorities (those with less clout), and whites do not regard Latinos and African Americans in the same way. Regarding the effects of racial context, I find that the racial threat hypothesis largely explains foreign-born Latinos' and blacks' racial attitudes. When Latino immigrants and blacks feel racially threatened (such as by residing in a predominantly black county for immigrants and residing in a growing Latino setting for blacks), they are more likely to perceive competition with the group that

TABLE 16. Findings for analyses of Latinos' perceptions of commonality and competition with blacks and whites using 2006 LNS and 2010 CCES data

	Commonality with		Competition with	
	Blacks	Whites	Blacks	Whites
Social contact with blacks	+	−	+ (f.b.)	
Social contact with whites	+ and − (n.b.) − (f.b.)	+		
Percentage black in county, perception of the number of blacks in county			+ (f.b.)	
Percentage white in county, perception of the number of whites in county		+ (f.b.)		−
Education level (county)	− (n.b.)		+ (f.b.) − (n.b.)	
Poverty rate (county)	− (n.b.)		+ (f.b.)	
Unemployment rate (county)	−	+ (n.b.)	+ (f.b.)	
Latino legislator			− (n.b.)	
Democratic congressional district				
State ballot initiatives, political referenda			− (f.b.)	
Identification with blacks		+	+ (f.b.)	
Identification with whites	+			

Note: Only findings that are statistically significant at the p level of 0.05 or less are presented. "F.b." signifies that a relationship only exists for foreign-born Latinos; "n.b." signifies that a relationship exists only for native-born Latinos.

surrounds them. Racial context can also have interactive effects—whites who perceive that they live near many whites are more likely to feel close to Latinos and are less likely to perceive economic competition with them.

As for the effects of economic and political context, I find support for Lawrence D. Bobo and Hutchings's (1996) modified group position theory. When Latinos and African Americans (though not whites) feel threatened economically, they are less likely to feel close to and are more likely to perceive competition with the other minority group (McClain et al. 2011; Nteta 2013). Threat can also explain the effects of political context on Latinos', blacks', and whites' racial dispositions. When Latinos do not feel threatened politically (e.g., residing in a state with direct democracy provisions and residing in a majority-minority district), they are less likely to regard African Americans as competitors. African Americans who are represented by a Latino are less likely to feel close to Latinos, and southern blacks represented

TABLE 17. Findings for analyses of blacks' perceptions of closeness and competition with Latinos and whites using 2004 NPS and 2010 CCES data

	Closeness with		Competition with	
	Latinos	Whites	Latinos	Whites
Social contact with Latinos	+	−	− (non-South)	− (non-South)
Social contact with whites		+	− (South)	− (South)
Percentage Latino in county, perception of the number of Latinos in county	+		+	
Percentage white in county, perception of the number of whites in county	−			+
Education level (county)				−
Poverty rate (county)			+ (non-South)	+ (non-South)
Unemployment rate (county)	−	+		
Black legislator				
Latino legislator	−		+ (South)	
Democratic congressional district				
State ballot initiatives, political referenda	−			
Identification with Latinos		+	− (South)	
Identification with whites	+			

Note: Only findings that are statistically significant at the p level of 0.05 or less are presented. "South" signifies that a relationship is only statistically significant among blacks in the South; "non-South" signifies that a relationship is only statistically significant among blacks in the non-South.

by a Latino legislator are more inclined to regard Latinos as rivals. Being represented by a nonwhite legislator may have positive effects on whites' attitudes toward Latinos and blacks since I find that whites with black or Latino legislators are more prone to perceive economic commonality with blacks and Latinos, respectively. Interestingly, whites in a largely Democratic district are less inclined to regard Latinos as economic competitors. These results reveal that when Latinos and blacks feel that the other minority group is encroaching on their status (and thus they are losing power), they respond negatively to the other group (McClain et al. 2011). Yet, threat does not seem to similarly explain the relationship between political context and whites' attitudes toward Latinos and blacks. Residing in a politically weak context actually may not have detrimental effects on whites' racial dispositions, thus providing some hope for improved white/black and white/Latino relations as minorities gain greater political clout.

TABLE 18. Findings for analyses of whites' perceptions of closeness and competition with Latinos and blacks using 2004 NPS and 2010 CCES data

	Closeness		Competition	
	Latinos	Blacks	Latinos	Blacks
Social contact with Latinos	+		+	
Social contact with blacks		+		−
Social contact with whites		+	+	−
Percentage of whites in county, perception of the number of whites in county	+		−	
Low percentage of Latinos in county × High percentage with high school degree in county	+		−	
High percentage of Latinos in county × Low percentage with high school degree in county	+			
Low percentage of blacks in county × High percentage with high school degree in county				
High percentage of blacks in county × Low percentage with high school degree in county				
Education level (county)	+	−	−	
Poverty rate (county)	+			
Unemployment rate (county)				
Black legislator		+		
Latino legislator	+			
Reside in a majority-minority district		−	+	+
Democratic congressional district			−	
State ballot initiatives, political referenda	+			
Identification with Latinos		+		−
Identification with blacks	+			−
Identification with whites				

Note: Only findings that are statistically significant at the p level of 0.05 or less are presented.

Feelings of identification with one's own racial group or others also structure black, white, and Latino racial attitudes. My quantitative analyses reveal that the more blacks and whites identify with another racial group, the less likely they are to regard them as rivals. As for Latinos, I find that Latino immigrants who identify with African Americans are more inclined to perceive competition with them. Nonetheless, I find robust support for the fact that identifying with one racial group increases the likelihood that whites, blacks, and Latinos perceive commonality with another group. Latinos who identify with blacks sense greater commonality with whites. African Americans who identify with Latinos feel closer to whites. The more whites identify with Latinos/blacks, the more they perceive closeness with blacks/Latinos, respectively. While identifying with one group may improve relations with another, an alternative explanation for this finding is that some individuals may not consider race or ethnicity when determining whether they perceive commonality with another group (as found in my focus group analyses).

Coalition and Policy Implications

In addition to shedding light on the complexities of interracial attitudes and accounting for the disparities among blacks, whites, and Latinos, the findings presented above develop our comprehension of the strengths and limitations of our laws and the likelihood that inter-race coalitions will form. Given that increased social contact can augment blacks', whites', and Latinos' sense of closeness toward each other, desegregation laws have the ability to improve race relations. Notwithstanding this, it is important to recognize that desegregation may not automatically lead to greater alliances across all groups. Latinos' and blacks' increased contact with each other heightens their hostility toward whites. This may be due to the fact that greater interaction with other minorities, particularly in settings where blacks and Latinos have limited sociopolitical power, can foment blacks' and Latinos' resentment toward whites, a group with generally greater sociopolitical opportunities. Further, desegregation laws may not lead to coalitions between blacks and Latinos since African Americans are more likely to regard Latinos as rivals in an emerging Latino context, and Latino immigrants in a largely black setting perceive greater competition with blacks. Zoning laws, however, may not be at the core of black/Latino tensions. As found in my focus groups of blacks in New Orleans, blacks regard Latinos as economic threats because they perceive that whites favor Latinos over blacks and place Latinos as direct competitors to blacks for jobs. Thus, in New Orleans (and possibly in other parts of the United States), the root cause of black/Latino tensions (according to blacks) may not be greater interaction with Latinos but rather whites' response to an emergent Latino population.

My findings regarding the effects of economic and political contexts on racial attitudes develop our understanding of the implications of this nation's economic and electoral policies. Since I find that blacks and Latinos in a weak economic environment (resulting in feelings of diminishing power) are more likely to regard each other as rivals, we now know that policies associated with increasing the minimum wage and developing job opportunities have the potential to depress conflict between Latinos and blacks and can even provide an opportunity for the two groups to form coalitions to work toward policy change. Further, policies that crackdown on racial discrimination among employers may depress racial hostility, especially between African Americans and Latinos. As for political contexts, Latinos' propensity to form alliances with blacks is high if Latinos reside in environments where they feel empowered such as in states with ballot initiatives and/or political referenda or living in majority-minority districts (for native-born Latinos). The likelihood that alliances form between blacks and Latinos would most likely not be as high if blacks were to reside in a district represented a Latino. Thus, increased political clout for Latinos through descriptive representation may not translate to greater black/Latino alliances, and African Americans may not be ready or willing to form coalitions with Latinos to elect a Latino representative. As to whites, since I find that whites represented by nonwhites are more likely to perceive commonality with Latinos and blacks, increasing the number of minority legislators who run and win elections may improve whites' perceptions of blacks and Latinos. Moreover, in the future, whites may not be so reluctant to elect representatives who are nonwhite.

The Effects of the Supreme Court Ruling on Arizona's S.B. 1070 and Multiracial Coalitions

Latinos', blacks', and whites' responses to immigration legislation can reveal the extent to which racial alliances can form among these three groups. Several states in the last few years have taken immigration issues into their own hands. The most controversial state law, S.B. 1070, was passed in Arizona in 2010 restricting immigration in a variety of ways. Some of the law's key provisions included allowing local police departments and federal immigration enforcement officers to coordinate immigrant deportations; permitting law enforcement officers to arrest an individual without a warrant if the officer has probable cause that the individual had performed a public offense resulting in deportation; and prohibiting illegal immigrants from searching for employment or working (Project Vote Smart 2010). After S.B. 1070 was passed, Latinos, blacks, and whites responded to this legislation in various ways. Many Latino civil rights organizations and groups in Arizona and throughout the country responded with protests, rallies, and boycotts. Several Latino leaders and organizations in Arizona launched a national boycott against the state, encouraging businesses, organizations, and individuals not to do business there. Among blacks, some responded negatively toward S.B. 1070. Reverend Al Sharpton referred to this legislation as an act of racism and injustice, and strongly called for individuals to be "Freedom Walkers" (drawing parallels to the Freedom Riders from the civil rights movement) and openly protest this legislation (Sharpton 2010). LaWana Mayfield, a leader in a North Carolina grassroots organization, has dedicated a significant portion of her time to educating blacks about S.B. 1070 and immigration reform. Not all African Americans, however, feel as strongly against Arizona's S.B. 1070 as Mayfield and Sharpton. Mayfield has actually observed that while some black leaders publicly support her pro-immigration efforts, almost no rank-and-file black leaders publicly support pro-immigration events (Persinger 2010). Limited support against S.B. 1070 among blacks may not be surprising since, as this study shows, many blacks feel that they have been adversely affected by increased immigration. As to whites, some have strongly protested against Arizona's law, and others have openly endorsed it. Many white Republican legislators pushed for the creation and enactment of S.B. 1070, stressing the economic strains of increased immigration and the importance of responding to those who broke the law to come to this country. Tea Party supporters even held rallies in Arizona to show support for the legislation (Fernandez 2010). On the other hand, some whites have participated in nationwide boycotts and rallies protesting S.B. 1070. Others, including many white business owners in Arizona who originally supported the law but have been adversely affected by the national boycott of Arizona, have urged political leaders in Arizona to reconsider the law given its negative economic impact on the state (Fernandez 2011).

In June 2012, the Supreme Court of the United States addressed the law's constitutionality. The Court struck down all of the law's provisions except the most controversial one: state law enforcement may determine the immigration status of anyone if they have reason to believe that the individual does not have legal status (Liptak 2012). The Court's ruling has given rise to more talks of leaving it up to the federal government to address immigration by passing comprehensive immigration reform. While comprehensive immigration reform has not been passed (as of the time of this writing), it is critical to determine the extent to which Latinos, whites, and blacks might form coalitions to bring about policy change. A few days after the Supreme Court's ruling, a Latino Decisions poll (commissioned by the Center for America's Progress Action Fund and America's Voice) of Latinos and non-Latinos examined individuals' preponderance to form alliances with others. The survey took place from July 7–16, 2012, with a margin of error of +/-4.4%. Table 19 presents the descriptive results of Latino, black, and white respondents' answers to those questions.

Individuals' answers to the questions presented in table 19 reveal several interesting findings. The majority of Latinos, whites, and blacks believe that

TABLE 19. Latino, black, and white responses to coalition questions post–SCOTUS ruling on S.B. 1070, by percentage

	Latinos	Whites	Blacks
"When an issue or problem needs to be addressed, would you work through it with existing organizations or groups to bring people together or would you get together informally or would you do nothing about this matter?"			
Use existing organizations	38.4	36.5	41.2
Get together informally	35.8	38.5	41.2
Both	4.1	1.9	1.9
Do nothing	21.8	22.9	15.7
N	565	405	51
If individuals responded "use existing organizations," "get together informally," or "both," they were further asked, "How would you describe these groups or individuals? Would they be . . ."			
Mostly Latino	24.1	3.2	2.3
Mostly black	1.6	6.4	16.3
Mostly Asian	0	0.4	0.0
Mostly white	3.7	20.0	4.7
An equal mix	70.3	68.6	76.7
Other	0.2	1.4	0.0
N	428	280	43
If individuals responded "an equal mix" to the previous question, they were further asked, "Okay, would you describe the groups as . . ."			
	7.9%	3.1%	—
Mixed Latino and black	3.0	3.1	3.0
Mixed Latino and Asian	0.7	—	—
Mixed white and black	1.7	4.2	6.1
Mixed white and Asian	6.0	1.6	3.0
An equal mix of all groups	79.7	84.4	81.8
Other	0.3	0.0	0.0
N	301	192	33

Source: July 7–16, 2012, Latino Decisions 2012a.

in order to address a problem, they must work with an existing organization or get together informally with others. Blacks are less supportive of doing nothing (15.7%) than Latinos (21.8%) and whites (22.9%). When it comes to the racial group that they would mostly work with (in existing organizations or informal networks), most blacks, whites, and Latinos would work with an equal mix of individuals. The second largest group that all groups would work with, however, would be those primarily belonging to their own racial/ethnic group, with Latinos being the most willing to work with their own group (24%). Interestingly, Latinos (3.7%) and blacks (4.7%) do not favor working with mostly white groups over those of their own race or ethnicity. When further probing who would make up the equal mix of individuals that they would work with to bring about change, the majority of Latinos, blacks, and whites emphasized that they would form a coalition with an equal mix of all groups. Yet, more Latinos asserted that their group would mostly consist of Latinos and whites (7.9%) rather than Latinos and blacks (3.0%). Further, more whites and blacks said that their coalitions would consist of whites (4.2%) and blacks (6.1%) rather than Latinos and members of their racial group (white/black).

What do these results as well as the key findings from this project suggest? In her analysis of multiracial coalitions, Karen Kaufmann (2007) argues that given the limited political resources and opportunities that blacks and Latinos have, it is in their best interests to form political coalitions with whites rather than with other minorities. This argument counters the rainbow coalition theory, which states that minorities should form alliances in order to successfully advance their sociopolitical clout (Kaufmann 2003). While my findings suggest that Latinos, blacks, and whites are more inclined to create alliances with members of their own groups than with others, my findings lend support to Kaufmann's (2007) thesis that blacks and Latinos are more willing to build alliances with whites and their racial counterparts than with other minority groups. Further, while previous analyses illustrate that some blacks regard Latinos more favorably than whites, blacks' and Latinos' limited influence and continuous economic struggles may impede them from forming rainbow coalitions. Notwithstanding this, future efforts made by the Democratic and Republican parties to enact comprehensive immigration reform and laws that do not disenfranchise individuals but boost the economic and political power of *all* U.S. residents may present opportunities for individuals regardless of status, race, and ethnic background to form multiracial partnerships.

Appendix

Chapter 2

Dependent Variables

2006 LATINO NATIONAL SURVEY (LNS)

In this study, I present two general measures of commonality: commonality with blacks and commonality with whites. The LNS includes questions that explore Latinos' commonality with whites and blacks on two dimensions: economic (e.g., employment opportunities, education level, and income) and political (e.g., political power and representation, and government services). The survey question that measures perceptions of economic commonality is, "Thinking about issues like job opportunities, educational attainment, or income, how much do Latinos/Hispanics have in common with other racial groups in the U.S. Would you say Latinos/Hispanics have a lot in common, some in common, little in common, or nothing at all in common with . . . [African Americans, whites]?" Political commonality with other racial groups is examined by asking: "Now I'd like you to think about the political situation of Latinos in society. Thinking about things like government services and employment, political power and representation, do Latinos/Hispanics have a lot in common, some in common, little in common, or nothing at all in common at all with . . . [African Americans, whites]?" The general commonality measures for whites, blacks, and Latinos are each composed of an additive index of economic and political commonality for each racial group. Hence, the additive commonality measures range from 0 (nothing at all in common with whites/blacks/Latinos regarding job opportunities, educational attainment, income, government services, employment, political power, and representation) to 6 (a lot in common with whites/blacks/Latinos as regards to socioeconomic and political clout).

The other main LNS dependent variable in this study is competition with blacks. Latinos' competition with whites was not assessed by the survey. Similar to perceptions of commonality, the LNS contains questions that assess Latinos' economic and political competition. The main survey question that examines Latinos' rivalry with blacks states, "Some have suggested that Latinos/Hispanics are in competition with African-Americans. After each of the next items, would you tell me if you believe there is strong competition, weak competition, or no competition at all with African-Americans? How about . . ." This question is repeated several times, yet the ending phrase alters in order to assess distinct types of competition: in getting jobs? getting jobs in city or state government? having access to education and quality schools? having Latino/Hispanic representatives in elected office? I create a general measure of competition with blacks that addresses Latinos' rivalry regarding general employment, employment in government, education, and political power.

2010 COOPERATIVE CONGRESSIONAL ELECTION STUDY (CCES)

The 2010 CCES also provides the opportunity to assess Latinos' perceptions of commonality and competition with whites and African Americans, though it does not assess Latinos' identification and competition with other Latinos. In order to assess Latinos' commonality with others, I rely on an economic commonality with blacks measure and an economic commonality with whites measure. The survey question that measures Latinos' perceptions of commonality with blacks and whites is, "Thinking about issues like job opportunities, educational attainment or income, how much do you have in common with the following groups [African Americans, Hispanics/Latinos, Whites, Asian Americans] . . . nothing, little, some, a lot, not sure?" Political commonality was not analyzed by the CCES. The variables that measure how much economic commonality Latinos have with blacks and whites range from 0 (nothing) to 3 (a lot). The other main CCES dependent variables that I employ in my analyses are perceptions of job competition with whites. Political competition with both groups was not assessed by the CCES. The employment competition with whites measure ranges from 0 (strongly disagree) to 4 (strongly agree) with a high score representing a perception of strong jobs competition with the relevant target group.

Independent Variables

2006 LNS

The following questions and descriptions detail the construction of the 2006 LNS independent variables for the ordinary least squares models.

Social contact. I explore social contact in a variety of settings: having black/white friends, having black/white coworkers, and participating in a majority black/white social, political, or civic group. Friendship with blacks is measured on a scale from 0 to 2 where 0 represents other/no black friends, 1 denotes mixed black friends, and 2 represents mostly black friends. Having black coworkers ranges from 0 (other/no black coworkers) to 2 (mostly black coworkers). Finally, participation in a black social, political, or civic group is measured on a three-point scale where 0 represents other/participation in a group with no blacks, 1 denotes participation in a mixed black group, and 2 represents participation in a mostly black group. Measures of social contact with whites are assessed in the same way. The questions used in the construction of the social interaction variables are: "How would you describe your friends? How would you describe your coworkers? Do you participate in the activities of one social, cultural, civic, or political group? How would you describe these groups?"

Identification with whites. This measure is included in my models as a dependent variable as well as an independent variable. It is operationalized in the same way as the dependent variable called "commonality with whites" mentioned previously.

Identification with blacks. This variable is also included in my models as a dependent and independent variable. It is coded in the same way as the dependent variable "commonality with blacks" mentioned previously.

General commonality with other Latinos. This variable is an additive measure of Latinos' sense of economic and political commonality with other Latinos. It ranges from 0 (nothing at all in common with other Latinos/Hispanics regarding job opportunities, educational attainment, income, government services, employment, political power, and representation) to 6 (a lot in common with other Latinos regarding economic and sociopolitical influence).

Time in the United States. "How many years have you lived in the United States?" This variable ranges from 0.5 to 91 years.

Foreign-born status. "Were you born in the mainland United States, Puerto Rico, or some other country?" My measure of foreign-born status is captured by a dummy variable where individuals who were not born in the United States or a U.S. territory were coded as a 1 and others were coded as a 0.

Linked fate with other Latinos. "How much does your doing well depend on other Latinos/Hispanics doing well? A lot, some, a little, or not at all?" I measure linked fate with Latinos on a scale from 0 (no linked fate) to 3 (a lot of linked fate).

English-language interview. "Would you prefer that I speak in English or Spanish?" The language that the respondent is interviewed in is coded 1 for English and 0 for Spanish.

Skin tone. "Latinos/Hispanics can be described based on skin tone or complexion shades. Using a scale from 1 to 5 where 1 represents very dark skin and 5 represents being very light, where would you place yourself on that scale?" Latinos' self-reported skin tones range from 0 (very dark) to 4 (very light).

South. My measure of residency in the South is captured by a dummy variable where Latinos who reside in Arkansas, Georgia, North Carolina, and Virginia were coded as a 1 and others were coded as a 0.

Age. "What year were you born?" Age is measured in terms of number of years ranging from 18 to 98 years.

Gender. Gender is coded 1 for females and 0 for males.

Education. "What is your highest level of formal education completed?" Education is coded using an eight-point scale ranging from 0 (none) to 7 (postgraduate degree).

Household income. "Which of the following describes the total income earned by all members of your household during 2004?" Household income is measured as a seven-point scale ranging from 0 (income less than $15,000 in 2004) to 6 (income greater than $65,000 in 2004).

Mexican. "Families of Latino/Hispanic origin or background in the United States come from many different countries. From which country do you trace your Latino heritage?" This is a dichotomous variable where 0 represents other and 1 represents Mexico/Mexican.

Partisan identification. "Generally speaking, do you consider yourself a Democrat, a Republican, an Independent, or some other party?" This variable ranges from −1 (Republican) to 0 (Independent, other) to 1 (Democrat).

2010 CCES

The following questions and descriptions detail the construction of the 2010 CCES independent variables for the ordinary least squares models in the appendix.

Social contact. Similar to the LNS, the 2010 CCES allows me to explore Latinos' social interaction in a variety of settings: having black/white friends, coworkers, and/or neighbors. Yet, since I am limited in the number of measures of contact that I can include in my model using CCES data, due to a small sample size of Latinos in the survey, I examine the effect of neighborhood makeup on racial attitudes since it was not examined by the LNS. Having black neighbors ranges from 0 (no black neighbors, other) to 2 (mostly black neighbors). Having white neighbors is measured similarly. The questions used in the construction of the social interaction variables are: "How would you describe the racial/ethnic mix for each of the following groups in your life? Neighbors" (Mostly Black, Mostly White, Mostly Latino, Mostly Asian, Mixed, Not sure).

Subjective racial context (perception of number of whites in county). Unlike the 2006 LNS, the 2010 CCES allows me to examine the effects of subjective contexts on Latinos' racial attitudes, using the question, "Thinking about the levels of diversity in the county in which you live, how many of each of the following groups would you say live in your county?" This variable is measured on a scale from 0 to 3 where 0 represents no whites and 3 represents a lot of whites.

RACIAL, ECONOMIC, AND INSTITUTIONAL CONTEXT VARIABLES

Racial context. Besides assessing the effects of variables included in the 2006 LNS and 2010 CCES, I collected racial context data from the U.S. Census website and merged these data to the 2006 LNS data set to assess the effects of racial context on Latino racial attitudes ("Stata FAQ" n.d.). I include two measures of racial context at the county level in my models: percent blacks and percent whites. These data are U.S. Census estimates for the year 2006.

Economic context. I also collected economic context data at the county level from the U.S. Census website and merged it to both data sets. For the models using 2006 LNS data, my measure of economic context are the percentage of individuals of all ages who live in poverty in 2007, residents' educational attainment (percentage of individuals over twenty-five years of age who have a high school degree) from 2006–10, and the percentage of unemployed individuals in 2008. For the models using 2010 CCES data, the only measure of economic context that I include is the percentage of individuals of all ages who lived in poverty from 2006–10. These data are estimates provided by the U.S. Census Bureau State and County QuickFacts. Since I could not obtain contextual data at the county level for just the years 2006 and 2010, I relied on data from the closest years or sets of years as a proxy for the ideal measures. It is important to note that given that the Great Recession began in 2008, I account for the poverty rate in 2007 and not from 2006–10 in my models using the 2006 LNS. Yet, the only unemployment rate data that I was able to obtain was for the year 2008, so I include these data in my models using data from the 2006 LNS.

Institutional context. In order to examine the effects of institutional context on Latino attitudes toward blacks and whites, I collected state congressional district data from the 2006 and 2010 *Almanac of American Politics* (Barone and Cohen 2005; Barone et al. 2009). The 2006 district data was merged onto the 2006 LNS by county, and the 2010 district data was merged onto the 2010 CCES by county. Due to a limited sample size of Latinos in the 2010 CCES, I am constrained in the number of institutional context measures that I am able to include in my model using data from the CCES. Thus, I only examine the effects of having a Latino legislator and residing in a state with provisions for direct democracy on Latinos' sense of economic commonality with blacks and whites and perceptions of employment competition with whites. I measure descriptive representation by determining whether an individual is represented by a Latino legislator. This variable is coded dichotomously with a 1 indicating that an individual is represented by a Latino and 0 indicating otherwise. Whether an individual resides in a majority-minority district is also measured dichotomously where 1 represents residing in a majority-minority district and 0 represents otherwise. I measure the political ideology of a district through the percentage of district votes cast in favor of the Democratic candidate in the previous presidential election (percentage of votes for Senator John Kerry for the 2004 presidential election for the LNS models). This variable ranges from 0 to 1. Another measure of institutional context is whether the state that an individual resides in allows for ballot initiatives and/or political referenda. This information was obtained from the National Council of State Legislatures and the Initiative and Referendum Institute at the University of Southern California. This measure is also coded dichotomously where 1 indicates that the respondent resides in a state that has provisions for direct democracy and 0 indicates otherwise.

Chapter 3

Focus Group Questions (in Spanish, translated to English)

1. Are you an immigrant or were you born in the U.S.? If you are an immigrant, when did you come to the U.S.?

2. Here in New Orleans, the majority of the population is black and white. How much contact do you have with blacks? For instance, do you have any neighbors, coworkers, or friends who are black?

3. How much in common do you have with blacks?

4. Do you think that competition exists between you and blacks? How much?

5. Based on the contact that you have with blacks, how does this affect your attitudes toward blacks? For instance, does contact affect your commonality and competition with blacks?

6. Now when it comes to another large group in New Orleans, whites, how much contact do you have with whites? For instance, do you have any neighbors, coworkers, or friends who are white?

7. How much in common do you have with whites?

8. Do you think that competition exists between you and whites? How much?

9. Based on the contact that you have with whites, how does this affect your attitudes toward whites? For instance, does contact affect your commonality and competition with whites?

10. How do you envision the future of race relations between you and blacks? Peaceful? Cooperative? Competitive?

11. How do you envision the future of race relations between you and whites? Peaceful? Cooperative? Competitive?

12. Well, that concludes our discussion. Is there anything else that you would like to add about your attitudes toward blacks and whites?

Questionnaire

First name or alias _____

Gender _____   Age _____   Employed (please circle): Yes   No

Occupation _____

Income (please check):

_____ $10,000 or less   _____ $25,001–$40,000

_____ $10,001–$25,000   _____ $40,001 or more

Education (please check):

_____ Elementary School (K–5th grade) but did not graduate

_____ Elementary School diploma

_____ Middle School (6–8th) but did not graduate

_____ Middle School diploma

_____ High School (9–12th) but did not graduate

_____ High School diploma

_____ College but did not graduate

_____ College diploma

_____ Graduate school or higher

_____On a scale from 0 to 10 (10 having a lot in common and 0 having nothing in common), how much in common do you think you have with blacks?

_____On a scale from 0 to 10 (10 having a lot in common and 0 having nothing in common), how much in common do you think you have with whites?

_____On a scale from 0 to 10 (10 having a lot of competition and 0 having no competition), how much competition do you think exists between you and blacks?

_____On a scale from 0 to 10 (10 having a lot of competition and 0 having no competition), how much competition do you think exists between you and whites?

Chapter 4

Dependent Variables

Closeness to whites. "How close do you feel in your ideas, interests and feelings to White people?" This variable ranges from 0 (not close at all) to 3 (very close).

Closeness to blacks. "How close do you feel in your ideas, interests and feelings to black people?" This variable ranges from 0 (not close at all) to 3 (very close).

Closeness to Latinos. "How close do you feel in your ideas, interests and feelings to Hispanic people?" This variable ranges from 0 (not close at all) to 3 (very close).

Employment Competition with whites. "More good jobs for Whites means fewer good jobs for people like me." This variable ranges from 0 (strongly disagree) to 3 (strongly agree).

Employment competition with Latinos. "More good jobs for Hispanics means fewer good jobs for people like me." This variable ranges from 0 (strongly disagree) to 3 (strongly agree).

Political competition with whites. "The more influence Whites have in politics, the less influence people like me will have in politics." This variable ranges from 0 (strongly disagree) to 3 (strongly agree).

Political competition with Latinos. "The more influence Latinos have in politics, the less influence people like me will have in politics." This variable ranges from 0 (strongly disagree) to 3 (strongly agree).

2010 CCES

Economic commonality with whites. "Thinking about issues like job opportunities, educational attainment or income, how much do you have in common with the following groups [Whites] . . . nothing, little, some, a lot, not sure?" This variable ranges from 0 (nothing) to 3 (a lot).

Economic commonality with Latinos. "Thinking about issues like job opportunities, educational attainment or income, how much do you have in common with the following groups [Latinos] . . . nothing, little, some, a lot, not sure?" This variable ranges from 0 (nothing) to 3 (a lot).

Employment competition with whites. "More jobs for whites means less jobs for people like me." This variable ranges from 0 (strongly disagree) to 4 (strongly agree).

Employment competition with Latinos. "More jobs for Latinos means less jobs for people like me." This variable ranges from 0 (strongly disagree) to 4 (strongly agree).

Independent Variables

2004 NPS

Social contact. I explore social contact in a variety of settings: having Latino/white friends, Latino/white coworkers, and Latino/white neighbors. Friendship with Latinos is measured on a scale from 0 to 2 where 0 represents other/no Latino friends, 1 denotes mixed Latino friends, and 2 represents mostly Latino friends. Having Latino coworkers ranges from 0 (other/no Latino coworkers) to 2 (mostly Latino coworkers). Having Latino neighbors ranges from 0 (other/no Latino neighbors) to 2 (mostly Latino neighbors). Measures of social contact with whites are assessed in the same way. The questions used in the construction of the social interaction variables are: "How would you describe the ethnic mix of your friends? Would you say your friends are mostly white, mostly black, mostly Hispanic, mostly Asian, or mixed? How would you describe the ethnic mix of your coworkers? Would you say your coworkers are mostly White, mostly black, mostly Hispanic, mostly Asian, or mixed? How would you describe the ethnic mix of your neighbors? Would you say your neighbors are mostly white, mostly blacks, mostly Hispanic, mostly Asian or mixed?"

Perceptions of discrimination. "Do you think the following groups face a lot of discrimination, some, a little, or no discrimination at all: Blacks?" This variable ranges from 0 (no discrimination) to 3 (a lot).

Negative stereotypes of Latinos. "Where would you rate Hispanics in general on a scale of 1 to 7, where 1 indicates lazy, 7 means hardworking?" This variable ranges from 0 (hardworking) to 6 (lazy).

Working class. "What is the highest grade or level of school that you have completed?" Class is measured dichotomously where 1 represents not having a college degree or higher and 0 represents other.

South. Residence in a southern state (Alabama, Arkansas, Georgia, Kentucky, Louisiana, Mississippi, North Carolina, South Carolina, Tennessee, Virginia, or West Virginia). This variable is measured dichotomously, 0 (other) to 1 (residence in a southern state).

Identification with whites. "How close do you feel in your ideas, interests and feelings to White people?" This variable ranges from 0 (not close at all) to 3 (very close).

Identification with Latinos. "How close do you feel in your ideas, interests and feelings to Hispanic people?" This variable ranges from 0 (not close at all) to 3 (very close).

Identification with blacks. "How close do you feel in your ideas, interests and feelings to African Americans?" This variable ranges from 0 (not close at all) to 3 (very close).

2010 CCES

Social contact. Similar to the LNS, the 2010 CCES allows me to explore blacks' social interactions in a variety of settings: having Latino/white friends, Latino/white coworkers, and Latino/white neighbors. The coding of these measures is the same as those for the 2004 NPS variables. The questions used in the construction of the social interaction variables are: "How would you describe the racial/ethnic mix for each of the following groups in your life?" (Mostly Black, Mostly White, Mostly Latino, Mostly Asian, Mixed, Not sure).

Subjective racial context. Unlike the 2004 NPS, the 2010 CCES allows me to examine the effects of subjective context (i.e., perceived numbers of whites/Latinos in blacks' counties) on blacks' racial attitudes. "Thinking about the levels of diversity in the county in which you live, how many of each of the following groups would you say live in your county?" This variable is measured on a scale from 0 to 3 where 0 represents no whites/Latinos and 3 represents a lot of whites/Latinos.

Economic commonality with whites. "Thinking about issues like job opportunities, educational attainment or income, how much do you have in common with the following groups [Whites] . . . nothing, little, some, a lot, not sure?" This variable ranges from 0 (nothing) to 3 (a lot).

Economic commonality with Latinos. "Thinking about issues like job opportunities, educational attainment or income, how much do you have in common with the following groups [Latinos] . . . nothing, little, some, a lot, not sure?" This variable ranges from 0 (nothing) to 3 (a lot).

CONTEXT VARIABLES

Racial context. I collected racial context data from the U.S. Census website and merged these data to the 2004 NPS and 2010 CCES data sets to assess the effects of racial context on black racial attitudes ("Stata FAQ" n.d.). I include two measures of racial context at the county level in my models: percent Latino and percent white. These data are U.S. Census estimates for the years 2004 and 2011.

Economic context. I also collected economic context data at the county level from the U.S. Census website and merged it to both data sets. For the models using 2004 NPS data, my measure of economic context are the per-

centage of individuals of all ages who live in poverty in 2007, residents' educational attainment (percentage of individuals over twenty-five years of age
who have a high school degree) from 2000, and percentage of unemployed
individuals in 2008. These data are estimates provided by the U.S. Census
Bureau State and County QuickFacts. Since I could not obtain contextual
data at the county level exactly for the year 2004, I relied on data from the
closest year or set of years as a proxy for the ideal measures. It is important
to note that given that the Great Recession began in 2008, I account for the
poverty rate in 2007. Yet, the only unemployment rate data that I was able
to obtain was for the year 2008 so I include these data in my models. For
the models using 2010 CCES data, my measures of economic contexts are
residents' educational attainment (estimated percentage of individuals over
twenty-five years of age who have a high school degree) from 2006–10 and
the estimated percentage of unemployed individuals from 2006–10.

Institutional context. In order to examine the effects of institutional context on black attitudes toward Latinos and whites, I collected state congressional district data from the 2004 and the 2010 *Almanac of American Politics.*
The 2004 district data were merged onto the 2004 NPS by county, and the
2010 data were merged onto the 2010 CCES by county.

The race of the legislator is measured with having a Latino legislator and
having a black legislator. These measures are coded dichotomously with a 1
indicating that an individual is represented by a Latino/black/minority and
0 indicating otherwise. I measure the political ideology of a district through
the percentage of district votes cast in favor of the Democratic candidate in
the previous presidential election (percentage of votes for Al Gore for the
2000 presidential election for the NPS models; votes for Barack Obama for
the 2008 presidential election for the CCES models). This variable ranges
from 0 to 1. Another measure of institutional context is whether the state in
which an individual resides has provisions for direct democracy such as ballot initiatives and/or political referenda. This information was obtained from
the National Council of State Legislatures and the Initiative and Referendum
Institute at the University of Southern California. This measure is also coded
dichotomously where 1 indicates that the respondent resides in a state that
has ballot initiatives and/or political referenda and 0 indicates otherwise.

Chapter 5

Focus Group Questions

1. Here in New Orleans, a large portion of the population is white. How
much contact do you have with whites? For instance, do you have any neighbors, coworkers, or friends who are white?

2. How much in common do you have with whites?

3. Do you think that competition exists between you and whites? How much?

4. Based on the contact that you have with whites, how does this affect your attitudes toward whites? For instance, does contact affect how much in common and competition that you have with whites?

5. Now when it comes to another minority group in New Orleans, Hispanics, how much contact do you have with Hispanics? For instance, do you have any neighbors, coworkers, or friends who are Hispanic?

6. How much in common do you have with Hispanics/Latinos?

7. Do you think that competition exists between you and Hispanics/Latinos? How much?

8. Based on the contact that you have with Hispanics/Latinos, how does this affect your attitudes toward Hispanics? For instance, does contact affect your commonality and competition with Hispanics?

9. How do you envision the future of race relations between blacks and whites? Peaceful? Cooperative? Competitive?

10. How do you envision the future of race relations between blacks and Hispanics? Peaceful? Cooperative? Competitive?

11. Well, that concludes our discussion. Is there anything else that you would like to add about your attitudes toward whites and Hispanics?

Questionnaire

First name or alias _____

Gender _____   Age _____   Employed (please circle): Yes   No

Occupation _____

Income (please check):

____ $10,000 or less   ____ $40,001–$55,000

____ $10,001–$25,000   ____ $55,001–$70,000

____ $25,001–$40,000   ____ $70,001 or more

Education (please check):

____ Elementary School (K–5th grade) but did not graduate

____ Elementary School diploma

____ Middle School (6–8th) but did not graduate

____ Middle School diploma

____ High School (9–12th) but did not graduate

____ High School diploma

____ College but did not graduate

____ College diploma

____ Graduate school or higher

____On a scale from 0 to 10 (10 having a lot in common and 0 having nothing in common), how much in common do you think you have with whites?

____On a scale from 0 to 10 (10 having a lot in common and 0 having nothing in common), how much in common do you think you have with Latinos?

____On a scale from 0 to 10 (10 having a lot of competition and 0 having no competition), how much economic competition do you think exists between you and whites?

____On a scale from 0 to 10 (10 having a lot of competition and 0 having no competition), how much economic competition do you think exists between you and Latinos?

____On a scale from 0 to 10 (10 having a lot of competition and 0 having no competition), how much general competition do you think exists between you and whites?

____On a scale from 0 to 10 (10 having a lot of competition and 0 having no competition), how much general competition do you think exists between you and Latinos?

Chapter 6

Dependent Variables

2004 NPS

Closeness to blacks. "How close do you feel in your ideas, interests and feelings to black people?" This variable ranges from 0 (not close at all) to 3 (very close).

Closeness to Latinos. "How close do you feel in your ideas, interests and feelings to Hispanic people?" This variable ranges from 0 (not close at all) to 3 (very close).

Employment competition with blacks. "More good jobs for Whites means fewer good jobs for people like me." This variable ranges from 0 (strongly disagree) to 3 (strongly agree).

Employment competition with Latinos. "More good jobs for Hispanics means fewer good jobs for people like me." This variable ranges from 0 (strongly disagree) to 3 (strongly agree).

Political competition with blacks. "The more influence Whites have in politics, the less influence people like me will have in politics." This variable ranges from 0 (strongly disagree) to 3 (strongly agree).

Political competition with Latinos. "The more influence Latinos have in politics, the less influence people like me will have in politics." This variable ranges from 0 (strongly disagree) to 3 (strongly agree).

2010 CCES

Economic commonality with whites. "Thinking about issues like job opportunities, educational attainment or income, how much do you have in common with the following groups [Whites] . . . nothing, little, some, a lot, not sure?" This variable ranges from 0 (nothing) to 3 (a lot).

Economic commonality with Latinos. "Thinking about issues like job opportunities, educational attainment or income, how much do you have in common with the following groups [Latinos] . . . nothing, little, some, a lot, not sure?" This variable ranges from 0 (nothing) to 3 (a lot).

Independent Variables

Social Contact. I explore social contact in a variety of settings: having Latino/White friends, coworkers, and/or neighbors. Friendship with Latinos is measured on a scale from 0 to 2 where 0 represents other/no Latino friends, 1 denotes mixed Latino friends, and 2 represents mostly Latino friends. The same scale is used for having Latino coworkers or neighbors. Measures of social contact with whites are assessed in the same way. The questions used in the construction of the social interaction variables are: "How would you describe the ethnic mix of your friends? Would you say your friends are mostly White, mostly black, mostly Hispanic, mostly Asian, or mixed? How would you describe the ethnic mix of your coworkers? Would you say your coworkers are mostly White, mostly Black, mostly Hispanic, mostly Asian, or mixed? How would you describe the ethnic mix of your neighbors? Would you say your neighbors are mostly White, mostly Black, mostly Hispanic, mostly Asian or mixed?"

CONTEXT VARIABLES

Racial context. I collected racial context data from the U.S. Census website and merged these data to the 2004 NPS data set to assess the effects of racial context on black racial attitudes ("Stata FAQ" n.d.). I include three measures of racial context at the county level in my models: percent Latino, percent black, and percent white. These data are U.S. Census estimates for the year 2004.

Economic context. I also collected economic context data at the county level from the U.S. Census website and merged it to both data sets. For the models using 2004 NPS data, my measure of economic context are the percentage of individuals of all ages who live in poverty in 2007, residents' educational attainment (percentage of individuals over twenty-five years of age who have a high school degree) from 2000, and the percentage of unemployed individuals in 2008. These data are estimates provided by the U.S. Census Bureau State and County QuickFacts. Since I could not obtain contextual data at the county level exactly for the year 2004, I relied on data from the closest year or set of years as a proxy for the ideal measures. It is important to note that given that the Great Recession began in 2008, I account for the poverty rate in 2007. Yet, the only unemployment rate data that I was able to obtain was for the year 2008 so I include these data in my models.

Institutional context. In order to examine the effects of institutional context on white attitudes toward Latinos and blacks, I collected state congressional district data from the 2004 *Almanac of American Politics.* The 2004 district data was merged with the 2004 NPS data set by county. The race of the legislator is measured for having a Latino legislator or a black legislator. These measures are coded dichotomously with a 1 indicating that an individual is represented by a Latino/black/minority and 0 indicating otherwise. Whether an individual resides in a majority-minority district is also measured dichotomously where 1 represents residing in a majority-minority district and 0 represents otherwise. I measure the political ideology of a district through the percentage of district votes cast in favor of the Democratic candidate in the previous presidential election (percentage of votes for Al Gore for the 2000 presidential election for the NPS models). This variable ranges from 0 to 1. Another measure of institutional context is whether the state in which an individual resides has provisions for direct democracy, that is, ballot initiatives and/or political referenda. This information was obtained from the National Council of State Legislatures and the Initiative and Referendum Institute at the University of Southern California. This measure is also coded dichotomously where 1 indicates that the respondent resides in a state that has ballot initiatives and/or political referenda and 0 indicates otherwise.

CONTROL VARIABLES

Perceptions of discrimination. "Do you think the following groups face a lot of discrimination, some, a little, or no discrimination at all: Whites?" This variable ranges from 0 (no discrimination) to 3 (a lot).

Negative stereotype of Latinos. "Where would you rate Hispanics in general on a scale of 1 to 7, where 1 indicates lazy, 7 means hardworking?" This variable ranges from 0 (hardworking) to 6 (lazy).

Negative stereotype of blacks. "Where would you rate Whites in general on a scale of 1 to 7, where 1 indicates lazy, 7 means hardworking?" This variable ranges from 0 (hardworking) to 6 (lazy).

South. Residence in a southern state (Alabama, Arkansas, Georgia, Kentucky, Louisiana, Mississippi, North Carolina, South Carolina, Tennessee,

Virginia, or West Virginia). This variable is measured dichotomously, 0 (other) to 1 (residence in a southern state).

Age. Ranging from 17 to 100 years.

Education. "What is the highest grade or level of school that you have completed?" This variable ranges from 0 (less than a high school degree) to 4 (graduate school).

Household income (log). "How much did you and all the members of your family living with you receive in the year 2003 before taxes?" I obtained the log (mathematical data transformation) of the income values.

Partisan identification. This variable ranges from −3 (strong Democrat) to 3 (strong Republican).

2010 CCES

Social contact. Similar to the LNS, the 2010 CCES allows me to explore blacks' social interaction in a variety of settings: having Latino/white friends, coworkers, and/or neighbors. The coding of these measures is the same as those for the 2004 NPS variables. The questions used in the construction of the social interaction variables are: "How would you describe the racial/ethnic mix for each of the following groups in your life? (Mostly Black, Mostly White, Mostly Latino, Mostly Asian, Mixed, Not sure)."

Subjective racial context. Unlike with the 2004 NPS, the 2010 CCES allows me to examine the effects of subjective context (i.e., perceived number of whites/Latinos in blacks' counties) on blacks' racial attitudes. "Thinking about the levels of diversity in the county in which you live, how many of each of the following groups would you say live in your county?" This variable is measured on a scale from 0 to 3 where 0 represents no whites/Latinos and 3 represents a lot of whites/Latinos.

Chapter 7

Focus Group Questions

1. Here in New Orleans, a large portion of the population is African American. How much contact do you have with blacks? For instance, do you have any neighbors, coworkers, or friends who are black?

2. How much in common do you have with blacks?

3. Do you think that competition exists between you and blacks? How much?

4. Based on the contact that you have with blacks, how does this affect your attitudes toward blacks? For instance, does contact affect how much in common and competition that you have with blacks? If so, in a positive way or negative way?

5. Now when it comes to another minority group in New Orleans, Hispanics, how much contact do you have with Hispanics? For instance, do you have any neighbors, coworkers, or friends who are Hispanic?

6. How much in common do you have with Hispanics/Latinos?

7. Do you think that competition exists between you and Hispanics/Latinos? How much?

8. Based on the contact that you have with Hispanics/Latinos, how does this affect your attitudes toward Hispanics? For instance, does contact affect your commonality and competition with whites? If so, in a positive way or a negative way?

9. How do you envision the future of race relations between you and blacks? Peaceful? Cooperative? Competitive?

10. How do you envision the future of race relations between you and Hispanics? Peaceful? Cooperative? Competitive?

Well, that concludes our discussion. Is there anything else that you would like to add about your attitudes toward blacks and Hispanics?

Questionnaire

First name or alias _____

Gender _____ Age _____ Employed (please circle): Yes No

Occupation _____

Income (please check):

_____ $10,000 or less   _____ $55,001–$70,000

_____ $10,001–$25,000   _____ $70,001–$85,000

_____ $25,001–$40,000   _____ $85,001 or over

_____ $40,001–$55,000

Education (please check):

_____ Elementary School (K–5th grade) but did not graduate

_____ Elementary School diploma

_____ Middle School (6–8th) but did not graduate

_____ Middle School diploma

_____ High School (9–12th) but did not graduate

_____ High School diploma

_____ College but did not graduate

_____ College diploma

_____ Graduate school or higher

_____On a scale from 0 to 10 (10 having a lot in common and 0 having nothing in common), how much in common do you think you have with Hispanics/Latinos?

_____On a scale from 0 to 10 (10 having a lot in common and 0 having nothing in common), how much in common do you think you have with blacks?

_____On a scale from 0 to 10 (10 having a lot of competition and 0 having no competition), how much competition do you think exists between you and Hispanics/Latinos?

_____On a scale from 0 to 10 (10 having a lot of competition and 0 having no competition), how much competition do you think exists between you and blacks?

Notes

Introduction

1. I employ the terms "black" and "African American" interchangeably in this study.

2. Some may argue that self-selection (such as having the opportunity to choose one's friends or neighbors) creates biased results. Contact, however, is still a key determinant of racial attitudes even after controlling for self-selection of the respondents (Powers and Ellison 1995; Oliver and Wong 2003; Pettigrew and Tropp 2006). Specifically, Pettigrew and Tropp (2006) conduct a meta-analysis exploring the effect of contact on prejudice and find that a negative relationship between contact and intergroup prejudice sustains even when taking into consideration participant selection. Moreover, Oliver and Wong (2003) assert that self-selection does not influence the relationship between contact (neighborhood ethnic mix) and attitudes toward out-groups. Although whites are the only group that participates in racial self-selection, white self-selection does not completely explain prejudice toward out-groups (578).

3. When referring to the New Orleans metro area in this circumstance, I am referring to Orleans and Jefferson parishes. A parish is the equivalent of a county.

1. A Triangular Theory of Contact, Context, and Identification

1. Some may state that contact and perceptions of closeness are intertwined and very similar. If one has commonality with another, then he or she surely has contact with that individual. How can individuals perceive closeness with another without actuality getting to know them? I argue that closeness and contact are neither similar nor interrelated. For instance, individuals can perceive that they are close or have something in common with a racial group by learning about the group through other individuals, the news media, or a documentary and never once experiencing indirect or direct contact with that particular group.

2. The exception to this hypothesis is the relationship between descriptive representation and rivalry with blacks. I posit that Latinos who are represented by a Latino legislator are more likely to perceive competition with blacks. Descriptive representation is a more tenuous form of power for Latinos than other measures of political clout. Further, descriptive representation for Latinos can create divisions between blacks and Latinos.

3. I do not pose a directional hypothesis as to the relationship between residing in a predominantly Democratic district and Latinos' sense of commonality with blacks. Although living in a fairly strong Democratic setting can empower Latinos and decrease their closeness with blacks, African Americans' significant support and allegiance to the Democratic Party may influence the effect of living in a strong Democratic district and affinity toward blacks.

2. Latinos' Perceptions of African Americans and Whites

1. In addition to the CCES Common Content, I also make use of data from questions added to the study by Jim S. Krueger, Franciso I. Pedraza, and myself. While I recognize that there are other national surveys with large samples of Latinos that I could assess to test my theory, many of these data sets do not employ questions regarding perceptions of commonality, closeness, competition, and social interactions.

2. I acknowledge that the original collectors of these data and Inter-university Consortium for Political and Social Research (ICPSR) are not responsible for the use of this data or for interpretations or inferences based on such uses.

3. The correlation coefficient for economic and political commonality with whites is 0.510, and the coefficient for economic and political commonality with blacks is 0.441. The Cronbach's alpha score for the general commonality with blacks measure is 0.609, and the score for the general commonality with whites measure is 0.673.

4. The 2010 CCES does not assess Latinos' perception of commonality with other Latinos.

5. The 2010 CCES Latino employment competition with blacks and whites indexes range from 0 (strongly disagree that more jobs for blacks/whites results in fewer jobs for Latinos) to 4 (strongly agree). The mean of the competition with blacks measure for Latinos is 1.63, and the mean of the competition with whites measure is 1.96.

6. I checked for multicollinearity in all of the models estimated in this chapter by obtaining the variance inflation factor scores and did not find any problems.

7. The analyses in table 5 do not examine the effects of residing in a growing black county on Latinos' perceptions of commonality with blacks and whites because including this measure would create collinearity in my models and I do not develop hypotheses as to the specific effects of this measure on Latino' identification with blacks and whites.

8. The predicted probabilities for figures 3–7 were calculated holding all other predictors at their mean value and based on ordered logit estimates in tables 5–7 using CLARIFY software (King et al. 2000).

9. It is important to mention that other analyses reveal that foreign-born and native-born Latinos in a predominantly black setting are more likely to perceive commonality with blacks.

10. Due to space limitations, these findings are not reported in table 6. Please contact the author for further information regarding these results.

11. The models in table 7 do not examine the effects of residing in a growing white county on Latinos' perceptions of competition with blacks because including this measure would create collinearity in my models. Furthermore, I do not develop hypotheses as to the specific effects of this measure on Latinos' perceptions of competition with blacks.

12. The CCES predicted probabilities were calculated holding all other predictors at their mean value and based on ordered logit estimates in table 8 using CLARIFY software (King et al. 2000).

3. Latinos Discuss Race Relations in New Orleans

1. Jefferson Parish includes the following cities: Avondale, Bridge City, Grand Isle, Gretna, Harahan, Harvey, Jefferson, Kenner, Lafitte, Marrero, Metairie, River Ridge, Terrytown, Timberlane, Wagamann, and Westwego.

2. The New Orleans metro area includes the following seven parishes: Jefferson, Orleans, Plaquemines, St. Bernard, St. Tammany, St. Charles, St. John the Baptist, and Washington.

3. At the beginning of my research, I did not pose clear directional hypotheses and specific ideas of what I wanted the participants to say. I knew I wanted the participants to discuss their attitudes toward blacks and whites, so I led the discussion with a focus on social contact and perceptions of commonality and competition, and asked questions regarding the effect of contact on these perceptions.

4. I continued conducting focus groups until I began to receive little to no new information (ideas and arguments) by Latino participants (Krueger 1994, 88).

5. I obtained Institutional Review Board (IRB) approval from Louisiana State University (IRB E3570) to conduct this study.

6. In the beginning of each discussion, I gave the participants the opportunity to answer the questions in English or Spanish, and they chose Spanish. All of the focus groups were conducted in Spanish. Hence, I have done my best to translate the discussions directly and have changed a couple of words around in order not to lose the meaning behind the statements.

Before each focus group began, participants were asked to fill out questionnaires assessing their demographic characteristics in addition to their perceptions of commonality and competition with blacks and whites. As it pertains to Latinos' identification with African Americans, participants were asked to portray how much in common they have with blacks on a scale from 0 (nothing) to 10 (a lot in common). This attitudinal question along with others was placed in the questionnaire in order to obtain a better understanding of Latinos' attitudes since I may not be able to capture all of the participants' attitudes in an hour-long focus group. Another reason for doing this is to examine whether the actual focus group process influenced individuals' attitudes or the portrayal of their views. I can state that Latinos' attitudes toward African Americans and whites expressed in the questionnaires do not differ very much from what they expressed throughout the focus groups. Nonetheless, I noticed that a couple of participants were cautious in the ways that they talked about African Americans, particularly regarding how much they have in common with them. In two focus groups, there were some heated exchanges regarding blacks. Individuals who expressed negative stereotypes of blacks were corrected to a certain extent by one or two other participants who stated something like, "not all are like that" and "there are some blacks who are bad and some that are good." After that, the responses of those who expressed the negative views became more neutral. In general, the results of the survey questions reveal that Latino focus group participants have little to some commonality with blacks.

7. Each participant's name has been changed in order to protect his or her identity.

8. Even though being a minority does not directly imply being a victim of discrimination, some research suggests that it does (Bonilla-Silva 2004; Kaufmann 2007; Abrajano and Alvarez 2010).

9. After asking what participants meant by "cultural level," many said that it was adopting family values, having a drive to succeed and a desire to work hard, the way that they behave, and having a high education level.

10. Often referred to as "cultural level" in the focus groups.

4. African Americans' Perceptions of Latinos and Whites

1. A restrictive immigration ballot initiative in California that attempted to deny undocumented immigrants access to social services, nonemergency healthcare, and education.

2. Some studies exploring black/Latino relations discuss zero-sum situations where gains by one group result in losses for the other (Telles et al. 2011). Recent research such as Telles et al. (2011) and Hutchings et al. (2011) argue that zero-sum scenarios are less applicable to relations between Latinos and African Americans. Furthermore, there are numerous contextual and demographic factors—which I account for in this study—that affect whether this occurs.

3. While Allport (1954) stated that the necessary conditions for the positive effects of contact to occur are direct equal-status contact, cooperation, and opportunities for social-izing, several studies (Welch and Sigelman 1993; Pettigrew 1998; Welch et al. 2001; Oliver and Wong 2003) suggest that all of these conditions do not need to be met in order for contact to counteract negative attitudes. Oliver and Wong (2003) declare that even casual exposure to out-groups can decrease the in-group's racial resentment and competition.

4. I would provide a hypothesis for the relationship between residing in a largely black context and blacks' attitudes toward Latinos, but I am not able to do so because of prob-lems with collinearity since I control for the effects of percent white and percent Latino to test other hypotheses. Further, testing this relationship is not central to this study.

5. I would test and provide a hypothesis for the relationship between being descrip-tively represented and blacks' attitudes toward Latinos, but I am not able to do so because of problems with collinearity (I control for the effects of being represented by a Latino legislator to test other hypotheses). Testing this relationship is not central to this study.

6. The correlation coefficient between employment and political competition with Latinos is 0.44. The correlation coefficient between employment and political competi-tion with whites is 0.41. The Cronbach's alpha score for the variables that compose the general competition with Latinos measure is 0.61, and the alpha score for the variables that make up the general competition with whites measure is 0.58.

7. While I recognize that social contact can be greatly related to racial context, I differ-entiate the two in that context refers to individuals' surroundings at the larger aggregate level such as the county or the metropolitan area, and social contact refers to direct interactions such as at the neighborhood or workplace level (see Hutchings et al. 2011).

8. I checked for multicollinearity in all of this chapter's analyses by obtaining the variance inflation factor scores and did not find any problems.

9. To somewhat address the extent to which racial context moderates the relation-ship between economic context and blacks' attitudes toward Latinos as discussed by Gay (2006), I created an interaction measure of county percent Latino and the unemploy-ment rate. I examined its effect on blacks' perceptions of closeness and competition with Latinos, and found that it is not a statistically significant predictor of black attitudes.

10. I conducted other analyses examining the effect of a change in Latino population (the difference in percent Latino in county between the years 2004 and 2000) to deter-mine if a direct growth in the number of Latinos in a county structure black attitudes. My results for these analyses were quite similar to those presented in table 9.

11. The predicted probabilities for figures 11–16 were calculated holding all other predictors at their mean value and based on ordered logit estimates in tables 9–12 using CLARIFY software (King et al. 2000).

12. I conducted other analyses examining the effect of a change in Latino population (the difference in percent Latino in county between the years 2004 and 2000) to deter-mine if a direct growth in the number of Latinos in a county structures black attitudes. My results for these analyses were quite similar to those presented in table 10.

I do not control for the effects of leading predictors of blacks' racial attitudes in my analyses since they depressed the sample size of the model significantly, and I am restricted in the number of variables that I can control for in each model. Table 11 presents the general competition models controlling for the effects of leading predictors on black racial attitudes.

13. I am only able to analyze blacks' economic competition with blacks since CCES data does not analyze blacks' political competition with Latinos and whites.

5. African Americans Discuss Race Relations in New Orleans

1. At the beginning of my research, I did not pose clear directional hypotheses and specific ideas of what I wanted the participants to say. I wanted the participants to discuss their attitudes toward Latinos and whites so the interviewer led the discussion with a focus on social contact, perceptions of commonality, and competition, and asked questions regarding the relationship between social contact and their perceptions.

2. Given that I am a light-skinned Latina and thus interviewer effects can influence the study's findings, I hired a dark-skinned African American professor with significant experience leading focus groups to conduct the interviews. I was not present during the focus group discussions. The only interaction that the focus group participants had with me was during the recruitment process, providing them directions to the study room (if necessary), and at the end of the focus group when they were compensated. The limited interaction that the participants had with me did not seem to affect the answers that they provided to the interviewer. It is important to emphasize, however, that other African American participants' long exposure to me did not seem to affect their responses. The interviewer and I have collaborated on another focus group project in which we conducted two pilot focus groups where she was the interviewer and I was present in the room for three-quarters of the interview as the note-taker. After I left the room, the interviewer continued the focus group discussion as if nothing occurred. Her last question examined whether the presence of the note-taker influenced individuals' responses. The participants in both pilot focus groups strongly denied that the presence of the note-taker influenced their responses.

3. We conducted focus groups until we began to receive little new information (ideas and arguments; Krueger 1994, 88). It is common for focus group studies to have small sample sizes since an insignificant amount of new information emerges after the first few interviews (Morgan 1996, 144–46).

4. I obtained IRB approval from the IRB office at Wake Forest University and Loyola University New Orleans (IRB 00001194) to conduct this study.

5. I speculate that the employment rate of the participants is lower because individuals who work full-time jobs were less willing and able to participate in a focus group than those who are unemployed.

6. Before each focus group began, participants were asked to fill out questionnaires assessing their demographic characteristics as well as their perceptions of commonality and competition with Latinos and whites. These attitudinal questions along with others were placed in a questionnaire in order to obtain a comprehensive view of black attitudes since I may not be able to capture all of the participants' attitudes in an hour-long focus group. Another reason for doing this is to examine whether the actual focus group process influenced individuals' responses to the interview questions. I can state that blacks' racial dispositions expressed in the questionnaires do not differ very much from what they

expressed throughout the focus groups. Still, I noticed that a couple of participants were cautious in the ways that they talked about how much in common and how much competition existed between blacks and Latinos. In two focus groups, there were some heated exchanges as to whether Latinos were a minority status group like blacks or whether they had greater socioeconomic clout than blacks, since Latinos disadvantaged blacks economically and whites favored Latinos over blacks. Individuals who believed that Latinos were like blacks were corrected a few times by one or two other participants who argued that Latinos were taking jobs away from blacks, that whites preferred Latino employees over blacks, and that Latinos thought that they were better than blacks. After the heated exchanges, those who believed that Latinos were very similar to blacks were less likely to express their views thoroughly to other questions. Nonetheless, the results of the survey questions as well as the focus group discussions generally reveal that black focus group participants have greater commonality and competition with whites than with Latinos.

7. Each participant's name has been changed in order to protect his or her identity.

6. Whites' Perceptions of Latinos and African Americans

1. It is important to recognize that the previous chapter on black racial attitudes, as well as several studies on racial attitudes and coalition behavior, suggest that Latinos and blacks do not clearly regard each other as natural allies and coalition partners (McClain et al. 2006; Kaufmann 2007; McClain et al. 2011; Morin et al. 2011).

2. While it may be fruitful to explore whites' perceptions of closeness and competition with Latinos relative to those of other whites, in order to explore how whites regard Latinos in comparison to other whites, creating a relative scale of Latino/white closeness and black/white closeness is statistically not possible given that the appropriate Cronbach's alpha scores for these scales (Latino/white closeness: 0.25; black/white closeness: 0.31) reveal that it is not appropriate to create an additive scale for whites' perceptions of closeness with Latinos/blacks relative to those of whites. This suggests that whites may not associate their views toward their racial counterparts with those toward Latinos and, thus, regard Latinos differently than whites.

3. Some studies exploring white/black/Latino relations discuss zero-sum situations where gains by one group result in losses for the other (Telles et al. 2011). Recent research such as Telles et al. and Hutchings et al. (2011) argues that zero-sum scenarios are less applicable to relations between Latinos and whites. Furthermore, there are numerous contextual and demographic factors—which I account for in this study—that affect whether this occurs.

4. While Allport (1954) stated that the necessary conditions for the positive effects of contact to occur are direct equal-status contact, cooperation, and opportunities for socializing, several studies (Pettigrew 1998; Welch et al. 2001; Oliver and Wong 2003) suggest that all of these conditions do not need to be met in order for contact to counteract negative attitudes.

5. In this study, "nonwhites" refers to Latinos and African Americans.

6. I would provide a hypothesis for the relationship between residing in a largely white context and whites' attitudes toward African Americans, but I am not able to do so because of problems with collinearity since I control for the effects of percent black in a county to test other hypotheses. Further, testing this relationship is not central to this study.

7. The correlation between economic and political competition with Latinos is 0.55.

The correlation between economic and political competition with blacks is 0.50. The Cronbach's alpha score for the economic and political competition with Latinos measure is 0.72, and the alpha score for the economic and political competition with blacks measure is 0.67.

8. The Cronbach alpha score (0.67) reveals that it is appropriate to create a relative Latino/black closeness scale.

9. The Cronbach's alpha score (0.84) reveals that it is appropriate to create a relative Latino/black commonality measure.

10. The Cronbach's alpha score (0.89) reveals that it is appropriate to create a relative Latino/black competition measure.

11. This scale does not range from –4 to 4 because apparently there are no whites who perceive strong competition with blacks and minimal competition with Latinos. The Cronbach's alpha score (0.94) reveals that it is appropriate to create a relative Latino/black employment competition measure.

12. On a 0 to 3 scale of perceptions of closeness, the mean for whites' closeness with other whites was 2.3 while their mean scores for closeness with Latinos (1.6) and African Americans (1.8) were lower.

13. While it may be fruitful to create a relative scale of Latino/white closeness and black/white closeness, I am not able to do so since Cronbach's alpha scores for these scales reveal that whites' closeness with Latinos and whites and closeness with blacks and whites are not closely related.

14. Whites' perceptions of competition with other whites were not assessed by the 2004 NPS and the 2010 CCES, therefore I am not able to report on these attitudes.

15. I checked for multicollinearity in all of the models by obtaining the variance inflation factor scores and did not find any problems.

16. I recognize that the sample size indicated in all of the tables in this chapter is lower than the sample size of the original data set. The numbers decreased since not all respondents chose to answer the questions (e.g., household income), some did not know the answers to the questions or said they did not apply, and not all were asked the same questions.

17. The predicted probabilities for figures 19–23 were calculated holding all other predictors at their mean value and based on ordered logit estimates in tables 13–15 using CLARIFY software (King et al. 2000).

18. In other analyses, I controlled for the effects of percent change in Latino and black populations from 2000 to 2004 and found comparable results.

19. While I recognize that the percent Latino variable does not have a natural zero point, in the next few paragraphs I discuss findings from predicted probabilities for closeness with Latinos in order to do a better job of shedding light on the extent to which education context conditions the relationship between racial context and whites' perceptions of Latinos. I do the same for the interaction term including percent black and education context.

20. Given that the standard errors for the percent Latino measure is based on the point where education context is zero, and the standard error for the percent high school degree measure is based on the point where percent Latino is zero, the standard error for the percent Latino term is larger than it is over the observed range of measures since it does not have a natural zero point. The same applies for the standard error of percent black in model 2 of this table (see Branton and Jones 2005, 367).

21. Please contact the author for further information about these analyses.

22. Unlike the 2004 NPS, the CCES assesses whites' perceptions of the number of Latinos, whites, and blacks in the counties in which they live. I do not test my racial and economic threat hypothesis with these data and instead focus on the extent to which subjective context structures white's racial attitudes. Please contact the author for further information about these analyses.

23. I do not control for the effects of having a black friend in these models because of high multicollinearity. After removing the black friend coefficient from these models, however, the variance inflation score for each model reveals that I have very minimal collinearity in my analyses.

24. I checked for multicollinearity in all of the models by obtaining the variance inflation factor scores and did not find any problems.

25. While I recognize that the percent Latino variable does not have a natural zero point, in the next few paragraphs I discuss findings of predicted probabilities for closeness with Latinos in order to do a better job of shedding light on the extent to which education context conditions the relationship between racial context and whites' perceptions of Latinos. I do the same for the interaction term including percent black and education context.

26. Given that the standard errors for the percent Latino measure is based on the point where education context is zero, and the standard error for the percent high school degree measure is based on the point where percent Latino is zero, the standard error for the percent Latino term is larger than it is over the observed range of measures since it does not have a natural zero point. The same applies for the standard error of percent black in model 2 of this table (see Branton and Jones 2005, 367).

27. For further information about these analyses, contact the author.

28. For further information about these analyses, contact the author.

7. Whites' Perceptions of an Established Minority and a New Minority in New Orleans

1. A significant portion of Orleans Parish is the city of New Orleans.

2. In this study, "nonwhites" refers to Latinos and blacks.

3. I conducted focus groups until I began to receive little new information (ideas and arguments; Krueger 1994, 88). It is common for focus group studies to have small sample sizes since an insignificant amount of new information emerges after the first few interviews (Morgan 1996, 144–146).

4. I obtained Institutional Review Board (IRB) approval from the IRB office at Louisiana State University (IRB E3570) to conduct this study.

5. Before each focus group began, participants were asked to fill out questionnaires assessing their demographic characteristics as well as their perceptions of commonality and competition with Latinos and whites. These attitudinal questions along with others were placed in a questionnaire in order to obtain a comprehensive view of black attitudes since I may not be able to capture all of the participants' attitudes in an hour-long focus group. Another reason for doing this is to examine whether the actual focus group process influenced individuals' responses to the interview questions. I can state that whites' attitudes expressed in the questionnaires did not differ very much from what they expressed throughout the focus groups, yet I noticed that several participants were cautious in the ways that they talked about African Americans in general. In two focus groups, there

were a few friendly disagreements regarding blacks. When one individual (over the age of forty) described blacks as lazy and as taking advantage of the resources given to them, another (younger than thirty years old) responded by stating that some whites are racist and do not understand why blacks act the ways that they do. In another focus group, after hearing that blacks should not wear their pants so far down and that they are lazy when speaking, one individual (younger than thirty years old) responded by stating that blacks have a legitimate reason for wearing their pants down and for speaking in a lazy manner. Moreover, for many years, blacks have been "neglected, they've been put down and forced in the ghettos, projects." Throughout the focus groups, younger generations seemed to have less discriminatory views of blacks than older individuals.

6. Each participant's name has been changed in order to protect his or her identity.

7. While I am a light-skinned Latina, I do not think that my physical appearance affected respondents' answers in any way. Most individuals believe that I am white when they meet me. Further, focus group participants did not ask me any questions about my ethnic origins or background, and seemed quite comfortable expressing strong negative stereotypes of Latinos and blacks in my presence.

8. It is important to note that in other parts of the focus groups, several participants mentioned that they are trying to learn Spanish and try to speak it, but others stated that Latinos must learn English.

9. This finding is supported to a certain extent by my quantitative results of whites' perceptions of closeness with Latinos where I find that closeness with blacks and whites has a positive effect on whites' closeness with Latinos. Some people may think of closeness in terms of having specific attributes or experiences in common and not about race as a determining factor.

10. I recognize that this comment may decrease the applicability of this study's results for the entire United States and be more relevant to race relations in the South.

11. It is important for me to mention that all of the individuals who mentioned this were under thirty years of age. Hence, age may play a mitigating factor in determining whites' sense of competition with blacks and whites' awareness or recognition of white-on-black discrimination. In addition, this statement is supported by my statistical models of whites' job and political competition with Latinos and blacks. The older whites are, the more job and political competition they believe they have with Latinos and blacks.

12. I find that southern and non-southern whites sense marginally greater competition with Latinos than African Americans.

References

Abrajano, Marisa A., and R. Michael Alvarez. 2010. *New Faces, New Voices: The Hispanic Electorate in America.* Princeton, N.J.: Princeton University Press.

Allport, Gregory W. 1954. *The Nature of Prejudice.* New York: Doubleday Books.

Alvarez, Lizette. 2012. "Justice Department Investigation Is Sought in Florida Teenager's Shooting Death." *New York Times,* March 16.

Alvarez, Lizette, and Cara Buckley. 2013. "Zimmerman Is Acquitted in Trayvon Martin Killing." *New York Times,* July 13.

Ansolabehere, Stephen. 2010. "CCES Common Content, 2010." Version 3. http://hdl .handle.net/1902.1/17705.

Banducci, Susan A., Todd Donovan, and Jeffrey A. Karp. 2005. "Effects of Minority Representation on Political Attitudes and Participation." In *Diversity in Democracy: Minority Representation in the United States,* edited by Gary M. Segura and Shaun Bowler, 193–215. Charlottesville: University of Virginia Press.

Barone, Michael, and Richard E. Cohen. 2005. *The Almanac of American Politics, 2006.* Chicago: National Journal Group.

Barone, Michael, Richard E. Cohen, and Jackie Koszczuk. 2009. *The Almanac of American Politics, 2010.* Chicago: National Journal Group.

Barreto, Matt. 2012. "Who Out-Latino'd Who?: Assessing the RNC and DNC Conventions' Latino Outreach." Latino Decisions, September 12. www.latinodecisions.com /blog/2012/09/12/who-out-latinod-who-assessing-the-rnc-and-dnc-conventions -latino-outreach/.

Barreto, Matt. 2013. "What the GOP Has to Gain—and Lose—among Latinos When It Comes to Immigration Reform." Latino Decisions, March 21. www.latinodecisions .com/blog/2013/03/21/what-the-gop-has-to-gain-and-lose-among-latinos-when -it-comes-to-immigration-reform/.

Barreto, Matt, and Gabriel Sanchez. 2008. "Social and Political Competition between Latinos and Blacks: Exposing Myths, Uncovering New Realities." Paper presented at the Latino National Survey Conference, Ithaca, New York.

Bishin, Ben, Karen Kaufmann, and Daniel Stevens. 2011. "Turf Wars: Local Context and Latino Political Development." *Urban Affairs Review* 48(1): 111–37.

Blow, Charles. 2012. "The Curious Case of Trayvon Martin." *New York Times,* March 16.

Blumer, Herbert. 1958. "Race Prejudice as a Sense of Group Position." *Pacific Sociological Review* 1: 3–7.

Bobo, Lawrence D. 1999. "Prejudice as Group Position: Microfoundations of a Sociological Approach to Racism and Race Relations." *Journal of Social Issues* 55(3): 445–72.

Bobo, Lawrence D., and Franklin D. Gilliam, Jr. 1990. "Race, Sociopolitical Participation, and Black Empowerment." *American Political Science Review* 84(2): 377–93.

Bobo, Lawrence, and Vincent L. Hutchings. 1996. "Perceptions of Racial Group Competition: Extending Blumer's Theory of Group Position to a Multiracial Social Context." *American Sociological Review* 61(6): 951–72.

Bonilla-Silva, Eduardo. 2004. "From Bi-racial to Tri-racial: Towards a New System of Racial Stratification in the USA." *Ethnic and Racial Studies* 27: 931–50.

Borjas, George. 1999. "The Economic Analysis of Immigration." In *Handbook of Labor Economics*, edited by Orley Ashenfelter and David Card, 3A:1697–1760. New York: North-Holland.

Branton, Regina P., and Bradford Jones. 2005. "Reexamining Racial Attitudes: The Conditional Relationship between Diversity and Socioeconomic Environment." *American Journal of Political Science* 49(2): 359–72.

Brians, C. L., L. Willnat, J. B. Manheim, and R. C. Rich. 2010. *Empirical Political Analysis*, 8th edition. New York: Pearson.

Carrero, Jacquellena. 2012. "Latinos Elected to State Legislatures in 36 States." NBC Latino, November 9. http://nbclatino.com/2012/11/09/latinos-elected-to-state-legislatures-in-36-states/.

Casellas, Jason. 2011. *Latino Representation in State Houses and Congress*. New York: Cambridge University Press.

Citrin, Jack, Beth Reingold, and Donald P. Green. 1990. "American Identity and the Politics of Ethnic Change." *Journal of Politics* 52(4): 1124–54.

Dawson, Michael. 1994. *Behind the Mule: Race and Class in African-American Politics*. Princeton, N.J.: Princeton University Press.

DeNavas-Walt, Carmen, Bernadette D. Proctor, and Jessica C. Smith. 2011. "Income, Poverty, and Health Insurance Coverage in the United States: 2010." U.S. Census Bureau, September. www.census.gov/hhes/www/income/.

Dunham, Richard. 2013. "Cruz Takes His Place in Senate, History." *Houston Chronicle*, January 3.

Eaton, Leslie. 2005. "Storm and Crisis: The Workers in Louisiana, Worker Influx Causes Ill Will." *New York Times*, November 4.

———. 2006. "Study Sees Increase in Illegal Hispanic Workers in New Orleans." *New York Times*, June 8.

Ellison, Christopher G., and Daniel A. Powers. 1994. "The Contact Hypothesis and Racial Attitudes among Black Americans." *Social Science Quarterly* 75:385–400.

Espenshade, Thomas J., and Katherine Hempstead. 1996. "Contemporary American Attitudes toward U.S. Immigration." *International Migration Review* 30(2): 535–70.

Fernandez, Valeria. 2010. "Thousands Protest SB1070 in Phoenix Rally." *La Prensa San Diego*, June 4.

———. 2011. "SB 1070 Casts Shadow on Arizona's New Anti-Immigrant Bills." *La Prensa San Diego*, March 25.

Fetzer, Joel S. 2000. *Public Attitudes toward Immigration in the United States, France and Germany.* Cambridge: Cambridge University Press.

Fraga, Luis R., John A. Garcia, Rodney Hero, Michael Jones-Correa, Valerie Martinez-Ebers, and Gary M. Segura. 2006. Latino National Survey (computer file). ICPSR20862–v1. Miami: Geoscape International. Ann Arbor, Mich.: Inter-university Consortium for Political and Social Research, 2008-05-27.

———. 2010. *Latino Lives in America: Making It Home.* Philadelphia: Temple University Press.

Fussell, Elizabeth. 2007. Mexican Mobile Consulate Survey. http://libarts.wsu.edu /soc/people/fussell/Final%20Report-Mexican%20consulate%20survey.pdf.

Gay, Claudine. 2001. "The Effect of Black Congressional Representation on Political Participation." *American Political Science Review* 95(3): 589–602.

Gay, Claudine. 2006. "Seeing Difference: The Effect of Economic Disparity on Black Attitudes toward Latinos." *American Journal of Political Science* 50(4): 982–97.

Gilliam, Frank, and Karen Kaufmann. 1998. "Is There an Empowerment Life Cycle?: Long-Term Black Empowerment and Its Influence on Voter Participation." *Urban Affairs Review* 33(6): 741–66.

Glaser, James. 1994. "Back to the Black Belt: Racial Environment and White Racial Attitudes in the South." *Journal of Politics* 56: 21–41.

Gomez, Alan. 2012. "Hispanics Feel Harassed under Alabama's Immigration Law." *USA Today*, July 22.

Goyette, Braden. 2013. "Cheerios Commercial Featuring Mixed Race Family Gets Racist Backlash (VIDEO)." Huffington Post, May 31. www.huffingtonpost.com /2013/05/31/cheerios-commercial-racist-backlash_n_3363507.html.

Guidi, Ruxandra. 2012. "Kendrec McDade's Shooting Revives Longstanding Tensions between Blacks and Latinos in LA." Southern California Public Radio, April 11. www.scpr.org/news/2012/04/11/31987/tensions-between-blacks-and-latinos -l-and-difficul/.

Hero, Rodney E., and Caroline J. Tolbert. 2004. "Minority Voices and Citizen Attitudes about Government Responsiveness in the American States: Do Social and Institutional Context Matter?" *British Journal of Political Science* 34: 109–21.

Hibbing, John R., and Elizabeth Theiss-Morse. 1995. *Congress as Public Enemy.* New York: Cambridge University Press.

Hood, M. V., III, and Irwin L. Morris. 1997. "Amigo o Enemigo?: Context, Attitudes, and Anglo Public Opinion toward Immigration." *Social Science Quarterly* 78: 309–23.

———. 1998. "Give Us Your Tired, Your Poor, . . . But Make Sure They Have a Green Card: The Effects of Documented and Undocumented Migrant Context on Anglo Opinion toward Immigration." *Political Behavior* 20: 1–15.

Hopkins, Daniel. 2010. "Politicized Places: Explaining Where and When Immigrants Provoke Local Opposition." *American Political Science Review* 104(1): 40–60.

Horwitz, Sari. 2012. "George Zimmerman Is Charged with 2nd-Degree Murder in Trayvon Martin Shooting." *Washington Post*, April 11.

Hunter, M. L. 2002. "If You're Light You're Alright: Light Skin Color as Social Capital for Women of Color." *Gender and Society* 16(2): 175–93.

Hutchings, Vincent L., Cara Wong, James Jackson, and Ronald E. Brown. 2011. "Explaining Perceptions of Competitive Threat in a Multiracial Context." In *Race, Reform, and Regulation of the Electoral Process: Recurring Puzzles in American Democracy*, edited by Guy-Uriel E. Charles, Heather K. Gerken, and Michael S. Kang, 52–74. Cambridge: Cambridge University Press.

Jackson, James S., Vincent L. Hutchings, Ronald Brown, and Cara Wong. 2004. National Politics Study. ICPSR24483–v1. Ann Arbor, Mich.: Inter-university Consortium for Political and Social Research, 2009-03-23.

Johnson, James H., Jr., Martin C. Farrell, and Chandra Guinn. 1997. "Immigration Reform and the Browning of America: Tensions, Conflicts and Community Instability in Metropolitan Los Angeles." *International Migration Review* 31(4): 1055–95.

Jones-Correa, Michael. 2011. "Commonalities, Competition and Linked Fate." In Telles, Sawyer, and Rivera-Salgado, *Just Neighbors?*, 63–95.

Kaufmann, Karen. 2003. "Cracks in the Rainbow: Group Commonality as a Basis for Latino and African-American Political Coalitions." *Political Research Quarterly* 56: 199–210.

———. 2007. "Immigration and the Future of Black Power in U.S. Cities." *Du Bois Review* 4(1): 79–96.

Kim, Claire Jean. 2000. *Bitter Fruit: The Politics of Black–Korean Conflict in New York City*. New Haven, Conn.: Yale University Press.

King, Gary, Michael Tomz, and Jason Wittenberg. 2000. "Making the Most of Statistical Analyses: Improving Interpretation and Presentation." *American Journal of Political Science* 44(2): 341–55.

Kochhar, Rakesh. 2012. "Employment Gains by Race, Ethnicity, Gender and Nativity: The Demographics of the Jobs Recovery." Pew Hispanic Center. www.pewhispanic.org/2012/03/21/ii-the-economic-recovery-for-hispanics-and-non-hispanics/.

Krueger, Richard A. 1994. *Focus Groups: A Practical Guide for Applied Research*. Thousand Oaks, Calif.: Sage Publications.

Latino Decisions. 2012a. "CAP/AV/LD SB1070 Supreme Court Decision Poll–July 19." Poll with Center for American Progress and America's Voice. www.latinodecisions.com/recent-polls/2012-poll/.

Latino Decisions. 2012b. "Obama Wins 75% of Latino Vote, Marks Historic Latino Influence in Presidential Election." November 11. www.latinodecisions.com/blog/2012/11/07/obama-wins-75-of-latino-vote-marks-historic-latino-influence-in-presidential-election/.

Levin, D., and M. R. Banaji. 2006. "Distortions in the Perceived Lightness of Faces: The Role of Race Categories." *Journal of Experimental Psychology* 135:501–12.

Liptak, Adam. 2012. "Blocking Parts of Arizona Law, Justices Allow Its Centerpiece." *New York Times*, June 25.

Lopez, Mark Hugo, and Ana Gonzalez-Barrera. 2013. "Inside the 2012 Latino Electorate." Pew Research Hispanic Trends Project, June 3. www.pewhispanic.org/2013/06/03/inside-the-2012-latino-electorate/.

Lopez, Mark Hugo, Ana Gonzalez-Barrera, and Danielle Cuddington. 2013. "Diverse Origins: The Nation's 14 Largest Hispanic-Origin Groups." Pew Research Hispanic Trends Project, June 19. www.pewhispanic.org/2013/06/19/diverse-origins-the-nations-14-largest-hispanic-origin-groups/.

Mack, Vicki, and Elaine Ortiz. 2013. "Who Lives in New Orleans and the Metro Area Now?" Greater New Orleans Community Data Center. www.gnocdc.org/Demographics/index.html.

Mansbridge, Jane. 1999. "Should Blacks Represent Blacks and Women Represent Women?: A Contingent Yes." *Journal of Politics* 61(3): 628–57.

Marrow, Helen. 2011. *New Destination Dreaming: Immigration, Race and Legal Status in the Rural American South.* Stanford, Calif.: Stanford University Press.

McClain, Paula D. 1996. "Coalition and Competition: Patterns of Black-Latino Relations in Urban Politics." In *The Politics of Minority Coalitions,* edited by Wilbur C. Rich, 53–63. Westport, Conn.: Praeger.

McClain, Paula D., Niambi M. Carter, Victoria M. DeFrancesco Soto, Monique L. Lyle, Jeffrey D. Grynaviski, Shayla C. Nunnally, Thomas J. Scotto, J. Alan Kendrick, Gerald F. Lackey, and Kendra Davenport Cotton. 2006. "Racial Distancing in a Southern City: Latino Immigrants' Views of Black Americans." *Journal of Politics* 68(3): 571–84.

McClain, Paula D., and Albert K. Karnig. 1990. "Black and Hispanic Socioeconomic and Political Competition." *American Political Science Review* 84(2): 535–45.

McClain, Paula D., Gerald F. Lackey, Efren O. Perez, Niambi M. Carter, Jessica Johnson Carew, Eugene Walton, Jr., Candis Watts Smith, Monique L. Lyle, and Shayla C. Nunnally. 2011. "Intergroup Relations in Three Southern Cities." In Telles, Sawyer, and Rivera-Salgado, *Just Neighbors?*, 201–41.

McClain, Paula D., Monique L. Lyle, Niambi M. Carter, Victoria M. DeFrancesco Soto, Gerald F. Lackey, Kendra Davenport Cotton, Shayla C. Nunnally, Thomas J. Scotto, Jeffrey D. Grynaviski, and J. Alan Kendrick. 2007. "Black Americans and Latino Immigrants in a Southern City: Friendly Neighbors or Economic Competitors?" *Du Bois Review* 4(1): 97–117.

McClain, Paula D., Monique L. Lyle, Efrén O. Peréz, Jessica Johnson Carew, Gerald F. Lackey, and Shayla C. Nunnally. 2009. "Black and White Americans and Latino Immigrants: A Preliminary Look at Attitudes in Three Southern Cities." Paper presented at the American Political Science Association Conference, Toronto.

McClain, Paula D., and Joseph Stewart, Jr. 2002. *"Can We All Get Along?": Racial and Ethnic Minorities in American Politics.* Boulder, Col.: Westview Press.

———. 2013. *"Can We All Get Along?"*: *Racial and Ethnic Minorities in American Politics*. 2nd edition. Boulder, Col.: Westview Press.

Meier, Kenneth J., and Joseph Stewart, Jr. 1991. "Cooperation and Conflict in Multi-racial School Districts." *Journal of Politics* 53(4): 1123–33.

Mindiola, Tatcho, Jr., Yolanda F. Niemann, and Nestor Rodriguez. 2002. *Black-Brown Relations and Stereotypes*. Austin: University of Texas Press.

Mladenka, Kenneth R. 1989. "Blacks and Hispanics in Urban Politics." *American Political Science Review* 83: 165–91.

Mollenkopf, John. 1997. "New York: The Great Anomaly." In *Racial Politics in American Cities*, edited by Rufus I. Browning, Dale Rodgers Marshall, and David H. Tabb, 75–87. New York: Longman.

Morgan, David L. 1996. "Focus Groups." *Annual Review of Sociology* 22: 129–52.

Morgan, David L., and Richard A. Krueger. 1993. "When to Use Focus Groups and Why." In *Successful Focus Groups: Advancing the State of the Art*, edited by David L. Morgan, 3–19. Thousand Oaks, Calif.: Sage.

Morin, Jason L., Gabriel R. Sanchez, and Matt A. Barreto. 2011. "Perceptions of Competition." In Telles, Sawyer, and Rivera-Salgado, *Just Neighbors?*, 96–124.

Morris, Irwin. 2000. "African American Voting on Proposition 187: Rethinking the Prevalence of Interminority Conflict." *Political Research Quarterly* 53(1): 77–98.

National Council of State Legislatures. N.d. Ballot Measures Database. www.ncsl .org/legislatures-elections/elections/ballot-measures-database.

National Conference of State Legislatures. 2014. "Undocumented Student Tuition: State Action." www.ncsl.org/research/education/undocumented-student -tuition-state-action.aspx.

Nteta, Tatishe Mavovosi. 2006. "Plus Ca Change, Plus C'est la Meme Chose?: An Examination of the Racial Attitudes of New Immigrants in the U.S." In *Transforming Politics, Transforming America: The Political and Civic Incorporation of Immigrants in the United States*, edited by Taeku Lee, Kathrick Ramakrishnan, and Ricardo Ramirez, 194–216. Charlottesville: University of Virginia Press.

———. 2013. "United We Stand?: African Americans, Self-Interest, and Immigration Reform." *American Politics Research* 41(1): 147–72.

Nteta, Tatishe M., and Kevin Wallsten. 2007. "Two Peas in a Pod?: Latino Attitudes toward African Americans." Paper presented at the Latino National Survey Junior Scholars Conference, Ithaca, New York.

Oliver, J. Eric, and Tali Mendelberg. 2000. "Reconsidering the Environmental Determinants of White Racial Attitudes." *American Journal of Political Science* 44(3): 574–89.

Oliver, J. Eric, and Janelle Wong. 2003. "Inter-group Prejudice in Multiethnic Settings." *American Journal of Political Science* 47(4): 567–82.

Ortiz, Elaine, and Allison Plyer. 2012. "Who Lives in New Orleans and the Metro Area Now?" Greater New Orleans Community Data Center. www.gnocdc.org /Demographics/index.html.

Passel, Jeffrey S., and D'Vera Cohn. 2008. "U.S. Population Projections: 2005–2050."

Pew Research Hispanic Trends Project. www.pewhispanic.org/reports/report
.php?ReportID=85.

———. 2009. "A Portrait of Unauthorized Immigrants in the United States." Pew
Research Hispanic Trends Project. www.pewhispanic.org/2009/04/14/a-portrait
-of-unauthorized-immigrants-in-the-united-states/.

Passel, Jeffrey S., D'Vera Cohn, and Mark Hugo Lopez. 2011. "Hispanics Account for
More than Half of Nation's Growth in the United States." Pew Research Hispanic
Trends Project. www.pewhispanic.org/reports/report.php?ReportID=140.

Persinger, Ryanne. 2010. "Black Voices Muted in Immigration Debate." *Charlotte
Post*, August 5, 1A–2A.

Pettigrew, Thomas F. 1998. "Intergroup Contact Theory." *Annual Review of Psychology*
49: 65–85.

Pettigrew, Thomas F., and Linda R. Tropp. 2006. "A Meta-Analytic Test of Intergroup
Contact Theory." *Journal of Personality and Social Psychology* 90: 751–83.

Pew Hispanic Center. 2011. "A Statistical Portrait of Hispanics in the U.S., 2009." Pew
Research Hispanic Trends Project. www.pewhispanic.org/factsheets/factsheet
.php?FactsheetID=70.

Planas, Roque. 2012. "Sheriff Joe Arpaio Ethnic Discrimination Case Goes to Court."
Fox News Latino, July 19. http://latino.foxnews.com/latino/news/2012/07/19
/sheriff-joe-arpaio-ethnic-discrimination-case-goes-to-court/.

Plyer, Allison. 2011. "Homeownership, Household Makeup, and Latino and Viet-
namese Population Growth in the New Orleans Metro Based on 2000, 2010
U.S. Census Bureau Data." Greater New Orleans Community Data Center. www
.gnocdc.org/HomeownershipHouseholdMakeupLatinosAndVietnamese/index
.html.

Plyer, Allison, and Elaine Ortiz. 2009. "Who Lives in New Orleans and the Metro
Area Now?" Greater New Orleans Community Data Center. www.gnocdc.org
/2008Demographics/index.html.

Plyer, Allison, Elaine Ortiz, Ben Horwitz, and George Hobor. 2013. "New Orleans
Index at Eight." Greater New Orleans Community Data Center. www.datacenter
research.org/reports_analysis/the-new-orleans-index-at-eight/.

Powers, Daniel, and Christopher Ellison. 1995. "Interracial Contact and Black Racial
Attitudes." *Social Forces* 74(1): 205–7.

Preston, Jennifer, and Colin Moynihan. 2012. "Death of Florida Teen Spurs Outcry
and Action." *New York Times*, March 21.

Preuhs, Robert. 2012. "The Sea-Change in Colorado." Latino Decisions, December 4.
www.latinodecisions.com/blog/2012/12/04/the-sea-change-in-colorado/.

Project Vote Smart. 2010. "Arizona Key Vote: Expanding Undocumented Immigration
Enforcement." http://votesmart.org/issue_keyvote_detail.php?cs_id=29812.

Quinlan, Adriane. 2013. "Fat City to Host Food Trucks, Music on Oct. 14." *Times-
Picayune*, October 11.

Rainey, Richard. 2013. "Mayor Landrieu Vetoes New Orleans Food Truck Law, Says
Would Not Stand up in Court." *Times-Picayune*, May 1.

Rocha, Rene R., and Rodolfo Espino. 2008. "Racial Threat, Residential Segregation, and the Policy Attitudes of Anglos." *Political Research Quarterly* 20: 1–12.

Rodriguez, Nestor, and Tatcho Mindiola, Jr. 2011. "Intergroup Perceptions and Relations in Houston." In Telles, Sawyer, and Rivera-Salgado, *Just Neighbors?*, 155–76.

Roig-Franzia, Manuel, Tom Jackman, and Darryl Fears. 2012. "Who Is George Zimmerman?" *Washington Post*, March 22.

Sanchez, Gabriel R. 2008. "Latino Group Consciousness and Perceptions of Commonality with African Americans." *Social Science Quarterly* 89: 428–44.

Sanchez, Gabriel R., and Jason L. Morin. 2011. "The Effect of Descriptive Representation on Latinos' Views of Government and Themselves." *Social Science Quarterly* 92: 483–508.

Sawyer, Mark Q. 2011. "Politics in Los Angeles." In Telles, Sawyer, and Rivera-Salgado, *Just Neighbors?*, 177–200.

Segura, Gary M., and Sean Bowler. 2005. *Diversity in Democracy: Minority Representation in the United States.* Charlottesville: University of Virginia Press.

Sharpton, Rev. Al. 2010. "Arizona—Here Come the Freedom Walkers." *New York Amsterdam News*, April 29, 12.

Sigelman, Lee, and Susan Welch. 1993. "The Contact Hypothesis Revisited: Black-White Interaction and Positive Racial Attitudes." *Social Forces* 71: 781–95.

Spain, Daphne. 1979. "Race Relations and Residential Segregation in New Orleans: Two Centuries of Paradox." *Annals of the American Academy of Political and Social Science*, 441: 82–96.

"Stata FAQ: How Can I Merge Multiple Files in Stata?" N.d. University of California, Los Angeles, Academic Technology Services, Statistical Consulting Group. www.ats.ucla.edu/stat/stata/faq/multmerge.htm.

State Initiative and Referendum. N.d. Institute at the University of Southern California. www.iandrinstitute.org/ballotwatch.htm.

Stump, Scott. 2013. "Cheerios Ad with Mixed-Race Family Draws Racist Responses." *USA Today*, June 3.

Stutzman, Rene. 2012. "George Zimmerman's Father: My Son Is Not Racist, Did Not Confront Trayvon Martin." *Orlando Sentinel*, March 15.

Susman, Tina. 2010. "Racial Strife Escalates in Staten Island." *Los Angeles Times*, August 22.

Tate, Katherine. 1991. "Black Political Participation in the 1984 and 1988 Presidential Elections." *American Political Science Review* 85(4): 1159–76.

———. 2010. *What's Going On?: Political Incorporation and the Transformation of Black Public Opinion.* Washington, D.C.: Georgetown University Press.

Taylor, Marylee C., and Matthew B. Schroeder. 2010. "The Impact of Hispanic Population Growth on the Outlook of African Americans." *Social Science Research* 39(3): 491–505.

Taylor, Paul. 2010. "Aren't Many Millennials Just Being 'Politically Correct' in Answering Racial Questions?" Pew Research Center, July 19. www.pewresearch.org

/2010/07/19/arent-many-millennials-just-being-politically-correct-in-answering-racial-questions/.

Telles, Edward, Mark Q. Sawyer, and Gaspar Rivera-Salgado. 2011. *Just Neighbors?: Research on African American and Latino Relations in the United States*. New York: Russell Sage Foundation.

Thornton, Michael C., and Yuko Mizuno. 1999. "Economic Well-Being and Black Adult Feelings toward Immigrants and Whites, 1984." *Journal of Black Studies* 30(1): 15–44.

Thornton, Michael C., Robert Joseph Taylor, and Linda M. Chatters. 2012. "African American, Black Caribbean and Non-Hispanic White Feelings of Closeness toward Other Racial and Ethnic Groups." *Journal of Black Studies* 43(7): 749–72.

U.S. Census Bureau. 2013. "Orleans Parish." www.census.gov/quickfacts/table/PST045214/22071,00.

———. 2006–10. American Community Survey. American Fact Finder. http://factfinder2.census.gov/faces/tableservices/jsf/pages/productview.xhtml?pid=ACS_10_SF4_DP02&prodType=table.

———. 2011. American Fact Finder. http://factfinder2census.gov/faces/nav/jsf/pages/community_facts.xhtml.

Vargas, Ramon Antonio. 2009. "Many Hondurans in New Orleans Support Weekend Ouster of Their Country's President." *Times Picayune, June 30*.

Waller, Mark. 2006. "In the Wake of Katrina, Thousands of Spanish-Speaking People Are Migrating to New Orleans, Drawn by the Dream of a Better Life (El sueño de una vida mejor)." *Times-Picayune*, October 8.

———. 2007. "Jefferson Bans Taqueria Trucks." *Times Picayune,* June 20.

Wallsten, Kevin, and Tatishe M. Nteta. 2011. "Elite Messages and Perceptions of Commonality." In Telles, Sawyer, and Rivera-Salgado, *Just Neighbors?*, 125–54.

Wang, Wendy. 2012. "The Rise of Intermarriage Rates, Characteristics Vary by Race and Gender." Pew Research Center, February 16. www.pewsocialtrends.org/2012/02/16/the-rise-of-intermarriage/.

Warren, Christopher L. 1997. "Hispanic Incorporation and Structural Reform in Miami." In *Racial Politics in American Cities*, edited by Rufus I. Browning, Dale Rodgers Marshall, and David H. Tabb, 155–78. New York: Longman.

Welch, Susan, and Lee Sigelman. 2000. "Getting to Know You?: Latino-Anglo Social Contact." *Social Science Quarterly* 81: 67–83.

Welch, Susan, Lee Sigelman, Timothy Bledsoe, and Michael Combs. 2001. *Race and Place: Race Relations in an American City*. New York: Cambridge University Press.

Wieder, Alan. 1987. "The New Orleans School Crisis of 1960: Causes and Consequences." *Phylon* 48: 122–31.

Wilkinson, Betina Cutaia. 2007. "Understanding Latinos' Assimilation in the U.S." Paper presented at the Latino National Survey Conference, Cornell University.

———. 2009. "How Outsiders View Insiders: Exploring Latinos' Perceptions of Commonality and Competition toward Whites and Blacks." Paper presented at the Politics of Race, Ethnicity and Immigration Colloquium, University of California, Irvine.

Wilkinson, Betina Cutaia, and Natasha Bingham. 2013. "Getting Pushed Back Further in Line?: Examining the Effects of Perceptions of Discrimination and Powerlessness on African American Immigration Attitudes." Unpublished manuscript.

Wilkinson, Betina Cutaia, and Emily Earle. 2013. "Taking a New Perspective to Latino Racial Attitudes: Examining the Impact of Skin Tone on Perceptions of Commonality toward Blacks and Whites." *American Politics Research* 41(5): 783–818.

Wong, Cara, Jake Bowers, Daniel Rubenson, Mark Fredrickson, and Ashlea Rundlett. 2012. "Does the Context Fit the Outcome?: When (or Where) Racial Context Should Affect Politics." Paper presented at the Symposium on Politics, Immigration, Race, and Ethnicity (SPIRE) conference, Yale University.

Wong, Morrison G. 2012. "Model Minority or Perpetual Foreigner: The Political Experience of Asian Americans." In *Perspectives on Race, Ethnicity, and Religion: Identity Politics in America*, edited by Valerie Martinez-Ebers and Manochehr Dorraj, 153–73. New York: Oxford University Press.

Index

Page numbers in italics refer to tables.

African Americans (*continued*)
15, 123, 128, 135, 170–71, 199, 217n10;
whites' focus group expressions about,
167, 169–77, 216–17n5, 217n7, 217n11;
zero-sum scenarios in race relations
and, 100, 212n2
Alabama's H.B. 56, 7, 136
Allport, Gregory W., 21, 212n3, 214n4
Alvarez, R. Michael, 9, 48
Arizona's S.B. 1070, 7, 136, 187–88, *189*
Asian Americans, 3–4, 7

ballot initiatives, 30, 32, 196, 201. *See also*
political and institutional context of
race relations
Banducci, Susan A., 30
Barreto, Matt, 47, 53
Bingham, Natasha, 100–101
Bishin, Ben, 55
blacks. *See* African Americans
Blumer, Herbert, 100, 142. *See also* group
position theory
Bobo, Lawrence, 108, 142. *See also* group
position theory
Branton, Regina P., 25, 27–28, 42, 139,
141

California's Proposition 187, 94, 211n1
coalition building: among blacks and
Latinos, 91, 214n1; desegregation and,
186; economic context conducive to,
186–87; immigration reform and, 188,
190; institutional context and, 29;
multiracial coalitions and, *189*, 190; in
New York, 24, 47; political coalitions
and, 13–14; political context conducive
to, 187; precursors of, 138, 179; rainbow
coalition theory and, 15, 27, 190
commonality among racial and ethnic
groups: behavior and values versus race
and, 84, 90, 217n9; of blacks with Latinos, whites, and other blacks, 103–4,
104, 106, *107*, 108–10, *108–10*, 123–28,
135, 181–82, *184*, 212n9, 213–14n6;
closeness and, 118; coalition formation
and, 2, 11–12, 179; versus competition,
11, 33, 34–35, 132–33, 141; cultural

levels and perception of, 90; dependent
variables indicating, 191, 192, 198, 203,
204; desegregation and, 186; economic
context and, 27; identification and,
10–11, 100, 108, 185–86; independent variables and, 193; language and,
54; Latinos' focus group expressions
regarding, 82–84, 90, 211n6; of Latinos
with whites, blacks, and other Latinos,
47, 57–60, *58*, *61–63*, 62–67, *65*, *67*,
73–74, 82–84, 181, *183*, 210nn3–4,
210n9; linked fate and, 46; perceptions
of closeness and, 22, 209n1 (chap. 1);
policy implications and, 13; predictors
of Latino racial attitudes and, 52; racial
threat hypothesis and, 24–25; schol-
arship on, 3–5, 179–80; siding with
those with clout and, 182; skin tone
and, 53; of whites with Latinos, blacks,
and other whites, 141–43, 145–48, *146*,
148–52, 151–53, *154–55*, 155, 161–62,
168–72, 182, *185*, 215nn8–9, 215nn12–
13, 217n9
competition among racial and ethnic
groups: of blacks with Latinos, whites,
and other blacks, 91–93, 100–101,
103–5, *105*, 110, *111–12*, 112, *113*,
114–15, *114–17*, 118, 122–23, 125–26,
128–33, 135, 181–82, *184*, 212n9,
213–14n6; closeness and, 114, *116–17*,
117–18; coalition formation and, 2,
11–12, 179; versus commonality, 11,
33, 34–35, 132–33, 141; dependent
variables indicating, 191–92, 198–99;
discrimination and, 125–26, 129–30;
economic context and, 13, 26, 85–88,
120, 186–87; geographic location and,
54; in-group expectations of relative
status and, 29, 31; growing out-group
population and, 138–40; identification
and, 185; language and, 54; between
Latinos and blacks, 8; of Latinos with
blacks, whites, and other Latinos, 47,
57–60, *59*, 67, *68*, 69–74, *70–71*, *73*,
84–88, 181, *183*, 210n5; policy implications and, 13; political representation
and, 30; racial alienation and, 100;